Mapping, Measurement and Metropolis

Several persons had represented this city, as not deserving the attention of strangers, not being remarkable for any singularity, nor affording anything worthy of the curiosity of a traveller. But we see in this map, that *Dublin* is one of the finest and largest cities in Europe.

John Rocque, Index, *Exact survey of Dublin* (Dublin, 1756)

Mapping, Measurement and Metropolis

HOW LAND SURVEYORS SHAPED EIGHTEENTH-CENTURY DUBLIN

Finnian Ó Cionnaith

FOUR COURTS PRESS

Set in 10 on 12.5 point Bembo for
FOUR COURTS PRESS LTD
7 Malpas Street, Dublin 8, Ireland
www.fourcourtspress.ie
and in North America for
FOUR COURTS PRESS
c/o ISBS, 920 N.E. 58th Avenue, Suite 300, Portland, OR 97213.

© the author and Four Courts Press 2012

A catalogue record for this title
is available from the British Library.

ISBN 978–1–84682–348–0

SPECIAL ACKNOWLEDGEMENT
This publication has received financial support from Leica Geosystems,
Dublin City Council, Dun Laoghaire–Rathdown County Council,
Fingal County Council and Dublin City Council.

Printed in England
by CPI Antony Rowe, Chippenham, Wilts.

Contents

Acknowledgments

During the course of researching this book, I have met many individuals who have helped with information, advice, guidance and interest. I would like to thank them all for their support. I am deeply obliged to the directors and staff of numerous archives, both in Ireland and abroad: Ann Simmons of Marsh's Library, Dublin; Penny Woods of the Russell Library, NUI Maynooth; Colette O'Daly, Glenn Dunne, James Harte and Honora Faul of the National Library of Ireland; Aideen Ireland of the National Archives of Ireland; Tim Eggington of Whipple Library, University of Cambridge; Paul Ferguson of the Map Library, TCD; Sharon Sutton of the Digital Resources and Imaging Department, TCD; Rachel Bewley-Bateman of the Religious Society of Friends Library, Dublin; Tom Morgan of the National Portrait Gallery, London; Noel Healy of the Old Dublin Society; Bernadette Cunningham, Petra Schnabel and Sarah Gearty of the Royal Irish Academy; the staff of Libreia Nazionale Marciana, Palazzo Querini Stampalia and Centro di Rilievo, Cartografia ed Elaborazione, Venice; John Powel and Julia Reed, Newberry Library Chicago; Raymond Refaussé of the Representative Church Body Library; Louise Morgan, Andrew Moore, Sarah Montague, Niamh MacNally and Kerry Eldon of the National Gallery of Ireland; and Colum O'Riordan of the Irish Architectural Archive. I would very much like to thank Mary Clark and the staff of Dublin City Archives, especially Andrew O'Brien, for the help, interest, generosity and encouragement they have given throughout my research.

It is a pleasure to thank John Kerrigan and Rekha Voralia of Leica Geosystems for their generous financial support and enthusiasm for this project. I would like to thank the Heritage Officers of Dublin's four local authorities: Charles Duggan (Dublin City), Tim Carey (Dun Laoghaire–Rathdown), Gerry Clabby (Fingal) and Rosaleen Dwyer (South Dublin), in addition to Patrick Shine of the survey and mapping division (DCC), for their financial assistance.

As a land surveyor, I have had the pleasure and privilege of learning from many talented surveyors in the field during the course of my career. I would like to thank Mark Nicholls, Thomas O'Rourke, Geraldine Fitzgerald, James Keane, Shane McLoughlin and David O'Quigley for being mentors and teachers.

I am grateful to all those who aided me so much during my travels undertaken for this research; in Cambridge, Maureen and Brendan Donnelly for their hospitality, and in Venice, Gloria Correggiari of Università Iuav di Venezia for her advice and introductions.

It has been a great joy for me to cooperate with some former lecturers and colleagues, in addition to fellow researchers, working on the same era of history or similar topics. I would like to thank Alison Fitzgerald, Department of History, NUI Maynooth, Christine Casey, Department of History of Art and Architecture, TCD;

James Kelly and Ruth McManus of St Patrick's College, Drumcondra; John Montague of the Royal Irish Academy; Frank Prendergast, Department of Spatial Information Science, DIT Bolton Street; Malachy McVeigh; and Niall McKeith of the National Science Museum, NUI Maynooth for his help with gaining access to eighteenth-century instrumentation. I would like to express my deep appreciation and gratitude to Jacinta Prunty of the Department of History, NUI Maynooth. Her guidance, advice and passion for research have been invaluable in enabling me to develop the ideas in this book and to bring the work to completion. I would also very much like to thank Colm Lennon and Marion Lyons, Department of History, NUI Maynooth, for their interest and assistance.

This book would never have been possible in this form without the previous research conducted by John Andrews. I have had the pleasure of reading his extensive works and following in his research footprints, and now have the honour of him writing the foreword to this book. Nobody has done more to keep the subject of historical Irish land surveying alive than Professor Andrews, and I am very grateful for his tireless work and enthusiasm for the subject.

I am also deeply indebted to Dublin's surveyors of the eighteenth and nineteenth centuries. Over the course of the past few years, I have learnt about their lives – not only on a professional basis but also, occasionally, the joys and sorrows they experienced during their lives in Dublin. In my mind, each surveyor has his own face, his own personality, his own particular take on life. The delight I have experienced in discovering some new trait about them or their often unique and occasionally clashing characters has been the driving force behind this research. As a land surveyor, I passionately believe that these men deserve recognition for their life's work. My original and continuing aim for this research is for these men not to be forgotten and to ensure that their lives will live again, in some form, through a renewed interest in their wonderful and detailed measurements.

For Philomena and Fiachra

Abbreviations

CIRCE	Centro Cartografico Interdipartimentale, Venice
DCA	Dublin City Archive
DCC	Dublin City Council
DHR	*Dublin Historical Record*, Dublin, 1938–
DIT	Dublin Institute of Technology
GB	Google Books
IAA	Irish Architectural Archives
IGSB	*Bulletin of the Irish Georgian Society*
IHTA	Irish Historic Towns Atlas
IUAV	Università Iuav, Venice
J.T. Gilbert (ed.), *Ancient records*	*Calendar of ancient records of Dublin in the possession of the municipal corporation*, ed. J.T. Gilbert and R.M. Gilbert, 19 vols, Dublin, 1889–1944
ML	Marsh's Library, Dublin
NAI	National Archives of Ireland
NCAD	National College of Art and Design
NGI	National Gallery of Ireland
NLI	National Library of Ireland
NUI	National University of Ireland
RIA	Royal Irish Academy
RL	Russell Library, NUI Maynooth
RSL	Religious Society of Friends Library, Dublin
TCD	Trinity College Dublin
UCD	University College Dublin
WL	Whipple Library, University of Cambridge
WSC	Wide Streets Commission

Illustrations

PLATES (between p. 88 and p. 89)

Foreword

Let us begin with Finnian Ó Cionnaith's sub-title: 'how land surveyors shaped eighteenth-century Dublin'. First, who were these land surveyors? How were they recruited, what did they do, and how were they trained to do it? Who were their employers and how much were they paid? Ó Cionnaith, himself a fully qualified surveyor, answers all these questions clearly and comprehensively, with a wealth of original examples.

The idea of 'shaping' is more complicated. On the most literal interpretation, it means the laying out of new streets, walls, water pipes etc. that had first been delineated on accurate maps. As Ó Cionnaith makes clear, this was done by professional surveyors working for private landowners, for the city corporation and later for the Wide Streets Commission. A less direct kind of shaping was to demarcate the boundaries of estates and tenements by planimetric representation on maps made for landowners and lessees who could then develop their holdings by building on them. Irish surveyors spent much of their time admeasuring units of land-tenure by enclosing them with precisely determined distances and bearings, an operation implicit in Ó Cionnaith's unusually full descriptions of contemporary surveying instruments.

In a more figurative sense, by a kind of intellectual transfer or displacement 'shaping' is what happened when the whole of Dublin was portrayed on one map by a surveyor-cartographer like Charles Brooking, John Rocque or Thomas Sherrard. These events are the high points of Ó Cionnaith's narrative, leading us from utilitarian land measurement into the worlds of design, graphic embellishment, engraving, printing and publicity. All are dealt with in ample detail. Indeed, an alternative title for this book might be 'Dublin's role in the history of cartography'. Even then 'Dublin' would have to be interpreted broadly: there is a whole chapter on the mapping of the bay and harbour, and much attention is given to canals and roads converging on the city.

One commendable feature of *Mapping, measurement and metropolis* is its mastery of primary sources, from which we are given many verbatim extracts and a fine range of graphic illustrations. These create an impression of freshness, even with topics that have been treated by earlier writers. Not all Ó Cionnaith's lessons are positive, however. Much cartography consists of covering one's tracks. Although innumerable finished maps survive from the eighteenth century, the private surveyors of this period seem to have left no archival legacy of field notes, sketches, line diagrams, content plots, examination traces, name books or proof sheets comparable with those preserved later by the Ordnance Survey. If such documents existed, Ó Cionnaith would surely have told us about them. For all his erudition he never quite manages to follow in a surveyor's footsteps. In their non-professional lives, too, surveyors and cartographers guarded their privacy against the historian's intrusion. For many of them, it is only when engaged in controversy with their peers that their personalities come into focus. Ó Cionnaith has a sharp eye for such episodes, and for occasions of light relief in general. He goes as far as anyone could to humanize 'the men behind the maps'. Equally if not more important, his own writing is lively, lucid and refreshingly free from thesis-writer's jargon. He has the gift of readability.

This book will be widely used and enjoyed as an important addition to the literature of several subjects.

J.H. Andrews
Formerly Associate Professor,
Department of Geography
Trinity College Dublin
1 June 2012

Introduction

The night of 4/5 December 1687 was cold and wet in Dublin. A solitary carriage pulled by two horses travelled down a cobbled and lamp-lit Capel Street, its driver huddled in his heavy great coat against the incessant winter breeze as he made his uncomfortable journey south towards Essex Bridge. It had been raining for days and the River Liffey ran high with flood water. Already several sections of the city further up stream had been flooded, with houses being inundated by the river and stories told of boats floating loose in the streets. The driver pressed on towards the bridge, his empty carriage rocking and bouncing over the uneven road. The bridge had been constructed ten years earlier. The silhouette of its arched stony back and high oil lamps appeared before the driver, who looked out from under a sodden and increasingly damp hat, cursing his luck to be out in such foul weather. The carriage began to cross the empty bridge, the lights of the southern end appearing though the river mist. A crack. A shudder. Below the driver, the coach suddenly fell as a section of the bridge beneath him abruptly collapsed into the turbulent dark waters. The horses dragged violently against the ground as the carriage pitched into the river, hauling them kicking into the watery chasm, still strapped and harnessed. One of the horses by chance found itself free of the carnage in the river and, in a panicked state, was washed downstream to eventual safety. The driver and the other horse met their ends.

This tragic and bizarre accident had consequences for the city of Dublin that no one at the time could foresee. Indeed its after-effects are still felt by tens of thousands of the city's residents daily. A series of events stemming directly from this single incident led to the creation of much of Dublin's modern city centre, giving it a distinctly Georgian atmosphere that it embraces to this day. Bridges were built, streets were straightened and modernized. Important thoroughfares such as O'Connell Street, Parliament Street and Westmoreland Street appeared. This event was the catalyst by which the city was transformed from medieval disarray to Georgian homogeneity.

The damage caused to Essex Bridge in 1687 was not the last time that this structure collapsed. Immediately following the death of the coachman, the bridge was repaired. As was later discovered, however, the problem lay not with the bridge itself, but with its foundations. In February 1751, the same section of the bridge collapsed into the river, this time without any recorded fatalities. The city's population had expanded greatly in the sixty-four years since the original accident and this collapse denied them easy passage across the river on one of Dublin's few bridges. Essex Bridge at the time was the closest bridge to the mouth of the Liffey and the furthest point inland at which seagoing vessels could dock. Its loss brought logistical and financial chaos to the city's residents. Despite Dublin Corporation providing extra ferries across the river, a long-term solution was required.[1]

---

1 8 Dec. 1752: J.T. Gilbert (ed.), *Ancient records*, x, p. 53.

During a visit to the lord archbishop of Dublin in 1751, engineer George Semple became involved with rebuilding Essex Bridge. At the meeting, Semple listened to another of the archbishop's guests, Mr Prior, 'pathetically lament on the loss and inconvenience the public sustained by being near four months deprived of the use of Essex Bridge'.[2] At the time, two proposals were under review by Dublin Corporation for the repairing of the bridge – rebuilding with wood, taking five months and costing £500, or with stone, taking six months and costing £800. Shortly afterwards, Semple, accompanied by his brother, John, inspected the remains of Essex Bridge. The breach had occurred at the same location where the repairs had been made in 1687 and Semple suspected that the plinth below the breach had subsided slightly, causing the collapse.[3] The bridge needed to be demolished, redesigned and rebuilt, and Semple was determined that his new creation 'should last as long as the little adjacent mountain, called Sugar Loaf hill'.[4] Semple's reconstruction of the new Essex Bridge brought the words of Italian architect Leon Battista Alberti to his attention: 'a bridge must be made as broad as the street which leads to it'.[5]

Slowly, Semple and those around him began to direct their attention to the southern junction of Essex Bridge, which was a traffic black spot of narrow streets and difficult junctions. From their initial assessment, it was proposed to create a single street at this southern junction, to be called Parliament Street, covering the 120m from the bridge to the main thoroughfare of Dame Street.

Parliament Street was the first project for a group of wealthy landowners in the upper echelons of the city's hierarchy who, from 1757 until the mid-nineteenth century, redesigned and redeveloped large portions of Dublin's city centre, creating many of the city's most important streets and avenues. The body responsible for this work, the *Commissioners for making wide and convenient streets and passages*, or as they came to be known, the Wide Streets Commission (WSC), had a radical effect on how the modern city of Dublin looks and flows. The unfortunate and random death of the coach driver in 1687 had substantial, unpredicted and enduring consequences in shaping Dublin to what it is today.

THE MAKERS OF MAPS

Without land surveyors, the work of the commissioners would have been impossible. Indeed, this often-overlooked small group of artisans played a disproportionately large role in the city's evolution. Period architects and engineers are often remembered, and deservedly so, but surveyors, despite the frequent inclusion of their maps in historical publications, regularly escape the public's attention. These men provided Dublin, and the rest of the country, with mapping for every conceivable purpose; from the most important and far-reaching engineering works to determining rents

---

2 George Semple, *A treatise of building in water* (Dublin, 1786), p. 1.   **3** Ibid., p. 2.   **4** Ibid., p. 24.   **5** Ibid., p. 8.

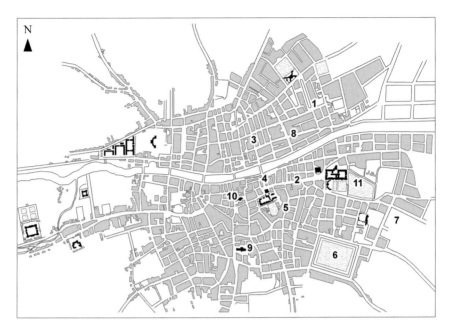

1.1 Dublin city, *c.*1775. 1: Sackville Street (modern O'Connell Street); 2: Dame Street; 3: Capel Street; 4: Parliament Street; 5: George's Street; 6: St Stephen's Green; 7: Merrion Square; 8: Abbey Street; 9: St Patrick's Cathedral; 10: Christ Church Cathedral; 11: Trinity College.

of the smallest tenant farms. Their maps are of immense cultural significance: they show our homes, our places of work, streets we use on a daily basis and ordinarily pay little attention to, in a manner that seems so familiar yet, in the same instance, so alien. They provide the backdrop against which some of the most momentous and fascinating stories of eighteenth-century Dublin are told. The maps and plans they produced may seem at first to be confined to libraries and historical collections, but this is not the case – they are alive everywhere in the city. This book charts the history of Dublin's land surveyors, the manner in which they conducted their business and the substantial effect they had on the development of the city and how it looks today.

Compared to the modern city, eighteenth-century Dublin was minuscule (figs 1.1, 1.2). Areas that now play such an intrinsic part in the life of the city, such as Kilmainham, Rathmines, Donnybrook, Glasnevin, Coolock and Sutton, were all rural villages. The city itself extended only as far as the modern North and South Circular Roads, and was a densely packed and vibrant place. This was a significant time for Dublin, as it expanded rapidly, urged on by both economic and social demands. As the centre of British rule in Ireland, a calmer socio-political environment removed the need for the city to retain its defensive medieval walls, allowing rapid urban growth. Its population increased from approximately 50,000 in 1700 to

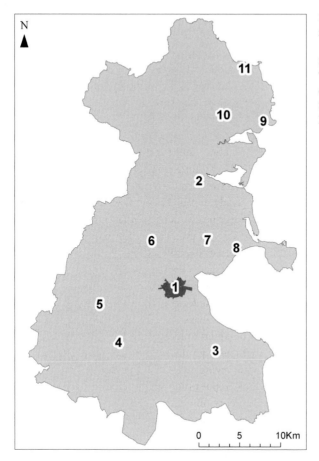

1.2 Co. Dublin: places mentioned in the text; 1: Dublin City; 2: Swords; 3: Dundrum; 4: Tallaght; 5: Clondalkin; 6: Finglas; 7: Coolock; 8: Sutton; 9: Rush; 10: Lusk; 11: Skerries.

nearly 200,000 by 1810,[6] making it one of the largest cities in the British Empire. Suburbs expanded in all directions, and the city began its gradual transformation to its present form.

This era gave the city many of its most important landmarks. Buildings north of the Liffey that trace their origin to this time include the Four Courts (1796), the Rotunda Hospital (1745), the Custom House (1791), Henrietta Street (1720s), and Parnell and Mountjoy Squares (1790s). Their south-side equivalents, Fitzwilliam and Merrion Squares (1792 and 1762) were joined by the current western façade of Trinity College (1751), Dublin Castle (redeveloped 1761), Leinster House (1745), the Houses of Parliament on College Green (1727) and Dublin City Hall (1779). These iconic structures represent Dublin during an era of confidence and development, when new designs and urban fashions were not restricted simply to Dublin's resi-

---

6 Patrick Fagan, 'The population of Dublin in the eighteenth century', *Eighteenth-Century Ireland/Iris an dá chultúr*, vi (1991), 121–56.

dents, but to the fabric of the city itself. An active port, Dublin's docks were frequented by ships from Britain, the Caribbean, India and throughout Europe. It was home to important figures such as author Jonathan Swift (1667–1745), composer George Frederic Handel (1685–1759), architect James Gandon (1743–1823) and politician Henry Grattan (1746–1820). Energy was everywhere. The streets were thronged by the powerful and penniless alike. The Ormond and Liberty boys, rival street gangs, fought running battles in Smithfield, vigorous and raucous debates took place in the Irish Houses of Parliament, soldiers paraded in their redcoat uniforms in the grounds of the Royal Barracks, Dublin's unfortunates crowded into the city's poorhouses, the actors of the Smock Alley theatre entertained the crowds, and in the Phoenix Park gentlemen faced off against each other in duels over matters of honour.[7] The north side of the city greatly expanded, the quays slowly took shape and the iconic four-story, redbrick Georgian townhouses that so embody Dublin of that time appeared with greater frequency and even greater uniformity.[8]

Built around a small core of professionals over the course of a century, Dublin's land-surveying industry was equally energetic during in this period. Surveyors provide a unique and unrivalled insight into eighteenth-century Dublin. They left behind them a rich cartographic history in the form of thousands of maps deposited in dozens of libraries and collections. These maps trace the development of the city during this time – from well-known buildings to ideas and schemes that were never realized. Research into how such maps were produced is scarce, and works concentrating on the practice and science of surveying during this period in Ireland are even rarer. The period covered by this book, 1690–1810, was a time of transformation in the surveying profession. Improvements in instrumentation, technology and surveying techniques drew Dublin's surveyors, some reluctantly, into the beginnings of the Industrial Revolution and into the modern world.

This time was the golden era of the freelance surveyor in Dublin. The industry had moved beyond the link between surveying and the military found so often in Ireland's cartographic past and had yet to face the dominance of the major mapping resources that the Ordnance Survey would bring to Ireland in 1824. Fragmented urban estates, expansive rural properties and engineering projects provided ample opportunity for the individual land surveyor to make his name, and money, by landing a major client. The surveyors themselves were an eclectic group consisting of professionals, amateurs, artists, frauds, rogues and cranks. Competition, usually cordial but occasionally hostile, was constant.

This book is the story of the land surveying industry at that time, as much as it is about Dublin. It follows the careers and lives of the surveyors, shedding light on the men behind the maps (fig. 1.3). In order to fully understand their work in

---

7 James Kelly, *That damn'd thing called honour: duelling in Ireland, 1570–1860* (Dublin, 1995).
8 Constantia Maxwell, *Dublin under the Georges* (Dublin, 1936), p. 100; Edel Sheridan, 'Designing the capital city' in J. Brady and A. Simms (eds), *Dublin, c.1660–1810* (Dublin, 2001), pp 66–136 at p. 66.

1.3 Engraving of
eighteenth-century
surveyors at work
(Dupain de Montesson,
L'art de lever des plans
(Paris, 1763)).

reshaping Dublin, it is first necessary to explore what it meant to be a surveyor at that time. Dublin was home to the great Irish surveying lineages of the Sherrard, Gibson and Neville families, renowned mapping military officers such as Charles Vallancey and his subordinates, troublemakers like Thomas Owen, and the creative cartographic artists Bernard Scalé and Samuel Byron. Surveying in Dublin attracted names well known in the eighteenth century outside of Ireland. Captain William Bligh, of HMS *Bounty* infamy, once applied his surveying skill to the shores of Dublin Bay. John (Jean) Rocque, the celebrated French Huguenot surveyor, in 1756 produced a masterpiece survey of Dublin, which once graced the rear of the late twentieth-century pre-Euro Irish £10 note – a unique feat for an Irish cartographic work. Even authors such as Mary Shelley were well versed in period surveying issues.

To understand the surveying industry is to understand how these practitioners helped the city evolve. They lived in a complex professional world often marred with disputes, both technical and personal, with their brethren as well as the city's landlords and tenants. A knowledge and understanding of the techniques they used, their methods of self-promotion, the instruments responsible for their detailed and precise measurements, and the art and skill applied to their mapping are vital to fully comprehend the surveyor's role in eighteenth-century Dublin.

The profession, business, science and technology of land surveying in Dublin during this period were all closely linked. The eighteenth century began with Irish surveying largely restricted; maps tended to contain simple geographic features, possessed relatively basic decoration and were presented in a style similar to the surveys conducted during previous centuries.[9] Instrumentation consisted of chains, plain tables and circumferentors,[10] all familiar to surveyors of the early seventeenth century. By the end of the eighteenth century, the situation had altered. Surveyors had branched out to high-precision engineering and urban redevelopment plans, contributing to scientific discussions along the way, while retaining their traditional and core practices.[11] Map decoration had begun to incorporate the fashionable baroque and rococo styles that grew in frequency through the latter half of the century. The development of new and more accurate surveying instruments had begun to push Irish surveyors forward.[12] Older instruments disappeared and newer ones took their place. Increasing technological sophistication within surveying reduced some instruments to the realm of virtual museum pieces; others were adapted, modified and retained. Greater demands from the cartographic consumer market, influenced by improvements in map production in England and France, led to Irish surveyors adapting new methods and practices to reach levels of accuracy and design previously unseen in the country.

Maps resemble reality – they do not replicate or mirror it, if they did they would be of infinite complexity and detail. They are our selective representation of the world around us, and, as such, they reflect the era and purpose in which they were created. One can often see the surveyor's initial objectives in the completed map. In essence, the man, like the world, was reflected in the map. The surveyors present in this book are still reflected in the streets of Dublin.

Land surveying was described by Dublin-based eighteenth-century surveyor Bernard Scalé as 'one of the most profitable and genteel professions'.[13] This book explores both the surveyors and the city. It looks at the surveying industry at that time, using examples of surveying in Dublin and occasionally further afield. It reviews a lively and dynamic profession that applied scientific principles and industrial techniques that have left a major impact on both the layout of the city and its cartographic heritage. It aims to give recognition to all those mentioned, for the lasting effect their work had on Dublin city and how, as a small group of individuals, they influenced the development of Ireland's largest city.

9 The cartographic design of William Petty's Down Survey (1655–6) heavily influenced Irish surveying for over a century. **10** The circumferentor is also known as a surveyor's compass. **11** For example, *Freeman's Journal*, 11 Oct. 1787: John Heylin, a land surveyor from Mount Wilson near Edenderry, Co. Offaly, contributed to an ongoing discussion about determining magnetic variation. **12** Arnold Horner, 'Cartouches and vignettes on the Kildare estate maps of John Rocque', *IGSB*, 14: 4 (1971), 57–71 at 28. **13** *Freeman's Journal*, 13 Jan. 1770.

Table 1 Timeline of Dublin surveyors. This list includes some of the most active surveyors operating in eighteenth-century Dublin. While it is not exhaustive, records from the listed surveyors are among the most frequently found in period map collections and minute books and are mentioned throughout this book.

Sir William Petty (b. 1623; d. 1687)	Supervisor of the Down Survey (1655–6), conducted in the wake of Oliver Cromwell's campaign in Ireland. This survey was held in high regard by eighteenth-century surveyors.
John Greene (active 1679–1724)	First holder of Dublin Corporation's 'city surveyor' position. Estate surveyor for the archbishop of Dublin.
Gabriel Stokes (b. 1682; d. 1768)	Deputy surveyor general, trained by Joseph Moland. Also known to have manufactured surveying instruments.
Joseph Moland (active 1698–1718)	Assistant city surveyor to John Greene. Became city surveyor in 1687. Produced survey of Dublin Bay and harbour.
Peter Duff (active 1700–25)	Surveyor to the Domville Estate and archbishop of Dublin.
Alexander Stewart (active 1705–24)	Surveyor to the Domville Estate.
Thomas Cave (active 1709–49)	Surveyor of the estate of Christ Church Cathedral and the Pembroke family, Dublin, during the 1740s.
James Ramsey (active 1718–35)	Dublin city surveyor responsible for the production of brass standard yards as a form of standardized measurement for civic use.
George Semple (b. 1700; d. 1782)	Accomplished engineer and architect. Rebuilt Essex Bridge after its collapse in the 1750s. Conducted early reconnaissance work for the Grand Canal Company and was first surveyor to the Dublin's Wide Streets Commission.
John Rocque (b. 1704; d. 1762)	Produced pioneering map of Dublin in 1756. Surveyor of the earl of Kildare's lands. Founder of the 'French School' of Irish surveying.
Thomas Reading (b. 1704; d. 1779)	Surveyor to the estate of the Hatch family and of Christ Church Cathedral.
Roger Kendrick (active 1735; d. 1778)	Verger of St Patrick's Cathedral, Dublin, and holder of the office of Dublin city surveyor. Attempted to produce city map in the 1750s in direct competition to John Rocque.
Bernard Scalé (b. 1739; active until 1790)	Apprentice to John Rocque. Established successful survey business based in Abbey Street. Known for well-executed map decorations.

Robert Gibson (active 1752–60)	Deputy surveyor general and author of *Treatise of practical surveying* (Dublin, 1763).
George Gibson (active 1754–65)	Son of Robert Gibson. Held position of deputy surveyor general and surveyor to the Wide Streets Commission. Surveyed Dublin Bay and harbour in 1756.
Jacob Neville (active 1754–82)	Produced map of Wicklow in 1750s. Progenitor of the Neville surveying family.
Thomas Mathews (active 1760–82)	Dublin city surveyor. Compiled book of the works of the city surveyor.
Andrew Skinner (active 1760–82)	Surveyor and military officer. Produced roads atlas of Ireland in 1770s. Saw active service during the American Revolutionary War (1775–83).
George Taylor (d. 1841)	Military officer and business partner of Andrew Skinner.
William Purfield (active 1762–94)	Measurer with surveying experience. Worked on the reconstruction of the façade of Trinity College. Second surveyor hired by the Wide Streets Commission.
Patrick Roe (active 1763–92)	Surveyor and grocer. Conducted extensive survey work on the Pembroke Estate.
William Cox (active 1767–80)	Estate surveyor who unsuccessfully applied for the position of surveyor to the Dublin Paving Board.
Francis Mathews (active 1767–1800)	Surveyor for the archbishop of Dublin.
Charles Vallancey (b. 1726; d. 1812)	Military officer. Conducted military survey of Ireland and was heavily involved with early canal surveying.
John Brownrigg (b. 1748; d. 1838)	Apprentice of Bernard Scalé and business partner of Thomas Sherrard. Conducted extensive estate and valuation surveys.
Richard Brassington (b. 1749; d. 1838)	Business partner of Thomas Sherrard. Family retained association with surveying in Dublin until late nineteenth century.
Thomas Sherrard (b. 1750; d. 1837)	Apprentice and assistant to Bernard Scalé. Surveyor and clerk to the Wide Streets Commission. Highly successful land-surveying and valuation business. Extensive work on the redevelopment of Dublin.
Thomas Owen (active 1774–87)	Surveyor to Dublin's Paving Board. Turbulent career with the board, eventually being dismissed.
John Longfield (active 1775; d. 1833)	Apprentice to John Brownrigg. Associated with a wide range of individual surveys thanks to the Longfield map collection.

Thomas Logan (active 1777–1820)	Surveyor to the archbishop of Dublin.
Samuel Byron (active 1782; d. 1795)	Dublin city surveyor. Trained by Bernard Scalé in England and known for the high artistic quality of his maps.
Arthur Richard Neville (active 1782–1837)	Dublin city surveyor. Unsuccessfully applied for the position of surveyor to Dublin's Paving Board.
John Roe (active 1789–1826)	Son of Patrick Roe. Surveyor to the Pembroke Estate.
D.B. Worthington (active 1790–1801)	Dublin city surveyor.
Arthur Neville Jr (active until 1852)	Civil engineer. Last holder of the position of Dublin city surveyor.
Clarges Greene (active 1813–66)	Apprentice and eventual business partner of Thomas Sherrard and Richard Brassington.

Part I
The profession

1 'That art which enables us to give a plan': defining the name of and the need for land surveying

Surveying is at the heart of eighteenth-century mapping. It is the physical measurement of land through the use of a wide variety of instruments, the calculation and transference of these measurements onto paper and the creation and decoration of a final product – a map. As such, it can be considered a science, an art and, with financial backing, a business. In reality, however, this fails to fully explore the rich diversity that existed in those that called themselves land surveyors during this time. It is necessary to examine how surveyors of the era viewed their profession and of what use such skills were to those that employed them.

In the many varied treatises and manuals written on the subject of land surveying during the eighteenth century, there is considerable divergence in the definition of the work of a surveyor. The eminent Irish surveyor, Robert Gibson, defined surveying in his 1763 treatise as

> that art which enables us to give a plan, or just representation, of any piece or parcel of land, and to determine the content thereof, in such measure as is agreeable and customary to the country or place where the land is.[1]

American surveyor Zachariah Jess followed the same lines as Gibson in 1799: 'surveying is the art of delineating and calculating the content of land, in acres, roods and perches, and consists in a knowledge of geometrical definitions and problems'.[2] As did Englishman Daniel Fenning in 1772:

> Surveying, or the art of measuring land, implies the act of taking the dimensions of any field, parcel, or tract of land, laying down the same in a map or draught, and casting up the content ... as this art is of the utmost importance to all owners and occupiers of land.[3]

The *London Tradesman*, published in 1774, defined a land surveyor as one

> employed in measuring land, and laying it out in gardens and other kinds of policy about gentleman's seats. [They are] to have a good taste ... he ought

---

1 Robert Gibson, *Treatise of practical surveying* (Dublin, 1763), p. 1.   2 Zachariah Jess, *A compendious system of practical surveying* (Wilmington, 1799), p. 1.   3 Daniel Fenning, *The young measurer's complete guide or a new and universal treatise of mensuration* (London, 1772), p. 49.

to travel to France and Italy, and to have a liberal education, but especially a thorough knowledge of geometry and designing. They may earn a guinea a day when employed in laying out, and are always esteemed above a mechanic.[4]

Yet, despite these useful if somewhat repetitive definitions, it is difficult to gain a true representation of the range of work undertaken by eighteenth-century Irish surveyors. Few period definitions of surveying make any reference to map making and even fewer refer to engineering. Dublin surveyors often had various skill-sets and were at times employed as engravers,[5] cartographers,[6] compilers, engineers,[7] publishers,[8] land agents, valuers[9] and, in the case of Patrick Roe of Smithfield, a grocer.[10]

To complicate matters, the title 'surveyor', when used in eighteenth-century contexts, did not universally refer to land surveyors. For example, the role of surveyor general would suggest the title of the most senior figure in land surveying, but in actuality this role was more concerned with engineering and architecture,[11] with the land surveying aspect often being covered by the deputy surveyor general. To add more confusion, estate managers, customs officials and naval supply officers were also grouped under the umbrella term 'surveyor' (these were of course distinct from land surveyors). Some land surveyors also chose to vary their own job title, as towards the end of the eighteenth century many Irish practitioners would refer to themselves as engineers or use the letters CE (civil engineer) after their name.[12]

Where did such name variation come from? Why did surveyors stray so far from the clinical definition given in treatises, with their strong emphasis on measurement and geometry? The explanation lies in the very real lack of regulation within the land surveying industry in eighteenth-century Ireland.

With no centralized governing body, Irish surveyors were free to define their job titles as they saw fit and to work in whatever industry they wanted. Surveying was very fluidic, with amateur surveyors cropping up time and again only to disappear as quickly as they appeared. The abundance of easily read surveying manuals allowed people to self-educate in surveying and they could then use these skills to supplement their regular income.[13] Surveying lacked guilds or licensing that controlled so many

4 R. Campbell, *The London tradesman* (London, 1747), pp 274–5. This is a good example of the higher end of the profession of surveying in the eighteenth century. Such cases were rare in the Irish industry. **5** John Rocque, *An exact survey of the city and suburbs of Dublin* (Dublin, 1756). **6** Herman Moll, *A set of twenty new and correct maps of Ireland* (London, 1728). **7** Semple, *A treatise on building in water.* **8** Bernard Scalé, *An Hibernian atlas* (London, 1776). **9** Bernard Scalé, *Tables for the easy valuing of estates* (Dublin, 1771). **10** Mary Colley, 'A list of architects, builders, surveyors, measurers and engineers extracted from Wilson's Dublin directories, 1760–1837', *IGSB*, 34 (1991), 7–68 at 56. **11** Frederick O'Dwyer, 'Building empires: architecture, politics and the Board of Works, 1760–1860', *IGSB*, 5 (2002), 108–75. **12** Arthur Neville, as listed in Colley, 'A list of architects', 48. **13** Peter Callan, *A dissertation on the practice of land surveying in Ireland* (Drogheda, 1758), p. 15;

other industries at the time and, consequently, it could occasionally be exploited by poor practitioners, fraudsters or criminals for their own nefarious needs.

At first glance, it may appear that this lack of centralized control could simply be an annoyance to professional surveyors, or that such discrepancy in career definition was a passing issue. However, land surveyors were intrinsically involved with Ireland's main form of revenue generation – land. The ownership, size and rental value of Ireland's fields, pastures, meadows and mountains were defined by the country's land surveyors. Therefore, anyone deriving their livelihood directly from agriculture, from tenant farmers to the wealthiest estate owners, had a vested interest in the quality of land surveyors. With no governing body regulating surveyors, the possibility of serious financial and legal repercussions, both to the individual and to the country as a whole, was very real. Peter Callan, a somewhat bad-tempered and vocal Drogheda-based surveyor, wrote extensively on the surveying industry in Ireland, of which, regulation was a genuine concern:

> Whereas the general regularity of the affairs of landlords and tenants in this kingdom chiefly depends on the skill, diligence and integrity of surveyors of land, since there are no judges, no magistrates or incorporated society who legally assume to themselves the power of administrating justice in matters of surveying: but every man who is pleased to undertake the occupation of land surveying (without any regular qualification) is at free liberty to impose on the public in the most important affairs, without any regular means of redress, but the liberty of the press, to expose to public view, the unaccountable proceedings of such surveyors as obstinately persist in known errors, to the general prejudice of landlords and tenants ...[14]

Others within professional surveying were not blind to this serious problem. In 1750, the deputy surveyor general, Gabriel Stokes, was tasked to help restore the public's confidence in the surveying industry, which had been dented by poor practitioners. The result was the creation of a certificate of proficiency – an official reference from the surveyor general's office that the holder of such a certificate was fully capable of performing surveying work to a high degree of accuracy. To support the certificate, Stokes published the following declaration:

> Whereas by decretal orders from His Majesty's high court of chancery, and court of exchequer, the surveyor general is frequently directed to appoint skilful surveyors; and as the surveyor general knows not (for want of examining, as was in the original institution of this office) who are skilful, gentlemen would do well for many other reasons, not to employ any surveyor, but such as have passed an examination, and obtained a certificate

J. Vaughan, *The gentleman and farmer's pocket assistant* (Shrewsbury, 1795), p. vi; Samuel Wyld, *The practical surveyor* (London, 1725), p. vii. **14** *Universal Advertiser*, 1 Dec. 1753.

from the surveyor general's office, of their qualifications for the business of surveying of land, and of tracing down surveys.[15]

Research conducted by historian J.H. Andrews shows that a total of twenty testimonials, such as the one above, were published in eighteenth-century newspapers and, of these, thirteen focused on the certificate-holder's ability to copy Down Survey maps.[16] The ability to copy from the main source of background data for the vast majority of the country, the Down Survey (1655/6), was of the utmost importance. A common solution to boundary disputes was for a surveyor to examine the area in question from the Down Survey,[17] and plot out on the ground the boundary lines using reference data from this source, much as Ordnance Survey mapping is used today.[18] Stokes' deputy, Robert Gibson, continued the surveyor general's certificates until 1760 and from 1765 by Robert's son, George.

The award of a certificate of proficiency from the surveyor general's office did not necessarily mean that a certified surveyor's measurements went unquestioned or that other surveyors respected the certificate. One surveyor defending a contested survey felt it necessary to assure the public that he had obtained a certificate and was therefore a skilled surveyor.[19] His opponent dismissed such a defence, referring to the mentioning of the certificate as 'the airs he puts on in newspapers'.[20] The certificate was not a legally binding document and, as such, it can be viewed as, at best, a very good reference or credential for an individual surveyor. The certificate system was discontinued in 1784.[21]

Callan was a particularly keen and highly vocal observer of the types of surveyors operating in Ireland. In his *Dissertation on the practise of land surveying* (Drogheda, 1758), he both categorized and presented a detailed but biased analysis of the levels of professionalism within Irish surveying as well as the many frauds and fakes operating in Ireland during the mid-eighteenth century.

Those who Callan classified as 'complete surveyors' were the most professional and honest surveyors working in Ireland at the time, being 'completely furnished with all necessary instruments'.[22] This group consisted of the majority of professional surveyors. 'Grand surveyors' appeared at first glance to be professionals, but they had a poor work ethic, were not averse to being bribed and too often they bullied their clients through bravado and boasting.[23] 'Bungling surveyors' were either honest men with poor equipment or training or dishonest men willing to alter measurements in favour of their clients. If two sets of opposing clients each hired a bungling surveyor, the consequences could be financially damaging to both:

---

15 *Dublin Journal*, 16 Dec. 1750.   16 J.H. Andrews, *Plantation acres* (Omagh, 1985), p. 100. 17 A general survey of Ireland (1655–6) conducted by Sir William Petty in the wake of Cromwell's campaign in Ireland.   18 Robert Gibson, *Treatise of practical surveying* (Dublin, 1762), p. 284.   19 *Universal Advertiser*, 26 July 1760.   20 Ibid.   21 Andrews, *Plantation acres*, p. 101.

[The bungling surveyors] likewise jarring and fighting for several days together, sometimes for several months, about a small piece of work, wasting the time, and consuming the substance of both landlord and tenant.[24]

Self-educated surveyors also felt Callan's criticism, perhaps somewhat undeservedly, being described as fops or 'town schoolboys, and self-conceited petty teachers of the mathematicks'.[25] He also drew attention to open criminality by some pretenders or conmen, who were not in fact surveyors, but claimed to be educated in an obscure but highly accurate method of measuring land. Such perpetrators would defraud their clients, 'which occasions the utter ruin of great numbers of industrious families'.[26] Callan's opinion must be treated as prejudiced, of course, as he has a recorded history of disputes with other surveyors.[27] Nonetheless, he provided a fascinating glimpse into the darker corners of the Irish surveying industry at the time.

Unsurprisingly, Callan developed his own theories of how the surveying profession could be regulated. He proposed that the industry could be more governable through a series of annual meetings where surveyors and their instruments would be appraised, and if they were deemed insufficient then they should be suspended.[28] Those performing such inspections were to be selected on a five-year basis from among members of the surveying community and that the members of the Dublin Society should be responsible for the inspector's appointment.[29] Each surveyor would be required to recite an oath at each annual meeting, stating that he would perform his duties in a diligent and impartial manner.[30] He also called for the standardization of the paralleled paper on which surveys were drawn, to eliminate it as a source of contention, and insisted that every map must have the surveyor's name upon it.[31] The surveying community in eighteenth-century Ireland never adopted Callan's ideas.

THE NEED FOR SURVEYS AND SURVEYORS

Apart from clinical and professional definitions of land surveying, a breakdown of the need for surveyors in Dublin during this period can help understand the industry in a real-world environment. The primary needs for land surveys were often based on disputes over landownership, establishing of rents according to the exact acreage of a property, and for planning and construction purposes. Maps can be considered the by-product of such measurements and calculations. Engineering surveys became increasingly common later in the eighteenth century, and several practitioners were also involved in notable city and nationwide mapping projects, although the vast majority of surveyors spent their careers establishing landownership through mapping and property surveys.

22 Callan, *A dissertation*, p. 12. **23** Ibid., p. 13. **24** Ibid. **25** Ibid. **26** Ibid., p. 17. **27** *Dublin Gazette*, 27 Sept. 1760. **28** Callan, *A dissertation*, p. 47. **29** Ibid., p. 45. **30** Ibid., p. 46. **31** Ibid., p. 47.

Infringements on property boundaries, whether intentional or accidental, were a relatively common source of employment for surveyors, and disputes regularly required surveys of the land in question. Irish surveyor Benjamin Noble quoted from the Bible to help highlight this issue in his book *Geodæsia Hibernica* (Dublin, 1768): 'cursed be he that removeth his neighbour's land-mark; and all the people shall say amen (Deut. 27.17)'.[32] A letter written in 1761 by John Firth to the Pembroke family highlights such a dispute:

> Ushers Quay, 11 August 1761
> My Dear Lord,
> We have been at some trouble in ascertaining & fixing the boundaries of your lands, from those of other people, & very probably, may in some parts of your estate find an opposition from particular men, who from time to time have encroached upon you, & who may contest it with you, upon finding you are resorted to take back what is *bona fide* your own. The mearings of Dundrum may be one of them; a *Manning*,[33] who is troublesome about some of your ground near Merrion Street may be another & a Mr Butler ... of whom I have heard but too much, is a third.

The legal loopholes that could be exploited by squatters or those altering land boundaries were also a concern for the Pembroke family, as highlighted in the same letter:

> Mr Butler, a tenant, for such a given parcel of land & that you also find Mr Butler has without lease or any authority, made use of another large parcel of land, close upon your own domestic domain, which you are now determined to wall ... There is a law in this country which realises any parcel of land to him, who has been quietly in possession of it, for 20 years. Mr Butler has gone on, upon this land seven or eight years, has paid no rent for it.

Of course, the role played by a land surveyor was vital in solving such issues by establishing the legal boundaries of land and therefore ownership:

> I have, therefore, had this whole parcel of land, surveyed & have ordered Mr Taylor ... to build the wall, which is to divide your lands from those of L. Trimblistown & Lady Allen & to comprehend, within wall, all the land, for which Mr Butler has no lease. Enclosed to you, a drawing of it, done from Mr [Jonathan] Barker's survey, by myself ... as soon as I see you, which will be soon, will further explain it.[34]

---

32 Benjamin Noble, *Geodæsia Hibernica* (Dublin, 1768), cover. **33** Mr Manning had previously caused trouble to the Fitzwilliam family in April 1761 over a plot on Merrion Street: 18 Apr. 1761, William Fitzwilliam, Dublin, to his brother, Viscount Fitzwilliam (NAI Pembroke papers, MSS 97/46/1/2/7/137). **34** 11 Aug. 1761: John Firth to Lord Fitzwilliam (NAI Pemborke papers, 97/46/1/2/6/8).

Such infringements often required the recognition of individual field boundaries, particularly around the periphery of an estate, on maps[35] and of more importance from a landlord's perspective, any disturbance to these boundaries.[36]

Re-surveys of lands were an additional method of determining any changes that had occurred on a landlord's property. They assisted landlords in establishing new rents based on the productivity of the land, for instance by increasing rents where unproductive land, such as bogs or marsh, had been drained and turned into pasture or arable land by the tenant. Classification of land, usually using a colour scheme or reference table within the map's border, can be found in a number of surviving eighteenth-century maps.[37] Such maps could also be submitted as evidence of a tenant's abuse of his lease, mainly with reference to the burning of land to increase its fertility in the short term, but to its overall detriment in the long term.[38]

The materials used for eighteenth-century maps meant that there was an obvious need to replace them periodically. Some surveyors attempted to avoid the quick decay of maps through the use of vellum – Peter Duff produced several maps of lands in Meath using this material,[39] as did Alexander Stewart[40] – yet its use is comparatively rare throughout the eighteenth century. Paper maps were also delivered via potentially destructive or damaging means, with Thomas Sherrard and Michael Kenny sending folded maps[41] as letters to their respective clients. The greater long-term importance of estate and lease maps, however, often meant that their rates of survival were far greater than engineering plans, as mentioned by Andrews: 'they were often kept as long as the property itself, and then transferred with it to the new owner and later in turn to his successor'.[42]

LANDLORD OR TENANT

Surveyors did not necessarily work exclusively on the side of landlords. One example is the Cork surveyor and diarist Joshua Wight who, in 1752, was approached by several tenants of an estate who requested him to survey their combined farms. Wight initially expressed reluctance, informing the tenants that if his results differed

---

35 John Longfield, 'Lands in Glasnevin' (1807) (NLI Longfield papers, MS 2789(110)), John Longfield, 'Lands in Simons Court' (1820) (NLI Longfield papers, MSS 2789–90(74)). **36** John Longfield, 'Lands in Kill o the Grange' (1814) (NLI Longfield papers, MSS 2789–90(32)), John Longfield, 'Lands in Loughlinstown' (1821) (NLI Longfield papers, MSS 2789–90(74)), John Longfield, 'Lands in Glasnevin' (1807) (NLI Longfield papers, MS 2789(110)). **37** Charles Frizzell, 'Lands in Deansgrange' (1791) (NLI Longfield papers, MSS 2789–90(25)), John Longfield, 'Lands in Kill o the Grange' (1814) (NLI Longfield papers, MSS 2789–90(32)). **38** 3 George III c.29: *Dublin Chronicle*, 19 Aug. 1788. **39** Peter Duff, 'Raleigh, Co. Meath' (1713) (NLI Domville papers, MS 11,937(42)), Peter Duff, 'Tallow, Co. Meath' (1718) (NLI Domville papers, MS 11,937(46)). **40** Alexander Stewart, 'Ballymun' (1705) (NLI Domville papers, MS 11,937(49)). **41** Sherrard and Brassington, 'Turnapin' (1803) (NLI Longfield papers, MS 11,937(16)), Michael Kenny, 'Glasnevin' (1804) (NLI Domville papers, MS 11,937(20)). **42** Andrews, *Plantation acres*, p. 129.

significantly from those of the surveyor employed by the landlord, then it may 'breed
a controversy and cause uneasiness'.[43] Wight eventually submitted to the tenants'
request, promising to survey their lands 'as carefully and exact as if their lands was my
own', but insisted on receiving his full pay before any map or catalogue of the lands
was handed over to the tenants. He proceeded to survey several small holdings,
apparently with the landlord's consent, and determined that many of them were actually smaller than the landlord's surveyor had previously stated. This error meant that
the landlord was overcharging his tenants. Upon procurement of the maps, the
tenants presented their evidence to the landlord, who seemed noticeably 'uneasy' at
this revelation. He immediately sent for his surveyor, referred to by Wight as Mr K—y,
who examined Wight's new maps. Wight, the landlord and Mr K—y retired to a
nearby public house to discuss the discrepancies further. Wight, upon finding 'the
surveyor [K—y] being much in liquor' and 'stark drunk', tried to leave, at which
point he was subjected to a verbal assault from K—y, who, after calling him a dunce,
determined that Wight would 'soon see who was right'. Wight then informed K—y
that he would only be free to look at the matter further the following week and not
a moment before. This reply provoked the intoxicated K—y, who

> in a great rage … said he would compel me and that he would follow me,
> wherever I went if would not meet him, there or upon the spot, he would
> post me up [in the] Gazette … and he would make me pay the rents.[44]

At this point, the landlady of the public house, finding her husband was not present,
requested a patron of the pub to forcibly remove Wight's antagonist from the premises. Wight reflected on the incident later, concluding that 'I was never so abused
before'.

Examining his opponent's surveys, Wight found that K—y had not included
either a scale bar or a north arrow in any of these maps and that K—y had calculated
his acreages from 'tables of difference of latitude and long[itude]'. Wight's criticisms
of this method were based on the fact that 'numbers were inflexible, paper was flat,
but land ruff and attended with [deviations]'. It appears from Wight's diary that this
was the point that caused K—y to respond in such an aggressive and violent manner.
After the crisis had passed, Wight informed the landlord that 'I made a good vow for
I never would have another conversation with him right, nor wrong and I disap-
proved of his method … I would have nothing to do, or to say with him'.[45] Several
days later, a friend of the landlord approached Wight and asked him to come and
resurvey the lands as the landlord was anxious to determine the exact acreage in his
possession and to determine if the original difference was 'a simple mistake or a wilful
one'. Wight offered the tenants to resurvey their land, with their assistance, and said
that 'if I did not make my returns the same within a trifle, I would pay them back
their money'. The tenants refused Wight's offer; they were satisfied with what he had

43 Diary of Joshua Wight, 25 Sept. 1752 (Friends Library, Dublin).   **44** Ibid.   **45** Ibid.

already done and stated that 'they have paid for more lands than they have in possession, & my surveys make it appears so'.[46] Wight's disagreement does not appear to
have been an isolated case, with Callan commenting that

> the landlords and tenants of this kingdom always complain of the wide differ-
> ence and intolerable jarrings which frequently happen between surveyors of
> land; especially of late, when swarms of pretenders to that art wander about
> the country, using several fraudulent means to raise variance between landlord
> and tenants, which prove troublesome to some landlords, and the entire ruin
> of several tenants.[47]

While it was not uncommon for surveyors to be in dispute with each other, relationships between tenant, landlord and surveyor were not always as amicable as the Wight
example. Opinions of surveyors from passers-by or affected parties ranged from
curious to cordial to hostile, but very rarely violent.[48] John Norden's fictional
dialogue between a seventeenth-century surveyor and a tenant somewhere in
England gives insight into how surveyors were treated and thought of while carrying
out their duties:

> Farmer: Sir, I am glad I have so happily met with you, for if I have not
>   been mistaken, you are a surveyor of land.
> Surveyor: Admit it so, Sir, what then?
> Farmer: I have heard much evil of the profession and to tell you my
>   conceit plainely, I thinke the same both evil and unprofitable.
> Surveyor: You seeme to be but a yong man in years and are you so deeply
>   seene in the abuse of this faculty, that you can so peremptorily
>   condemn it?
> Farmer: Call it you a faculty: What meane you by that word?
> Surveyor: Abilitie to performe a thing undertaken.
> Farmer: Then this faculty of yours, I say, is a vaine faculty, and a needless
>   worke undertaken.
> Surveyor: Speake you this by conjecture, by report of others, or by due
>   experience of your owne?
> Farmer: I speake indeede as induced to the opinion I hold, by all three
>   reasons.[49]

Another English surveyor, John Hammond, complained of often having to disguise
or hide his survey stations from local tenants due to attempts to sabotage his work:

46 Ibid. **47** Callan, *A dissertation*, p. 1. **48** Some took their resentment of surveyors
further than suspicion, with one seventeenth-century surveyor, Richard Bartlett, being
decapitated in Donegal: see J.H. Andrews, *The Queen's last map maker: Richard Bartlett in
Ireland, 1600–3* (Dublin, 2008), p. 29. **49** John Norden, *The surveyor's dialogue* (London,
1607), p. 1.

observing to conceal these plugs or marks from the county people, who in general, hating the practice of taking surveys of their grounds, will frequently remove the surveyor's marks, either to give him trouble or divert themselves.[50]

Surveyor and client relationships of course varied depending on the individuals involved and the circumstances related to the survey. Whether the surveyor was met with resentment or welcome, the need for land surveys was clear. The eighteenth-century Irish surveyor can be viewed as an individual who was technically qualified to gather data in the field with a variety of instruments, capable of working with existing maps in order to extract relevant information, as well as compiling data from various sources and able to take map data back to a real-world environment and plot it as required. Their work had a direct connection with Ireland's main source of income – land – and in this context they played a key role in defining ownership and authority over this asset. As the industry was so loosely controlled, all those who were involved in either the production of maps from the geographical data gathered by their own observations in the field – that is, surveyors – and those whose maps were produced from the compilation of the work of others – that is, cartographers – are grouped together, in this book, in the greater realm of the ever-changing surveying industry of eighteenth-century Dublin.

50 John Hammond, *The practical surveyor* (London, 1765), p. 61.

2 'Taste, ability and good connections': becoming a land surveyor in eighteenth-century Dublin

There was no single path for those who wanted to become a land surveyor in eighteenth-century Ireland. Men joined through a variety of means and for a variety of purposes. Regardless if this was through an apprenticeship, military service, mathematical school or family trade, the new surveyor's training revolved around the core themes of working with a wide assortment of surveying instruments and the performance of complex and often difficult geometry calculations.

Surveying opportunities in Dublin were limited by the amount of work available, which in turn helped maintain a stable, if small, surveying population. The surveying industry within the city was built around a core of approximately a dozen professionals at any given time during the eighteenth century, not including amateur or visiting surveyors.[1] Again, the lack of regulation within the industry prevents an exact figure to be determined, but with estimates of surveyor numbers being no more than one hundred for the entire island during the same period,[2] the Dublin figure appears reasonable. Surveyors tended to be based in the mercantile sections of the city, and occupied a social position of a professional skilled artisan. Unfortunately, no record exists describing a Dublin surveyor's workplace.

Recruitment for eighteenth-century surveying was in many ways radically different from that of the seventeenth century, mainly due to the changes in the political landscape over the course of these two centuries. Seventeenth-century surveyors active in Ireland were often affiliated with the operations of the English military. William Petty's Down Survey in the 1650s was a major source of income for surveyors following Cromwell's Irish campaign. This was followed at the turn of the eighteenth century by the Trustees Survey (1700–3), again for the re-division of land following the Williamite Wars (1689–91).[3] This sixty-year cycle of war and surveying not only led to the general population associating surveyors with the powers-that-be, but also acted as one of the major employers for the surveying community during this period.

The eighteenth century brought about a calmer socio-political landscape, particularly in the Dublin area,[4] leading to an increased availability of training and steady employment for surveyors. The cycle of war and land seizures had been broken, and

1 *Wilson's Dublin directory* (Dublin, 1737–1810). 2 Andrews, *Plantation acres*, p. 244; Callan, *A dissertation*, p. 18. 3 Richard Sims, *A manual for the genealogist, topographer, antiquary and legal professor* (Oxford, 1856), p. 147. 4 William Smyth, *Map making, landscape and memory* (Cork, 2006), p. 359.

rural property-holders could invest time and money in the development of their lands. Owners of estates, both lay and ecclesiastical, tended to retain a set group of surveyors through the life of the estate. For example, John Greene and Joseph Moland were the surveyors regularly employed by estates of the archbishop of Dublin between 1710 and 1720.[5] The liberty of Christ Church in Dublin retained the services of Thomas Cave throughout the 1740s, Thomas Reading during the 1750s and Samuel Byron during the 1780s, followed by John Brownrigg, while Michael Kenny was the preferred surveyor of the Domville Estate during the 1770s.[6] John Roe was the surveyor of choice of the Pembroke family during the early nineteenth century.[7] For these surveyors, this was an excellent opportunity to obtain regular work with the potential of new opportunities with other employers through the estate owner's recommendation. For the estate owner, there were obvious advantages to having a regular surveyor who would survey the same lands and be knowledgeable of their property history, yet there were also drawbacks to being reliant on one individual, as the owners of the Pembroke Estate discovered in a letter from their estate manager Richard Mathew:

> To all intents – Tuesday last was the day we appointed [land surveyor Thomas] Cave to be on the lands of Booterstown, he took a sudden disorder and is since dead, I shall have the lands please God survey'd and every holding as they now are occupied severally setforth and the avenue in a straight line from Mount Merrion to the sea as designed.[8]

AMATEURS

The basic art of surveying is relatively easy to learn. In the seventeenth century, Sir William Petty felt that one solid month's study of surveying manuals would be sufficient to conduct a reasonably accurate survey in the field,[9] whereas a nineteenth-century report on surveying and valuation suggested that four years would be preferable.[10] For the amateur, there was a wealth of surveying manuals and treatises from which the trade could be learnt.[11] Robert Gibson's *Treatise of practical surveying* (Dublin, 1752) stands out as the most widely distributed Irish written survey publication during this period, even being republished in the United States as late as

5 Raymond Refaussé and Mary Clark, *A catalogue of the maps of the estates of the archbishops of Dublin, 1654–1850* (Dublin, 2000).   **6** Michael Kenny, 'Book of maps of the estate of Charles Domville in the city of Dublin' (1778) (NLI Domville papers, 21F107).   **7** John Roe, 'Map of Ringsend and Irishtown, estate of the Rt Hon. Richard Lord Viscount Fitzwilliam' (Pembroke Estate papers, NAI 97/46/4/10).   **8** Letter of Richard Mathew, 1 May 1749 (NAI Pembroke papers, 97/46/1/2/5/64).   **9** William Petty, *The history of the survey of Ireland*, ed. Thomas Aiskew Larcom (Dublin, 1851), p. 2.   **10** *Report from select committee on survey and valuation of Ireland*, p. 73 [445], H.C. 1824, viii.79.   **11** Andrews, *Plantation acres*, appendix D.

1839.[12] Englishman Samuel Wyld's *The practical surveyor* (London, 1725), also available in Dublin, went into five separate editions during this period and was written with the amateur surveyor in mind:

> However, 'tis hop'd, the country farmer, who understands but so much of arithmetick, as to add, subtract, multiply and divide (with a little practice, the genuine part of perfection) by these plain directions, and with good instruments, will be enabled to find the content of each piece of land in his own occupation.[13]

A similar audience was the target of J. Vaughan's *The gentleman and farmer's pocket assistant* (Shrewsbury, 1795), which aimed to:

> enable a person, though he has no learning higher than the reading and understanding of words and figures, to find the contents of his field ... by the help of which every farmer may become his own land measurer.[14]

With a reasonable grasp of mathematics and geometry, a surveying treatise and access to a simple surveyor's chain, anyone, in theory, could practice surveying. There was, however, a limited market for the amateur surveyor. They tended to be either landowners or direct employees of landowners. They provided the flexibility to conduct very simple surveys that could help reduce the cost of land appraisal by removing the need to hire a professional, but lacked full technical expertise and were limited to simple surveys.

IMMIGRANTS

If one examines a list of surveyors operating in Dublin during the eighteenth century, the relative lack of traditional Gaelic names becomes evident. While the majority of these surveyors were in fact Irish, of British descent,[15] eighteenth-century Dublin provided definite employment opportunities for immigrant surveyors – and one visitor to the city in 1797 stated that 'a foreigner is always preferred by the Irish nobility'.[16]

Perhaps the most famous of all immigrant surveyors to work in Dublin was John Rocque (*c*.1709–62). Rocque was a Londoner of French Huguenot descent and had previous experience in publishing maps of London, Rome and Paris.[17] In 1754, he

---

12 Robert Gibson, *Treatise of practical surveying* (Hartford, CT, 1839).   **13** Wyld, *The practical surveyor*, p. vii.   **14** Vaughan, *The gentleman and farmer's pocket assistant*, p. vi.   **15** George Gibson, 'a citizen, son of a native', *Dublin Journal* (2 Nov. 1754).   **16** Anon., *Dublin and its vicinity in 1797* (London, 1797).   **17** John Varley, 'John Rocque, engraver, surveyor, cartographer and map-seller', *Imago Mundi*, 5 (1948), 83–91.

relocated to Dublin[18] to produce a map of both the city[19] and its surroundings.[20] It had been almost thirty years since Charles Brooking had produced the last original map of the city and, by the mid-eighteenth century, it was grossly out of date. At the same time as Rocque was beginning his venture, however, Dublin Corporation's 'city surveyor', Rodger Kendrick, announced that he was in the first stages of producing his own rival map.[21] In this case, Kendrick was far outclassed by Rocque, not only in cartographic skill but also in marketing and business savvy.[22] This cartographic battle also brought out some xenophobia within the Irish surveying community, albeit through some sense of loyalty towards the local Kendrick rather than out-and-out racism directed towards Rocque (see ch. four).[23]

Herman Moll was another surveyor of Continental extraction who was active on the Irish cartographic scene in the early eighteenth century. Moll, who was of German or Dutch origin, was so well known for his various atlases that he even appeared in *Gulliver's Travels* as a friend of the narrator.[24] Moll's Irish connections included Henry Pratt, an estate surveyor, whose assistance Moll acknowledged in his *New map of Ireland* (1714) as Pratt had done 'all the improvements ... viz. the roads, computed miles from town to town &c.'[25]

Not every immigrant surveyor made as big an impact as the distinguished Rocque and Moll however. Englishman James Pain produced only one small atlas and then completely disappeared from Irish surveying,[26] while Scotsman Peter May achieved even less impact with only one property being surveyed during his time in Ireland.[27] German-Jewish immigrant Richard Castle also commented that the foreign surveyor did indeed face difficulties moving and working in Ireland: 'as I lie under the disadvantage of being a stranger in this kingdom'.[28] Foreign surveyors often had to adjust to Irish surveying traditions if they wished to operate successfully. One early nineteenth-century surveyor described the differences between surveying in Ireland and England:

18 Rocque dedicated his map to his employers: 'to their excellencies Robert Viscount Jocelyn, Lord High Chancellor James earl of Kildare and Brabazon earl of Bessborough, lords justices general and general governors of Ireland. This plan is most humbly inscribed by their excellencies most dutiful and most obedient humble, John Rocque.' **19** Rocque, *An exact survey*. **20** John Rocque, *A map of Dublin and its environs* (Dublin, 1756). **21** *Dublin Journal*, 2 Nov. 1754. **22** Ibid., 14 Sept. 1754. **23** Ibid. **24** '... which thought I communicated many years ago to my worthy friend, Mr Herman Moll, and gave him my reasons for it ...': Jonathan Swift, *Gulliver's travels* (London, 1726), p. 191. **25** J.H. Andrews, 'New light on three eighteenth-century cartographers: Herman Moll, Thomas Moland and Henry Pratt', *IGSB*, 35 (1992–3), 17–22 at 17. **26** Royal Institution of Chartered Surveyors, *Five centuries of maps and map making* (London, 1953), p. 63. **27** Andrews, *Plantation acres*, p. 229. **28** Richard Castle, *Essay on artificial navigation* (Dublin, 1730), p. 1. Richard Castle, also known as David Richardo and Davide de Richardi, was raised in Dresden, while his father, Joseph Richardo, was a member of the court of Augustus, elector of Saxony/king of Poland in the 1690s: Loreto Calderón and Konrad Dechant, 'New light on no. 85 St Stephen's Green' in Christine Casey (ed.), *The eighteenth-century Dublin town house* (Dublin, 2010), pp 174–96.

> In Ireland, I was chiefly employed in measuring farms and smaller pieces of land, but in England I was engaged in enclosing lordships, which is considered most difficult as well as the most important branches of surveying ... In Ireland, plantation measure is used, with a two-pole chain of 14 yards, and in England statute measure with a four-pole chain of 22 yards; in measuring large tracts of land, a circumferentor is used with a chain by Irish surveyors, and the theodolite by English surveyors.[29]

The flow of surveyors was not only one way, with at least one Irish surveyor working for an English surveying business. The surveyor in question, however, David McCool of Derry, admitted in 1803 that such occurrences were rare: 'I being the first Irish surveyor ever employed by any of the London companies'.[30] McCool had been subcontracted by a London surveyor, Mr Crow, to survey Lord Donegal's lands, as 'Mr Crow ... did not come to Ireland, but wrote to me to see the whole business completed'.[31]

Despite their various opinions on the state of Irish surveying and Irish surveyors' reaction to them, immigrant surveyors to Ireland played a undeniably important role in the eighteenth-century surveying industry, by supplying the market with new cartographic styles and increased commercial competition.

FAMILY TIES

Family dynasties were present within the Dublin surveying industry throughout the eighteenth century. The names Neville, Sherrard, Gibson and Roe can be found in records that span the course of several professional generations and these families provided some of the most able and astute practitioners of the trade.

One the longest-serving surveying families operating in Dublin was the Nevilles. Jacob Neville first appeared in Wilson's *Dublin street directory* in 1772, describing himself as a land surveyor, but his career started decades earlier in Co. Wicklow. Having published a book on surveying in 1752, 'showing everything useful in the art of surveying',[32] Jacob then attempted to produce a map of Co. Wicklow in 1754. Running into financial difficulties in obtaining a satisfactory number of subscriptions from the very start, he struggled to complete the project and the final product did not appear until six years later.[33] Given the financial problems he encountered during the Wicklow project, it seems that the impact on Jacob's life may have been more than just professional disappointment. In 1761, he penned the following rhyme describing his financial woes:

29 *Report from select committee on survey and valuation of Ireland*, p. 84 [445], H.C. 1824, viii.79. **30** Evidence of David McCool (NLI Killadoon papers, MS 35,065(5)). **31** Ibid. **32** Andrews, *Plantation acres*, p. 431, appendix D. **33** *Dublin Journal*, 14 Mar. 1761.

As the county of Wicklow I did survey
I must now quit my hold for want of pay.[34]

Jacob's son, Arthur Richard Neville, or A.R. Neville as he signed himself in maps,[35] had his own thriving surveying, engineering and valuation practice from the 1780s onwards. Having unsuccessfully applied for the position of surveyor of the Paving Board in 1782,[36] he eventually became Dublin city surveyor in 1801.[37] A.R. Neville went into full partnership with his son Arthur junior in 1808 from their office in Camden Street.[38] The role of city surveyor was once more filled by a Neville when Arthur junior assumed the position in 1821.[39]

John Roe, who operated in surveying from the 1790s until the 1820s, succeeded his father, the previously mentioned grocer/surveyor Patrick Roe.[40] David Aher was also trained in surveying by his father, who was himself taught as part of Rocque's 'French School' style of surveying (fig. 2.1).[41] Such family connections could also skip a generation. John Kendrick, a possible grandson or great-grandson of the 1750s city surveyor Roger Kendrick, worked as a surveyor for the Post Office in the 1830s.[42] These surveying dynasties were not just an Irish phenomenon. In France, family names such as Cassini, Sanson and Delisle can be found operating in the realm of surveying and cartography throughout the eighteenth century.

One father and son who played a significant role in the city's surveying industry during this period were the Gibsons. A possible progenitor to the Gibson line may have been surveyor John Gibson, who was employed in the Trustees' Survey in the early eighteenth century.[43] Robert Gibson, who went on to become deputy surveyor general, described himself as a mathematician, but had also been active in land surveying since 1738.[44] Perhaps Robert's greatest achievement during his long career, apart from the certificate of proficiency that he initiated during his time with the surveyor general's office, was his influential *Treatise of surveying*, first published in 1752.[45] This book, which stands out among similar contemporary works for its practicality, clarity and structure, was still recommended reading over seventy years later, when the Ordnance Survey instructed its officers to study rules listed by Gibson.[46] Robert's son, George, followed his father not only into the surveying business but also into the role of deputy surveyor general, which he fulfilled from 1752 to 1760.[47]

---

34 Ibid., 12 Mar. 1761. **35** For example, A.R. Neville CS and Son, 'Map of Nettleton's holding on the east side of Kevin's Port' (1807) (DCA WSC/MAP/621). **36** 28 Aug. 1782 (DCA PB/Mins/10, p. 23): '... he was educated in this business under his father, who was very eminent: & has ten years practice which has matured his knowledge ...' **37** Gilbert (ed.), *Ancient records*, xiv, p. 398. **38** *Wilson's Dublin directory* (Dublin, 1808). **39** City surveyor maps, 'A map of small house ... on the east side of Lwr Exchange St.' (1821) (DCA C1/S1/22). **40** Colley, 'A list of architects', 56. **41** *Report from select committee on survey and valuation of Ireland*, p. 108 [445], H.C. 1824, viii.79. **42** *Wilson's Dublin directory* (Dublin, 1835). **43** *Dublin Intelligence*, 17 July 1708. **44** Robert Gibson, *Treatise of practical surveying* (Dublin, 1752), preface. **45** Ibid. **46** Andrews, *Plantation acres*, p. 274. **47** *Dublin Journal*, 25 July 1752, 19 Mar. 1765.

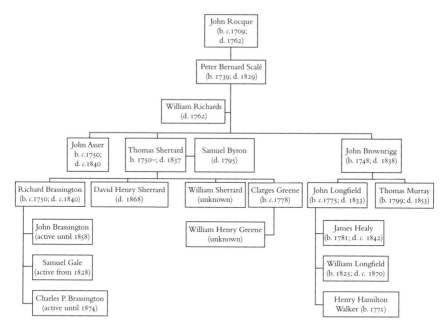

2.1 Partial French School lineage, 1709–1874

When examining father/son lineages for civic surveying positions, such as the Gibsons' occupation of the role of deputy surveyor general, the question of nepotism can naturally arise. While there is no direct evidence to show that this malpractice was common at the time for such surveying roles, the pattern of sons succeeding their fathers in official civic positions is found throughout these dynasties. One prominent example is that of William and David Henry Sherrard, who went on to replace their father, Thomas Sherrard, in the dual role of surveyor and secretary to the Wide Streets Commission after age and poor health caught up with Thomas in 1803.[48] Another is that of Thomas Owen, surveyor for the Dublin Paving Board, who at the time of his dismissal in 1787 was in the process of educating his son to assist him with his duties.[49] If nepotism had occurred or been encouraged by the boards of such organizations, the evidence of such is not contained within their official records and minute books.

APPRENTICES

Apprenticeships were another common method to join the industry. The requirements for surveying apprentices were, like many aspects of the surveying profession,

---

48 14 Jul. 1803 (DCA WSC/Mins/18, p. 321).   **49** 21 Feb. 1787 (DCA PB/Mins/19, p. 272).

loosely defined. Thomas Sherrard, when advertising for an apprentice in 1791, stated the qualities that he wished any potential candidate to possess: 'none need apply but a lad of taste, ability and good connections, who has been suitably educated'.[50]

No record exists of the duties or roles expected of a surveyor's apprentice in Dublin, again primarily due to the lack of regulation in the industry. Considering that an apprentice would have already been subject to formal education, as noted in Sherrard's advert, they may have been in their mid- to late teens before such an apprenticeship began. An apprentice would have received a traditional grounding in survey practice by accompanying the surveyor in the field and acting as his assistant and chainman. Area calculation and land valuation, instrument maintenance, the compilation of field observations and the production of maps and cartographic styles would have been core elements of this training.

Sherrard himself was a product of one of the most successful lines of masters and apprentices that existed in eighteenth-century Dublin. The founder of this lineage was John Rocque, who had begun his career with his elder brother, Bartholomew, designing stately gardens in 1730s England.[51] In 1754, Rocque arrived in Dublin to produce a map of the entire city with his various assistants and his teenage apprentice/brother-in-law Bernard Scalé (b. 1739).[52] Rocque's cartographic style was unique when it was introduced to Ireland during the mid-eighteenth century, with his level of planiformity, visual panache and overall clarity becoming an identifiable trademark in those who succeeded him. Indeed, so exceptional was this style within Irish surveying that the various apprentices that would follow in his wake were dubbed the 'French School' in honour of Rocque's Continental connections.[53] The French School was not a physical structure with an established curriculum, but rather a cartographic mode of thought and style that was passed down from Rocque to Scalé, who in turn passed it on to his apprentices. Before Rocque's arrival in Ireland, maps tended to follow traditional Irish cartographic formats with few surveyors successfully experimenting with new methods or applying popular design styles to the same degree of finesse that was common in other decorative arts. Period Irish mapping had an unfortunate tendency to appear basic, outdated and occasionally crude. Yet Rocque, with his distinctive rococo style,[54] attempted to represent the subject of his maps in as realistic a manner as possible. His work represented wider European cartographic and art fashions and shed a light on the often older methods being employed by Irish survey practitioners.

Rocque returned to London in the 1760s, but Scalé remained in Ireland and went into partnership with William Richards in 1762.[55] Scalé advertised himself as a

---

50 *Saunders' News Letter*, 12 Dec. 1791.   **51** Mauro Ambrosoli, *The wild and the sown: botany and agriculture in western Europe, 1350–1850* (Cambridge, 1992), p. 358.   **52** Sarah Bendall (ed.), *Dictionary of land surveyors and local map makers of Great Britain and Ireland, 1530–1850* (2 vols, London, 1997), ii, p. 460.   **53** J.H. Andrews, 'The French School of Dublin land surveyors', *Irish Geography*, 5 (1967), 275–92 at 278.   **54** Anne Hodge, 'A study of the rococo decoration of John Rocque's Irish maps and plans, 1755–1760' (BA, NCAD, 1994).   **55** Richards died in an accident in 1766 and Scalé reduced his work rate after the loss of 'topographer, after the manner of Mr John Rocque',[56] and updated and republished some of Rocque's work after his master's death. Scalé's time in Dublin was a fruitful one, with a flourishing business based in Lower Abbey Street, a cartographic style that was difficult to match by his contemporary rivals and the birth of six children.[57] With his business thriving, Scalé took on two apprentices in 1770 and 1771,[58] both of whom would become highly successful surveyors in their own right: Thomas Sherrard (1750–1837)[59] and John Brownrigg (1748–1838).[60] By 1774, the two young men had become integral elements of Scalé's business and he was pleased to announce in the *Freeman's Journal* that he had

> entered into partnership with two young gentlemen, Messrs Brownrigg and Sherrard … on whose perfect knowledge in every branch of surveying, those that are pleased to employ them may have the fullest reliance.[61]

This triple partnership between three unrelated men was a highly unusual occurrence in eighteenth-century Irish surveying. Considering that Scalé returned to live in England soon after, however, it seems a wise business move to leave his two trusted employees to run his firm for him.[62] Sherrard and Brownrigg appear to have toyed with the idea of following in Rocque's footsteps in the late 1770s, through selling compiled maps of cities or countries then in the news. In 1777, the two men advertised a coloured map of Ticonderoga, a fort in up-state New York that had been the site of a prolonged siege that summer during the American Revolutionary War.

Sherrard and Brownrigg moved to 60 Capel Street and operated a joint business there from 1783 until they parted company in 1800.[63] Like his professional 'grandfather', Rocque, Sherrard tried to grace Dublin's newspapers as often as possible – albeit with his adverts lacking the flair of Rocque's:

> Mr Sherrard respectfully acquaints the public that he has removed from Capel Street, to no. 1 Blessington Street, Dorset Street; and that the more effectually to enable him to fulfil his engagements, he has taken into partnership Mr Richard Brassington.[64]

---

his business partner.   **56** Scalé, *Tables for the easy valuing of estates*, preface.   **57** William Bernard (1766–9), Henrietta Anne (1767–1850), Bernard (1770–1852, vicar of Baintree, Essex), Charlotte (1772–3), Morley (b. & d. 1773) and Margaret Sophia (m. 1807): Bendall (ed.), *Dictionary of land surveyors*, ii, p. 25. Two of Scalé's children died in 1773 – Charlotte and Morley.   **58** *Freeman's Journal*, 13 Jan. 1770; 12 Sept. 1771.   **59** Bendall (ed.), *Dictionary of land surveyors*, ii, p. 26.   **60** Ibid., p. 461.   **61** *Freeman's Journal*, 19 Mar. 1774.   **62** '… instructions from persons residing in England or foreign parts, will be received by Mr Scalé, at Mangrove near Burnwood, Essex; domestic commands as usual by Mssrs Brownrigg and Sherrard at their house, Lower Abbey Street', *Dublin Journal*, 24 Sept. 1774.   **63** *Wilson's Dublin directory* (Dublin, 1783, 1800).   **64** *Saunders' News Letter*, 16 June 1800.

Based in a corner building at the junction of Blessington Street and Dorset Street, Sherrard's career went from strength to strength to include extensive estate surveys and land valuation, and his continual roles as secretary and surveyor to the Wide Streets Commission. He had previously taken on two apprentices in 1791,[65] as well as educating his sons William and David Henry in the art of surveying. Sherrard's work at times resembled that of a corporate body rather than a small practice, as alongside his surveying partnership he also advertised a land-valuation business with his son William from 1806 onwards.[66]

Brownrigg became one of Ireland's top canal surveyors, opening up a surveying practice at 63 Grafton Street,[67] next door to a relation, possibly his brother, Henry Brownrigg. His new apprentices included Thomas Murray and the eminent John Longfield. The Sherrard/Brownrigg partnership is a difficult one to judge on a personal level. Brownrigg and his wife, Catherine, named their son Thomas,[68] possibly after Sherrard, yet by the 1820s Brownrigg was openly criticizing his former partner for the high price of two guineas that Sherrard's company charged for a day's labour:

> If work coming from under their hands, was twice as well done as other people's, there would be no difficulty in the decision, but I have no idea this is the case! When Mr Sherrard and I lived together we were contented with one guinea per day clear of expenses![69]

Sherrard's company gained another associate in 1813 when assistant Clarges Greene was promoted to full partner. Sherrard, Brassington and Greene were once referred to as 'men of well-known skill, probity and abilities',[70] and appear to have been relatively large players in the Irish surveying and land-valuation scene in the early to mid-nineteenth century. Sherrard's valuation and surveying practices divided sometime near his death in 1837 – the valuation company of Sherrard (David Henry) and Spencer remained in business until at least 1856 and the surveying element, under the name of Brassington and Gale, was listed as operating from 52 Sackville Street Upper until 1893.

This French School legacy is not a complete history of Rocque's apprenticeship lineage, but rather an example of one of the longest traceable lines of master/apprentice relations in Dublin surveying. It runs from the 1730s, with Bartholomew Rocque, John Rocque's elder brother, until almost the twentieth century. To be a student of the French School was a mark of qualification and pride for those who had completed their apprenticeship under one of its masters and as noted by David

65 Ibid., 12 Dec. 1791.   66 *Wilson's Dublin directory* (Dublin, 1806).   67 *Wilson's Dublin directory* (Dublin, 1779).   68 Bendall (ed.), *Dictionary of land surveyors*, ii, p. 26.   69 Andrews, *Plantation acres*, p. 443.   70 Letter from Revd Moore Fishbourne to Thos. Spring Rice, 12 Apr. 1824: *Report from select committee on survey and valuation of Ireland*, p. 70, [445], H.C. 1824, viii.186.

Aher when being examined by the select committee on the survey and valuation of Ireland in 1824:

> In what school of engineer were you originally brought up?
> In the French School of Rocque.[71]

The French School's success was unmatched by any cartographic organization, albeit an unofficial one, until the establishment of the Ordnance Survey in the 1820s.

SURVEYING AND SCHOOLS OF MATHEMATICS

In order to approach the surveying industry, a potential surveyor required some sort of formal education. Knowledge of mathematics and geometry, as well as various sciences such as optics, astronomy, hydraulics and mechanics, were all necessary to a surveyor's career and subsequent success.

France and England were the two great cartographic powerhouses during the eighteenth century. The Irish surveying industry followed a similar trend to their English counterparts, with heavy emphasis on the practical elements of the industry. The fact that Irish practitioners followed this trend, however, did not necessarily mean that they were ignorant of French influences and advances, with one Irish surveyor commenting that 'it is generally admitted that in all the arts and sciences, we are at least one hundred years behind the French'.[72]

In Dublin, there had been a professor of mathematics at Trinity College since the plantation surveys conducted following Cromwell's campaign.[73] Mathematical schools were quite common, especially in seaports like Dublin, throughout the eighteenth century, with mathematical teachers regularly being listed in the commercial street directories. Benjamin Donn, who ran a mathematical academy in Bristol, listed a contemporary example of the curriculum of mathematical school students:

> At the Mathematical Academy in Library House, Kings Street Bristol, young gentlemen ... taught writing, arithmetic, book-keeping, navigation and geography – elements of algebra, altimetry, architecture, astronomy, chances, conics, decimals, dialling, fluxions, fortifications, gauging, geometry, gunnery, hydraulics, hydrostatics, levelling, mechanics, mensuration, optics, perspective, pneumatics, shipbuilding, surveying, trigonometry, plane and spherical; with the use of mathematical and philosophical instruments in a rational and expedition manner, according to new improvements – also courses of experimental philosophy read on reasonable terms.[74]

71 *Report from select committee on survey and valuation of Ireland*, p. 108 [445], H.C. 1824, viii.79. **72** Semple, *A treatise of building in water*, p. iii. **73** E. Evans, *Historical and bibliographical account of almanacs, directories etc. etc. published in Ireland from the sixteenth century* (Dublin, 1897), p. 36. **74** Benjamin Donn, *An epitome of natural and experimental philosophy*

Dubliner Samuel Byron was a product of the Dublin Society's drawing school, which, although mainly associated with the fine arts, also offered geographical, nautical, mechanical, commercial and military studies.[75] Specializing as a draughtsman, he eventually obtained the position of city surveyor in the 1780s and produced some of the most beautiful maps in eighteenth-century Dublin.

Adam Martindale, 'a friend to mathematical learning', specialized in teaching both mathematics and surveying to his students in northern England during the late seventeenth and early eighteenth centuries. His pupils avoided problems common to students of surveying by having partners available to assist them in handling surveying chains to prevent 'exposing of [their] unreadiness to the view of middlesome people' by gaining experience in a supervised environment.[76] There were times, however, when the lessons learnt by Martindale's students required practical demonstration in front of an audience:

> When I first began to instruct youths in mathematical learning in Warrington, some of my boys' parents desired a sensible demonstration of their sons proficiency in somewhat that they themselves could in some measure understand, and particularly ... upon measuring a piece of land: Whereupon I took four or five of my scholars to the heath with me, that had only been exercised within the walls of the school and never saw (that I know of) so much as a chain laid on the ground: and to the admiration of the spectators, and especially of a skilful surveyor then living in the town, they went about their work as regularly, and dispatched it with as much expedition and exactness, as if they had been old land-meters.[77]

No such school is recorded in eighteenth-century Dublin, but the presence of mathematical schools throughout this era greatly increases the likelihood that such lessons were taught to Dublin's young surveyors.

THE MILITARY

In the wake of skirmishes, musket fire and canon volleys, came the surveyors. Despite the political and sectarian fallout from various British military campaigns and subsequent mapping operations in Ireland over the previous three centuries, military surveyors played an important role in the Irish surveying industry.

The military was a relatively large supplier of surveyors to the Irish industry from the sixteenth century onwards. One of the earliest military surveyors of note was Richard Bartlett, who surveyed large sections of Ulster for Queen Elizabeth I from 1600 to 1603 before meeting a violent death in Donegal.[78] The majority of

including geography and the uses (London, 1769), endpaper.   **75** *Dublin Journal*, 1 July 1783.
76 Adam Martindale, *The country-survey-book* (London, 1702), p. 65.   **77** Ibid., p. 66.   **78** Andrews, *Queen's last map maker*, preface.

eighteenth-century military surveyors were officers, usually engineers, who received their training either at the Royal Military Academy at Woolwich or the Naval Academy at Portsmouth.[79] One former member of the corps of surveyors working in Ireland was a Mr Hyett, who later became professor of military drawing at the Royal Military Academy, instructing cadets in surveying and sketching the country.[80] It was rare for the military to train personnel to fulfil a role based purely on land surveying. A large part of military training was in fact based on calculating artillery ranges, the physical laws that affect falling heavy bodies (shells), the weight of shot by different gun bores and practical mathematics relevant to military operations.[81] Brigadier General James Douglas also emphasized artillery and 'bombarding in its general perfection' as a key subject for military surveyors.[82]

Among the most well-known military surveyors of the eighteenth century was the somewhat eccentric Charles Vallancey (1726–1812),[83] with his military survey of Ireland being his greatest cartographic achievement. Other military surveyors of note at the time include the Taylors: Major Alexander Taylor (1746–1828)[84] and Captain George Taylor (d. 1841).[85] The elder Taylor produced an extensive roads survey of Ireland[86] with fellow officer Captain Andrew Skinner in 1778.

Regardless of where a surveyor received his training, a universal rule can be applied. The surveyor had to have a good understanding of mathematics and geometry in order to measure areas and distances. Abstract thinking and spatial awareness were also important abilities.[87] What drew individuals to the surveying industry, whether through family heritage, desire to see the world, financial gain or scientific curiosity, is unfortunately nearly impossible to determine, as it was a matter of personal choice, and Dublin surveyors rarely recorded their private thoughts on paper. One rare but highly positive endorsement survives, penned by Scalé, who referred to surveying as being 'one of the most profitable and genteel professions'.[88]

79 D.W. Marshall, 'Military maps of the eighteenth century and the Tower of London drawing room', *Imago Mundi*, 32 (1980), 21–44.   **80** *Report from select committee on survey and valuation of Ireland*, p. 198 [445], H.C. 1824, viii.79.   **81** John Robertson, *A treatise of mathematical instruments* (London, 1775), appendices i–xvii.   **82** James Douglas, *The surveyor's utmost desire fulfilled* (London, 1727), p. 81.   **83** *Hibernian Journal*, Nov. 1812.   **84** Bendall (ed.), *Dictionary of land surveyors*, ii, p. 502.   **85** Ibid.   **86** George Taylor and Andrew Skinner, *Maps of the roads of Ireland* (Dublin, 1778).   **87** Callan, *A dissertation*, p. 11.   **88** *Freeman's Journal*, 13 Jan. 1770.

3 'Very great and actual labour': surveying fees, salaries and costs in eighteenth-century Dublin

The Earth does not owe gratitude only to those who create books, unite maps to the art of geography and fit lands to sky and sky to lands as with a plumb line; but also to those who persuade, urge, correct and increase these works, promote them with money and expense, strengthen the feeble, recover the lost, and give shape and polish to the deformed, so that the illustrious offspring can be born and reborn and appear with beauty into the light and faces of men.[1]

Money and mapping are intrinsically linked in this statement by seventeenth-century Dutch cartographer Johannes Blaeu. Enthusiasm to increase the knowledge of the world, and willingness to correct cartographic mistakes of the past, to push the science of surveying into new realms and to refine the art of map making, are all important and noble elements. Yet, aside from these majestic and righteous ideals, his fundamental point was the importance of patronage and financial support for surveyors – in essence, the business and finances of surveying. Surveying is often considered as an art and a science, but what is also important to remember is that its main function, especially to the surveying community, is as a business. Surveyors could not live on the gratification of knowing that their cartographic style was in fashion or that their surveying techniques were scientifically sound – they needed cold hard cash. The main driving force behind the entire surveying business was a client's need for cartographic data and his readiness to pay for it. Surveyors were the skilled specialists that could obtain this information for them. Such clients ranged from heads of state[2] and civic bodies[3] to private individuals,[4] with varied require-ments for each individual survey. Evidence of the cost of surveying is difficult to uncover, as the majority of surveying in eighteenth-century Dublin was conducted in a private capacity, away from the detailed record-keeping of local and central government. Therefore, determining an overview of surveying finances requires significant investigation.

1 Johannes Blaeu, *Atlas novus* (Amsterdam, 1654), trans. I. Cunningham, quoted in Charles W.J. Withers, *Geography, science and national identity: Scotland since 1520* (Cambridge, 2001), p. vii.   2 John Rocque described himself as 'chorographer to the prince of Wales', *Dublin in four parts* (Dublin, 1756).   3 Wide Streets Commissioners, Ballast Board, Dublin Corporation.   4 Bernard Scalé, 'Wynnsfield, Kildare' (1772): map produced for John Wynn Baker, landlord.

A surveyor's payment, mainly established through either a flat fee or by the amount of land included in a survey,[5] covered his wages as well as costs of transportation, assistants' fees, equipment charges and possibly food and board. The price charged for surveys therefore varied greatly, often depending on the individual surveyors. It is also difficult to determine which method of funding was the most lucrative during this period for Dublin surveyors, as professional and financial success varied from individual to individual.

SUBSCRIPTION

Securing funding for a major survey project was the first step towards completing a finished commercial cartographic product. One favourite funding method used in Dublin was subscription. Through this method, the surveyor would advertise a proposed mapping project. Interested parties had the opportunity to pay approximately half the total cost of the proposed final map as a deposit, thus enabling the surveyor to obtain funds to begin the work. The subscriber could be further enticed into handing over money by promises of a free copy or a special reduction in the price of the published map. Overall, this method tended to be a hit-and-miss affair, with the surveyor's knowledge of marketing and consumer confidence often being the deciding factor.

In 1754, both Roger Kendrick and John Rocque went in search of subscriptions for their respective Dublin maps, in direct competition with each other. Kendrick's subscription fee was half a guinea, which was to be paid to George Faulkner, a newspaper publisher, of Essex Street, or to Kendrick himself in Kevin Street.[6] In addition, if his subscribers were sufficiently encouraging, Kendrick was willing to extend the bounds of his map to four miles into the country surrounding Dublin. This tactic would, in theory, open up a wider market of subscribers as farmers and landed gentry in the immediate environs could have villas and estates included on the final map. Yet Kendrick's Dublin map was doomed to failure due to his inexperience of such large urban mapping projects compared to that of Rocque.[7]

Rocque planned two maps simultaneously – one of Dublin city and the other of the city and its environs.[8] Like Kendrick, he charged half a guinea for the initial subscription fee and the same amount eight months later when he assured the public that the map would be completed. Subscriptions were taken by several booksellers in Dublin, as well as by Rocque himself from his lodgings in Dame Street. He encouraged his subscribers to review his extensive back catalogue, which could be viewed anywhere that subscriptions for his map were taken.[9] Three-hundred-and-forty-four people subscribed to Rocque's map, including his fellow surveyors Jonathan Barker, Bernard Scalé and George Semple.

Lists of subscribers enable researchers to gain an idea of which sections of society

---

5 *Drogheda Journal*, 27 Aug. 1796: Michael McGawley charged 12*d*. per acre. **6** *Dublin Journal*, 31 Aug. 1754. **7** Ibid. **8** Ibid., 7 Sept. 1754. **9** Ibid., 31 Aug. 1754.

Table 3.1 Notable subscribers to Taylor and Skinner's
Maps of the roads of Ireland (Dublin, 1778).

Earls	54
Viscounts	20
Bishops	17
Lords	32
English subscribers	13
Scottish subscribers	9
Generals	4
Colonels	6
Lt Colonels	9
Majors	17
Captains	21
Lieutenants	17
Cornets	4
Ensigns	5
Surveyors	5

were actively supporting the cartographic arts. George Taylor and Andrew Skinner
produced their *Maps of the roads of Ireland* (Dublin, 1778) with extensive use of
subscriptions.[10] Taylor and Skinner's list of subscribers was eleven pages long and the
breakdown of the 'respectable noblemen and gentlemen' subscribers included the
lord lieutenant Earl Temple, the lord chancellor, the lord primate, the archbishops of
Dublin and Tuam, the duke of Leinster, the duke of Devonshire and the marquis of
Rockingham. A breakdown of notable subscribers is given in table 3.1. This is not a
complete listing of all of Taylor and Skinner's subscribers but it demonstrates the
range of those parties who took an interest in their project.

Maps were not the only product of surveyors to find funding through subscription. With a keen market from both professional and amateur surveyors in Ireland,
Jacob Neville (1752),[11] James Morphett (1760),[12] Thomas Power (1767),[13] Garrett
Heagerty (1783),[14] Anthony Divir (1786),[15] and Nicholas Walsh (with the assistance
of Thomas Sherrard; 1787)[16] all published various treatises, pamphlets and manuals by
subscription.

PRIVATE HIRE

Patronage served the surveyors' needs by supplying the gap left between subscriptions
and civic authorities. The majority of surveys were supplied to meet the private

10 Taylor and Skinner, *Maps of the roads of Ireland*. **11** 'A proposal for printing by
subscription: a treatise of practical surveying', *Dublin Journal*, 28 Mar. 1752.   **12** 'A complete
practical system of surveying', *Belfast News Letter*, 13 Mar. 1760.   **13** 'The universal land
surveyor', *Cork Evening Post*, 15 Oct. 1767.   **14** 'A new and curious method of surveying',
Cork Evening Post, 24 July 1783.   **15** 'The mariner and surveyors' companion', *Strabane
Journal*, 28 Aug. 1786.   **16** 'A treatise on surveying', *Dublin Evening Post*, 12 July 1787.

market, whether landlords, tenants or large bodies such as the church.[17] They were of such importance to surveyors that London-based Irish cartographer Braddock Meade (also known as John Green) wrote: 'indeed, without the patronage of the rich and the great, it is hardly possible that the sciences should ever thrive much in any place'.[18] Records of surveyors' expenses in a private capacity are more common than in archives and newspaper articles. Surveyors' charges usually followed one of two avenues: one was a charge by the number of days spent conducting the survey; the other related to the area of land being surveyed.

If a survey happened to be far from Dublin, it was possible for surveyors to advertise their proposed route and offer to survey lands along this route, as Jonathan Barker did in 1754 while making his way from Dublin to Cork via Waterford.[19] Generally speaking, the further the surveyor had to travel, the higher he could charge for his services. This was especially true for those held in high regard such as Barker. John Bannan, who was active in estate surveying in the early nineteenth century, was charging as high as several hundred pounds for a large estate, and as little as 6*d.* for a single field.[20] Some landlords, who were, for various reasons, unwilling to pay high fees to have their entire estate surveyed, could simply ask for an existing survey of their lands to be updated. Lord Abercorn followed this process in 1803 when he was quoted £500 for a complete resurvey of his estate, but instead asked for a revision of a previous survey conducted in the 1770s.[21]

Surveying prices, of course, had to move with the economic times and, as a surveyor's reputation grew, very often so did his fee. Thomas Sherrard, for example, charged a shilling per acre in 1792 but by 1820 he was charging two guineas per day as a flat fee. His former partner, John Brownrigg, strongly disagreed with Sherrard's high prices but did note that inflation had caused depreciation in currency since the time Brownrigg and Sherrard had worked together.[22]

Given the various rates and charges applied by surveyors, how much could an individual expect to make in a year? This figure naturally depended on how much work was available to the surveyor. The early nineteenth-century surveyor William Bald estimated that a surveyor could measure fifty to 150 acres depending on the day.[23] J.H. Andrews estimated that, considering the relatively little detail that Irish surveyors were expected to collect in the field, a figure of one hundred acres per day was not an unreasonable one. If, due to bad weather and office duties, a surveyor

17 Bernard Scalé, 'Lands belonging to Earl Clanbrasil, Dundalk' (1777), reproduced in Harold O'Sullivan, *Dundalk* (Irish Historic Towns Atlas, no. 16, Dublin, 2006), map 11. Francis Mathews, 'Map of lands in Templeogue' (1783), reproduced in Refaussé and Clark, *A catalogue of the maps*, pl. 32. John Roe, 'Map of the palace, Tallaght' (1811), reproduced in Refaussé and Clark, *A catalogue of the maps*, pl. 37, p. 85. 18 John Green, *Remarks in support of the new chart of North America in six sheets* (London, 1753), p. 3. 19 *Universal Advertiser*, 16 July 1754. 20 John Bannan, 'Bills for surveying, 1810–17' (NLI Rolleston Estate, MS 13794(6)). 21 J.H. Gebbie, *An introduction to the Abercorn letters as relating to Ireland, 1736–1816* (Omagh, 1972), p. 250. 22 Andrews, *Plantation acres*, appendix E, p. 443. 23 *Report from select committee on survey and valuation of Ireland*, p. 59 [445], H.C. 1824, viii.79.

could reasonably be expected to spend every other day at fieldwork, then an approximate yearly total of 15,000 acres could be covered comfortably. Based on Andrews' estimate for mid-eighteenth-century surveying pay rates, an annual income of £125 can be suggested.[24] Once again, the lack of centralized surveying authority meant that surveyors' charges were only kept in check by competitors.

SALARIED EMPLOYMENT

Apart from surveyor's private clients, there also existed the opportunity for salaried work to those with the right connections or skills or sheer good luck to obtain regular employment with a civic body.

One very profitable body for surveyors was Dublin's Wide Streets Commission. From its foundation in the 1750s, the WSC provided regular and well-paid work to several Dublin surveyors fortunate enough to be associated with them.[25] The WSC was radically reshaping Dublin's city centre during the late eighteenth century and required a regular flow of maps to assist with its projects. Surveying duties with the WSC consisted primarily of cadastral work – namely establishing property boundaries, assisting with valuations,[26] design of maps for the proposed streets,[27] and facilitating with the eighteenth-century equivalent of compulsory purchase orders.[28] The WSC finances came from a duty on imported coal and this was used to pay not only their surveyors, but also property owners affected by their work and grand juries. Occasionally, the costs for map engraving were paid for by the commissioners, such as the work conducted by engraver Edward Fitzgerald, who was awarded £12 4s. 4d. for his work on the commissioners' maps in 1802.[29]

Thomas Sherrard had some of the strongest capitalistic tendencies of any surveyor operating in Dublin at that time. His work with the WSC had the distinct benefit of supplying him with a regular flow of work, but also adversely reduced the amount of time he could spend looking after clients of his own successful private survey business. He was particularly astute in obtaining large, regular payments from the WSC, as epitomised by the following endorsement of his hard work written by the commissioners in 1791, which netted him almost £300:

> [We,] having found during the progress of their examination the very great and actual labour and close attention required to be performed by the said Thomas Sherrard in directing and superintending all the lines and levels of the new streets and building in the city of Dublin ... that notwithstanding the difficulties arising from the nature of the said business, and the clashing interests of individuals ... the said works have been executed and brought to

24 Andrews, *Plantation acres*, p. 240. **25** 1 May 1758 (DCA WSC/MINS/1, p. 3). **26** 15 Mar. 1762 (DCA WSC/MINS/1, p. 146). **27** 14 Feb. 1806 (DCA WSC/MINS/20, p. 17). **28** 10 Oct. 1810 (DCA WSC/MINS/22, p. 267). **29** DCA WSC/MINS/18, p. 110.

their state of perfection and we are happy to add to the public satisfaction under your orders, by the unremitting exertions of the said Thomas Sherrard for all of which labour and services he has made no charge whatever in his said accounts.[30]

In fact, Sherrard was perhaps one of the few eighteenth-century surveyors who thrived financially. His 1837 will stated that his estate was worth the princely sum of £8,571 12s. 2d., including £3,714 7s. 7½d. in securities and £1,456 15s. 5d. in other properties in Coolock, in addition to his Blessington Street home and horse and carriage.[31] In contrast, Sherrard's business partner Richard Brassington's net worth was estimated to have been £900 in 1837, including his home in Dominick Street, which was left to his wife Maria.[32]

Sherrard was not alone in his conflict between fulfilling his duties to the city and his work as a private surveyor. The office of Dublin city surveyor was created in 1679 to record the extents of city property out on lease by Dublin Corporation, with John Greene being the first to hold the post. Despite the regular income from this position, Greene found it difficult to balance his private and public work, and on many occasions was not present in Dublin,[33] likely surveying in a private capacity elsewhere in the country. Greene's continual absence from his official role and the subsequent frustration to the corporation led to the promotion of his assistant, Joseph Moland, as joint city surveyor in 1698.[34]

Over a century later, the holder of the same office, A.R. Neville, seemed to have the opposite of Greene's problems with civic cash flow. Neville was one of the most expensive surveyors to ever hold the post and seemed willing to try to extort as much money as possible from the city. Over the course of his nearly three-decade career as city surveyor (1801–28), Neville charged the city over £2,000. The city assembly became quite concerned with the amounts that Neville was charging, and in 1808 it was recommended that he be given a flat fee annually so as to 'prevent the bringing forward of any bills from the city surveyor in the future',[35] such as his unreasonable charge of ten guineas for simply examining maps at the town clerk's office.[36] While the recommendation of a flat fee was not accepted, the city assembly managed to restrict Neville's rampant charging by subtle methods such as making the tenants, rather than the city, pay for surveys of leased property.[37]

A flat fee was instigated for the role of surveyor of the Dublin Paving Board. This organization was established in 1774 to improve the paving, flagging and street maintenance throughout the city, and it employed a land surveyor to supervise work, map areas requiring improvements and pay contractors.[38] The position of surveyor to the

---

30 26 Oct. 1792 (DCA WSC/MINS/11, p. 106).   **31** Last will and testament of Thomas Sherrard (NAI IWR. 1837/F286).   **32** Last will and testament of Richard Brassington (NAI IWR. 1837/452).   **33** 20 Oct. 1690: Gilbert (ed.), *Ancient records*, v, p. 507.   **34** 24 Mar. 1706: Gilbert (ed.), *Ancient records*, vi, p. 49.   **35** 28 Apr. 1808: Gilbert (ed.), *Ancient records*, xvi, p. 87.   **36** 22 Apr. 1811: Gilbert (ed.), *Ancient records*, xvi, p. 253.   **37** Ibid. **38** 7 June 1776 (DCA PB/Mins/2, p. 138).

Paving Board was advertised in June 1774, with the set payment rate of £100 per annum.[39] Three surveyors applied for the position: Thomas Owen, Thomas Mathews and William Cox,[40] with a ballot among the members of the Paving Board being used to decide the outcome. Owen was elected and went on to have a somewhat difficult and turbulent relationship with his employers.[41] His payment was initially made on an irregular basis; however, by 1783, the board resolved that he would be paid each November[42] and that:

> the surveyor of this corporation shall not demand or accept any sum or sums of money, for measuring work done in the respective divisions [of the city], on pain of dismissal from his office.[43]

As a final point on surveyor's ideas on expenses, Bernard Scalé demonstrated that surveyors required a good business sense. He noted how even small expenses were watched and if possible the client was made pay rather than the surveyor: 'no letters will be attended to, unless free or post paid'.[44]

---

39 8 June 1774 (DCA PB/Mins/1, p. 4).   **40** Mathews was the then city surveyor and Cox was an accomplished estate surveyor. There is no known documentation relating to Owen. **41** See ch. 17 for more on Owen's employment with Dublin's Paving Board.   **42** 25 Apr. 1783 (DCA PB/Mins/10, p. 264).   **43** 27 June 1783 (DCA PB/Mins/11, p. 6).   **44** Scalé, *Tables for the easy valuing of estates*, appendix.

4 'The public may readily judge': surveyors and the media

November 1759; a pasture in rural Meath. Two surveyors face each other and a heated argument ensues. Fingers are pointed, insults thrown, tempers rise. This is a duel. It was played out on that rain-soaked field not with swords or pistols, as was common at the time, but with maths and measurements. At stake was something of immense value to both men – personal and professional honour. The cause of this professional contest was a series of newspaper debates about a disputed survey that had appeared in Dublin's newspapers in which both men tried their best to humiliate each other. The incident puts into perspective the key role that the media played in financial and professional success for the country's surveyors. An examination of surveyors and their relationships with media, particularly newspapers, puts flesh on the country's cartographic bones by adding the human element to the story of mapping during this time.

Most of what is known about the country's surveyors from this period is based on surviving maps. The newspaper adverts,[1] articles[2] and discussions (especially arguments)[3] related to Ireland's surveying community allow the surveyor's own words and opinions to be heard in a manner that is impossible to match through mapping. Such evidence demonstrates that there is often a story behind even the most simple and unassuming piece of eighteenth-century cartography. For example, few would guess that a simple and unremarkable cadastral survey conducted by Sherrard in 1799, would end up with the surveyor being the target of pick pockets and having to alert the public that 'the said map has been kept by some villain who foolishly supposes he might extort money'.[4] This chapter examines a number of surveying stories that graced newspapers at the time and demonstrates the surveyor's relationship with the media, for both good and bad.

DISPUTES

From the 1740s until the turn of the nineteenth century, a spate of land-surveying disputes appeared in Dublin's newspapers. The airing of dirty professional laundry for the world to see usually had one common cause – differences between two surveyors' measurements when calculating the area of a particular property. At first

1 Ibid., advertisement at rear of book. 2 Robert Gibson, *Dublin Journal*, 21 July 1752; John Hylin, *Freeman's Journal*, 11 Oct. 1787. 3 Peter Callan, *Dublin Gazette*, 27 Sept. 1760. 4 *Saunders' News Letter*, 19 Nov. 1799.

glance, this may appear to be a trivial issue, but rents for tenants, particularly in rural areas, were directly related to the acreage of the land they occupied. If a surveyor returned a result that was smaller than the landlord's figure, then the tenant could sue the landlord for the excess rent paid. The opposite was also true, and a tenant might find himself pursued by a landlord for extra and backdated rent if the land was found to be in excess of the original agreement. In such circumstances, legal and financial chaos could ensue for tenant and landlord, to the ruin of both. Surveyors had a direct and key role to play in this issue, and when two surveyors' area calculations failed to agree, the serious matters of professional pride and potential future employment were very much at stake for both.

In 1749, Kilkenny-based surveyor William Thornton was accused in the *Dublin Journal* not only of claiming an area of land was four acres larger than claimed by his opponent, surveyor John Noble, but also of deception by bringing an adjudicator, William Steel, to the wrong field to check the figures.[5] Thornton also appeared in the *Leinster Journal* nineteen years later, defending himself from more accusations by fellow surveyor Thomas Brown, but on this occasion he had the adjudicators' support.[6] The normally aloof Bernard Scalé was dragged into a dispute with Mathias Tannam relating to two surveys in Kildare and one in Meath in 1772.[7] Tannam claimed that Scalé was at fault and that all previous attempts to communicate with him had failed, however Scalé was more than willing to defend his junior partner, Sherrard, who had conducted the surveys: 'as to Mr Sherrard's return, I have accurately [calculated] it, and found the difference between it and my owner so trivial, as scarcely to admit notice'.[8]

A disputed survey between Richard Barry and William Higgins in 1784 was one of the less cordial to grace Ireland's newspapers, with Higgins challenging Barry to meet him on the field and re-conduct his survey:

> I will hold Barry or any of his friends a wager of twenty guineas that his survey is false … [and] pity him for his ignorance, despise him for his malice and think him unworthy [of] my notice.[9]

Unsurprisingly, surveyors were often reluctant to fight such battles alone and were more willing to call in a respected mediator to act on their behalf. The renowned Robert Gibson came to the aid of Charles and Richard Frizzell in 1758, during a dispute against fellow surveyor Andrew Conner,[10] backing their work and methods. Maurice Downer felt the need to remind Darby Dunne during an argument that he had already beaten Dunne with the help of the surveyor general in an earlier dispute and was willing to do the same again if he persisted with his acquisitions.[11] However heated such disputes may seem, they were generally limited to brief exchanges in

---

5 *Dublin Journal*, 16 Dec. 1749. **6** *Leinster Journal*, 20 July, 1768. **7** *Dublin Journal*, 1 Sept. 1772. **8** Ibid., 1 Dec. 1772. **9** *Hibernian Chronicle*, 3 May 1784. **10** *Dublin Journal*, 15 Aug. 1758. **11** Ibid., 22 Feb. 1757.

newspapers and can be seen as ill-humoured professional jostling rather than serious attempts to insult, harm or discredit opponents.

PETER CALLAN AND JOHN BELL, 1753–60

There was one incident that did not follow this trend, however. The longest, most stubborn and obnoxious surveying dispute to appear in Dublin's newspapers of the mid-eighteenth century was that between Peter Callan of Drogheda and John Bell of Co. Monaghan. A total of eighteen articles spread over seven years documented how a disagreement over a mere four acres of land spiralled out of control resulting in farcical accusations, absurd insults, attempted forgery, bitter law-suits and even threats of physical violence.

It began in 1753 when Peter Callan, author and surveyor, took it upon himself for reasons unknown to present to the public what he saw as the gross negligence of John Bell, an elderly surveyor who had been in the industry since the 1720s. Referring to Bell as one 'who by insinuating address, and want of opposition, has acquired the reputation of a good land surveyor',[12] Callan proceeded to list three separate incidents where he claimed surveys conducted by Bell in Co. Meath had resulted in incorrect measurements. Of particular note, in Callan's view, were lands in Gravelstown near Kells, which were owned by Bartholomew O'Brien and rented by tenant Bryan McConnell. These lands had been surveyed in 1731 by surveyor Garret Hogan, who had determined that they equated to 136 acres, which in turn determined the rent that McConnell would pay O'Brien. Bell had surveyed the same lands in 1747 and produced a figure of only 132 acres and, as a result, McConnell demanded a reduction in his rent as the land was smaller than originally thought. Callan challenged Bell to meet 'in order to make proper vindications in favour of his surveys, or submissive apologies for errors committed'.[13]

Not to be so insulted in the press, Bell accepted Callan's challenge so as to address the 'malicious and false advertisements ... so that justice may be done between land-lords and tenants'.[14] The two men, with their assistants, met on Monday 4 March and re-measured the land. There followed a lengthy gap, during which nothing more was heard of the matter in the media and one could thus assume that it had been fully addressed. This was not the case. Four years later, Bartholomew O'Brien, the landlord in question, published a harsh notice stating that Bell's poor surveying had been the reason that 'my affairs have been kept on one continual chain of trouble, these 11 years past'.[15] Apparently, during the resurvey in 1753, Callan had caught Bell and his nephew, also called John Bell, altering their chain and attempting 'several evasive tricks, which the said Callan immediately detected'.[16] After the survey, both parties went away to compile their results, but the Bells never returned and O'Brien demanded an apology, accusing them of being 'guilty of ... defects in capacity'.[17]

12 *Universal Advertiser*, 1 Dec. 1753. **13** Ibid. **14** Ibid., 24 Oct. 1753. **15** *Universal Advertiser*, 24 Oct. 1758. **16** Ibid. **17** Ibid.

Bell appears to have been genuinely taken aback by such accusations coming from O'Brien, who had been his former employer. He claimed that, following the resurvey four years previous, he had given his notes to two well-known surveyors and that they had agreed with him. Bell also suggested that at this stage perhaps the Dublin city surveyor or the surveyor general could be asked to mediate. More insinuations followed from O'Brien. He accused the younger Bell of stealing a map from the tenant McConnell and that the impartial newspaper reader would be easily able to tell if 'the said Bells have been judicious, honest men, in their occupation or fraudulent imposters'.[18] Such insinuations, or 'trumpery of rhapsody and sophistical questions',[19] as Bell called them, demanded addressing and Bell requested another survey with Callan of the lands, with witnesses present, to take place on 22 January 1759. The two Bells and their two witnesses waited in the cold for six hours at Gravelstown, but there was no sign of Callan.

At this juncture, fate dealt Bell a card he could not turn down. It appears that the articles submitted by O'Brien were in fact forgeries and had been penned and submitted by none other than Callan himself. When O'Brien had heard what Callan had attempted without his permission in such a virulent argument and one in which he had a serious financial and legal interest, he vowed he would 'horse-whip Callan for daring to make use of his name in so villainous a thing'.[20] Bell could afford to gloat in public about catching Callan red-handed, writing that 'the public may readily judge what kind of person Callan is', and that he ought to be persecuted and sued for deformation and damages.[21]

Callan, stubborn as ever, even with his attempted character assassination exposed, refused to acknowledge that he had done anything wrong. He claimed that O'Brien had originally asked him to use all means necessary to ensure that the matter was finished and that forging O'Brien's name had simply been one of his tactics.[22] He even went so far as to wager twenty guineas that he could prove Bell was wrong.

The continual arguments and deceitful behaviour by Callan was obviously beginning to exasperate Bell. In July 1759, he again challenged Callan to meet him 'notwithstanding all your false and malicious advertisements and mighty bravadoes.'[23] The meeting went ahead at 11am on 27 August, but Callan insisted on using a form of trigonometric calculation that neither of the Bells were familiar with, and the two parties left without the survey taking place but agreed to meet again in November.[24] Bell was obviously determined to make a final stand, as he had preformed the original survey almost twelve years previously and was resolute to defend it against 'any reputed crack-brained, crazy headed, lying splenetic pretender to surveying.'[25]

The November meeting eventually took place, but there was no sign of an end to the saga. Bell declared that 'the inclemency of the weather rendered it impracticable for such an old man as him to examine said survey at that time' and it was

18 Ibid., 21 Nov. 1758. **19** Ibid., 19 Dec. 1758. **20** Ibid., 7 Apr. 1759. **21** Ibid., **22** Ibid., 19 May 1759. **23** *Dublin Journal*, 21 July 1759. **24** *Dublin Gazette*, 20 Oct. 1759. **25** Ibid., 30 Oct. 1759.

delayed another nine months until August 1760, when, after seven years of fighting, insults and quarrelling, the resurvey finally took place. The survey party was joined by 'a teacher of mathematics, and a great number of surveyors and other gentlemen of curiosity'.[26]

The outcome for such a detracted battle was somewhat predictable – there was no definitive result. Bell still insisted that he was correct, had a statement signed by three mathematicians supporting his original value of 132 acres, and claimed that Callan had altered his surveyor's chains during the resurvey.[27] Callan doggedly insisted that his results were true and, in his own unique way, had the final word:

> we cannot expect propriety nor connection in the advertisements of a man who is inflicted with a compound of mental disorders as Mr John Bell ... for whom I cannot think of a better remedy than the use of St Patrick's [mental] Hospital.[28]

SURVEY OF DUBLIN: ROGER KENDRICK AND JOHN ROCQUE, 1754

Another clash of surveying interests fought out in the newspapers of 1750s, albeit in far more professional manner than the Bell/Callan debacle, was that of Dublin city surveyor Roger Kendrick and John Rocque. In 1754, both men were in the process of surveying for their respective maps of Dublin city, in direct competition with each other, with Rocque's clever and skilled use of media and marketing demonstrating clear advantages over Kendrick in such a large surveying undertaking. Rocque's map is still well received today, being subject to many reprints and reproductions in modern history publications. Kendrick's map, if it was even completed, has disappeared into obscurity.

Roger Kendrick was the verger of St Patrick's Cathedral[29] and held the office of Dublin city surveyor from 1735 to 1764, following the death of his predecessor James Ramsey.[30] In August 1754, Kendrick placed an advertisement in the *Dublin Journal*, stating that he aimed to produce a new map of Dublin and lambasted the previous dominant map of the city, the 1728 Charles Brooking survey, which he described as being full of gross errors. This was a clear attempt to show that Brooking's map was not only decades out of date, which was true, but that it was incorrect and that Kendrick's new map would not fall foul of the errors of the past. Aside from changing the scale, however, Kendrick's description of the area and decorations that were to be contained on his map sounded remarkably like Brooking's. Kendrick listed the intended boundaries of his map: 'to take in the Royal Hospital[Kilmainham] in the west, and Ringsend in the east; St George's Church or Summerhill in the North and St Stephen's Green in the south'.[31]

Each parish boundary was to be included, just as in Brooking's map, and Kendrick

26 Ibid., 13 Sept. 1760. **27** Ibid., 20 Sept. 1760. **28** Ibid., 27 Sept. 1760. **29** Roger Kendrick, 'Map of the liberty of Saint Patrick's' (1741). **30** 18 Jul. 1735: Gilbert (ed.), *Ancient records*, viii, p. 188. **31** *Dublin Journal*, 31 Aug. 1754.

proposed to incorporate perspective drawings of the most important buildings in the city – again exactly like Brooking's map. Using his position as city surveyor to his advantage, by having access to the latest maps of the city estates and lands, he stated that he already had a considerable part of the work completed and was seeking further subscriptions at a guinea a piece.[32]

The overall impression generated from Kendrick's initial advertisement is a continuation of Irish surveying traditions. His style and approach to design appear to recycle what had already come before him, showing no real ingenuity or uniqueness. It is interesting that Kendrick failed to mention his civic title as city surveyor in his initial advertisement.

John Rocque, on the other hand, made sure that the public knew who he was and in which cartographic circles he moved. Rocque became one of the most influential individuals in the Irish cartographic scene with his move to Dublin from London in 1754 and his foundation of the 'French School' of surveyors.[33] Referring to himself as 'Chorographer to His Highness the Prince of Wales', his initial advertisement stated that his employment in Dublin was at the request of the nobility and gentry of Ireland, who were enthusiastic for him to conduct a survey and plot a map of Dublin in the same style as his well-received maps of London and Rome.

Rocque's association with the powers-that-be in the country was as good a reference as any eighteenth-century surveyor could hope to get. Rocque stated that his map was to include the environs of the city (a good source for map sales to landed gentry) and the harbour (opening a market for traders, merchants and mariners), in addition to the surveying and charting of soundings from Dublin Bay, which in Rocque's own words would 'render it useful as well as ornate'.[34] Rocque seems to have ignored the Irish tradition of dismissing competitors or previous maps of the same area, preferring to focus on describing his own map's qualities in simple and relevant form.

Indeed, throughout the race between Rocque and Kendrick to produce their competing maps, Rocque's positive and enthusiastic adverts – a sound and logical marketing strategy showing Rocque's flair for self promotion and image management – stand in stark contrast to Kendrick's sombre notices. Rocque never once mentioned Kendrick in any of his adverts, thereby avoiding negativity by dismissing his opposition and simply not acknowledging Kendrick's existence, whereas Kendrick openly admitted that Rocque was his competitor, even once stating that Rocque's work was progressing at a faster rate than his own.[35] These announcements bear direct correlation to the two men's ability to organize a large and logistically complicated survey project in a competitive environment, while simultaneously conducting a marketing campaign. As the competition continued, this gap widened.

The following month, both Kendrick and Rocque appeared again in the *Dublin Journal*, although for very different reasons. In the first week of September 1754,

---

32 Ibid.   **33** Varley, 'John Rocque: engraver, surveyor, cartographer and map-seller', p. 83.
34 *Dublin Journal*, 14 Sept. 1754.   **35** Ibid.

Rocque and two assistants were measuring a baseline in the Irishtown area, which at the time was covered by mud-flats and marsh ground. Being unfamiliar with the tidal conditions in the area, the survey crew got into trouble and were caught in a rapidly rising tide. In proceeding back to shore via the shortest possible route, Rocque's two assistants found themselves in 'a deep pool; and had it not been for the timely assistance of some people gathering [on] shore, in all probability they [would] have been drowned'.[36] In submitting this article to the *Dublin Journal*, Rocque was following a dictum that is still familiar to spin doctors to this day – any publicity is good publicity. This incident, whether staged or not, had definite newsworthiness to it and, when published, would generate interest in those who may have been unaware of Rocque's work in Dublin.

In the same issue of the *Dublin Journal*, Kendrick also appeared, but with very different news than Rocque's. After initially trying to set out his city map on two sheets of imperial paper at twenty perches to an inch, Kendrick found that the paper was insufficient to show the full bounds of his project. He informed the public that his map would now be rescaled and his final product would appear on four sheets of imperial paper, minus the previously advertised profile drawing of the most important buildings in Dublin. As compensation to his customers, Kendrick reduced the cost of subscription to twelve English shillings, even though his paper costs would have doubled with the map now being produced on four sheets instead of two.[37]

At the end of his advert, Kendrick thanked the Dublin surveying fraternity for their support in his major cartographic project:

> N.B. He [Kendrick] has been offered the friendly assistance of several surveyors in order to expedite his work, for which he takes this opportunity to return his earthly thanks; for it might then not be deemed or looked upon as his own survey, and he was determined from the beginning to do the whole himself, if possible, he was on that account obliged to decline their friendly offers, and proposed to perform the whole himself. He therefore hopes that his great care will not turn out to his disadvantage, as he may thereby be behind Mr Rocque in point of time.[38]

There is evidence as to whom Kendrick was referring in his thankful message to Dublin's surveyors. Kendrick's associates in the wider Irish surveying fraternity would have seen the Rocque v. Kendrick battle as one in which they had a vested interest. George Gibson pointed out at that time that he, Gibson, was 'a citizen, son of a native',[39] possibly to stir up some patriotic loyalty in Irish surveyors. Writing in 1756, Rocque's own opinion of the Irish people, again ringing of a subtle marketing campaign, lacked the prejudicial rhetoric of his Irish contemporaries:

36 Ibid.   **37** Ibid.   **38** Ibid.   **39** Ibid., 2 Nov. 1754.

> The Irish keep up the most amiable society; are frank, polite, affable, make it
> their pleasure to live much with each other, and their honour to treat
> strangers with politeness and civility ... From my part, I have had the pleasure
> of being in Dublin above two years and have had all that time to be
> acquainted with the genius and temper of the people, and in the picture I
> have drawn of them I have only expressed the sentiments of my heart and
> paid to virtue the tribute that is ... due.[40]

Despite Rocque's threat to the status quo of Dublin surveying, Kendrick's own
admission of mistakes did not assist his reputation. Consumer confidence must have
taken quite a dip following the news that Kendrick had not initially planned his
project well enough to establish what sort of scale would suit his map. His removal
of the ornamental building façades would scarcely have assured the public that his
map 'will make both pleasing and in many respects very useful to the city' compared
to Rocque's death-defying surveying practices.

Rocque, however, was not infallible. On 2 November 1754, he published an
announcement in the *Dublin Journal*, stating that his original intention of showing
Dublin at the same scale that he had used for London and Rome could not be
produced in a one-sheet format as he had originally envisaged. Instead, the map
would be on two sheets, but he assured his existing subscribers that their costs would
not be increased. New subscribers would now, however, have to pay twenty-five
shillings initially, while the final map would cost one-and-a-half guineas. Possibly
sensing the potential harm that could be done to his business by the xenophobic atti-
tudes of his competition and the local press, Rocque made certain to state that he
used Irish labour in the survey and that he intended to employ an Irish engraver for
his final map.[41]

Kendrick's and Rocque's admission of errors are very similar. Both stated the
mistake made, both alerted the public to price changes and both assured their
customers that they would get the product out as soon as possible. For the modern
reader, however, the similarity of these mistakes and the manner in which the two
men dealt with them gives wonderful insight into their marketing strategies. Rocque
went a further step with his damage-limitation scheme. To avoid the public
becoming disenchanted with his work or believing that they had been deceived,
Rocque invited anyone who wanted to see what progress he had made to call to:

> see the original drawing in India inks (which are in great forwardness) and
> done in the same manner as they will be when engraved, he being willing to
> introduce the same method of engraving topographical maps in to this
> kingdom which he formerly brought into England.[42]

---

40 Rocque, *An exact survey*, quoted in B.P. Bowen, 'John Rocque's maps of Dublin', *Dublin
Historical Record*, 9 (Dec. 1947–Feb. 1948), 117–27. **41** *Dublin Journal*, 2 Nov. 1754.
42 Ibid.

This claim of a new method of engraving was another one of Rocque's marketing ploys that Kendrick simply could not match. Rocque's style was new to Ireland. Although those who had invited him to map Dublin would have already been familiar with it, it may have been relatively unknown to the general public. It was a break from the norm; a suitable medium to show Dublin in the same light as the major metropolitan centres of Rome, Paris and London. Rocque knew he had something different to offer, and he was more than willing to state this fact.

Rocque was the first to get his map on the market and his position in the cartographic history of the city was secured. His map marked a major turning point in eighteenth-century cartographic style and engraving techniques in Ireland and his works were met by enthusiastic approval by the city authorities:

> Last week, Mr John Rocque presented to their excellencies the lords justices his plan of the city of Dublin in four sheets, at which time there were present several of the nobility and gentry who approved of the plans as it was allowed to be the best of that kind ever published.[43]

Kendrick's map never materialized, and it is unknown whether a final version was ever completed. Rocque's marketing and clever use of the press cannot be seen as the sole source of his success in his cartographic battle with Kendrick, but it shows his flair for the dramatic and highlights the differences that existed between the European cartographic business mindset and that of the relative backwater of Ireland in the mid-eighteenth century.

SURVEYING TREATISES

Many surveyors expanded their publishing range far beyond mapping. One particular avenue followed by many Irish practitioners was the production of a surveying treatise or manual. Robert Gibson first advertised his seminal *Treatise of practical surveying* in the *Dublin Journal* in 1752, which demonstrated 'everything that is useful and curious in that art'.[44] Gibson focused his advertisements not only on its coverage of the most practical elements of surveying in Ireland, but also on four new techniques he had developed to measure the areas of right-lined figures and his observations on how to take measurements and tracings from the Down Survey. His target audience, in Gibson's own words, were 'persons who have any property in land, to lawyers in controverted surveys and to practical surveyors',[45] and he advised his subscribers that their pre-ordered copies were ready for collection on the presentation of a receipt. Gibson's book went on to become a success and was still in print as late as 1839.[46]

---

43 Ibid., 21 Sept. 1756. **44** *Dublin Journal*, 21 July 1752. **45** Ibid. **46** Robert Gibson, *The theory and practice of surveying* (Hartford, CT, 1839).

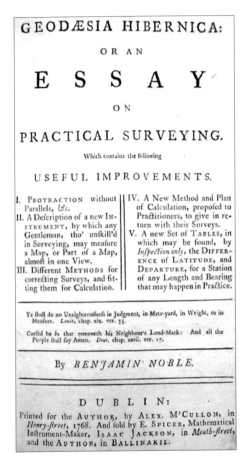

4.1 Cover of Dublin surveyor Benjamin Noble's *Geodæsia Hibernica* (Dublin, 1768) (courtesy of the National Library of Ireland © NLI).

Another highly popular surveying treatise from an Irish author was Benjamin Noble's *Geodæsia Hibernica*, presented as being of use to both professional and amateur surveyors (fig. 4.1). The publisher, Isaac Jackson of Meath Street, also felt the need to include a reference from the Dublin Society, who were:

> pleased to order that an honorary medal should be presented to the author, for his ingenious and useful performance, and that a number of the books should be purchased for the use of the society.[47]

Jacob Neville placed adverts for his treatises during the 1750s,[48] while Thomas Harding stated that his *Practical surveyor's best companion* would give 'a comparative view of Bourgh's [sic], Gibson's and Noble's methods, and the addition of two new

---

47 *Leinster Journal*, 13 Jul. 1768.   **48** *Dublin Journal*, 28 March 1752; 9 May 1752; 7 Sept. 1754; 2 Mar. 1762.

concise ones, never before printed'.[49] Harding's approach was not uncommon during this period. For example, *A treatise on surveying*, written by Nicolas Walsh and assisted by Thomas Sherrard, was advertised in the *Dublin Evening Post* in April 1787, in which he directly quoted magnetic variation calculations by Thomas Burgh (former surveyor general in the early seventeenth century) and Robert Gibson.[50] This association with well-known, already published treatises and their authors not only encouraged discussion of methods within the industry, but also, from a marketing viewpoint, directly connected a new and untested piece of literature with successful surveying manuals, thus encouraging sales.

Publication of surveying treatises also gave surveyors a captive audience to impress with their surveying capabilities. Benjamin Noble referred to his own skills and talent 'to survey land, as usual, for any gentleman &c. who is pleased to employ him'[51] in an advert placed in his *Geodæsia Hibernica*, and Peter Callan declared himself as a 'student and practitioner in the art of surveying'[52] in his *Dissertation on the practice of land surveying in Ireland*. In *Tables for the easy valuing of estates* (Dublin, 1771), Bernard Scalé went so far as to include a two-page advertisement for anyone who might have wished to hire him for his surveying and property valuation talents. Directing his advert at the gentry and landed nobles, particularly absentees living in England, Scalé claimed that his skills as a surveyor were so great that his client could in one view see:

> the topographical appearance of the whole; the quantity, quality and present value of each farm, with the exact account of the timber on the whole estate; by which return, the nobleman or gentleman becomes perfectly acquainted with the circumstances of his estate, the same as if resident thereon.[53]

His wide range of skills included

> old surveys copied and transferred into books in a very elegant and complete manner, for perpetuity; modern surveys examined, maps drawn for leases; demesnes and improvements surveyed and drawn with care and elegance; drawings and books of many thousand acres of different improvements may be seen.[54]

Scalé, aside from being an accomplished surveyor, also was able to partake in property valuations. In the same advert, he offered his skills to those who wanted to sell, purchase or mortgage lands or houses, offering to work 'with the greatest probity and punctuality and also with the utmost secrecy if required'. It seems that surveyor/client confidentiality was a service worthy of advertisement.

---

49 Ibid., 31 Aug. 1784.   **50** *Dublin Evening Post*, 14 Apr. 1787.   **51** Noble, *Geodæsia Hibernica* advert in full at end of book.   **52** Callan, *A dissertation*, p. i.   **53** Scalé, *Tables for the easy valuing of estates*, advert in full at end of book.   **54** Ibid.

Scalé was not above self-praise either. His 1776 *Hibernian Atlas* contained the following detailed and rather grand self-endorsement:

> In an age of dissipation and pleasure, when the instructive faculties are loos-
> ened by inattention, and the minds of the people in a great measure too much
> attached to trifling novelties, nothing but a work of extraordinary merit can
> reclaim the attention of the public to a subject of real utility, wherein novelty
> is blended with instruction, which at the same time amuses the imagination
> by mingling entertainment with genius. One stride towards the accomplish-
> ment of this great design is a judicious choice of proper subject. Amongst the
> first and most necessary of liberal arts is geography; by it we may form a better
> idea of any country than it is possible for us to conceive without its assistance,
> but how strange is it to reflect that no man has ever exhibited an actual survey
> of this ancient and of late cultivated fertile kingdom; but when it is considered
> how few [of] these are capable of the important undertaking, the wonder
> ceases, and had not the present design met with more than common encour-
> agement, joined with the extraordinary assistance of valuable materials and
> the author's constant residence and extensive practise for many years in every
> part of the kingdom, it never could have made its present progress.[55]

Marketing and self-advertising were central to the advancement of a land surveyor's career. Its execution often distinguished between those surveyors who were at the top of their profession and those who were not.

---

55 Scalé, *An Hibernian atlas*, preface.

Part II
The science

5 Manufacture and measurement: the scientific instrument trade and units of measurement

A land surveyor was only as good as his instruments and they, in turn, were only as good as their maker. The two core ethos that govern surveying – precision and accuracy – therefore originated in the work of the scientific and mathematical instrument maker. Such craftsmen, highly skilled, working with a mosaic of components and possessing elaborate metalwork skills, provided Dublin's surveyors with the tools they required to produce their cartographic works.

INSTRUMENT MANUFACTURING

The demand for scientific and mathematical instruments, in which land surveying equipment can be included, was small in eighteenth-century Dublin, compared to the demand for tools for other trades. Yet there was sufficient business available from surveyors, navigators, astronomers and institutions to keep a relatively healthy industry in operation throughout the century. The long working life of such instruments meant that only a few instrument traders could be supported comfortably, as reflected in business directories of the time.[1] The instrumentation industry did not work in an Irish vacuum, as Dublin was involved in the international trade in instruments. The English instrument maker Jesse Ramsden, for example, personally supervised the transportation of second-hand scientific instruments from London to Trinity College Dublin in 1793.[2]

The relationship between mathematical instrument makers and surveyors was generally cordial, with both parties interacting in a mutually beneficial way. Instrument makers often advertised themselves in surveying treatises, which were frequently written by surveyors with whom they had an existing working relationship. London-based instrument maker Jonathan Sission's advertisement at the beginning of Samuel Wyld's *The practical surveyor* is a typical example. Beginning by stating that the key to good surveying lies in accurate instruments, Sission assured the public that not only were his instruments accurate, but they also took advantage of the latest improvements available. The link between Wyld and Sission comes to light

1 William Wilson, *Wilson's Dublin directory* (Dublin, 1769–99), multiple editions. 2 N. Goodison, *English barometers, 1680–1860* (London, 1977), p. 64. 3 Wyld, *The practical surveyor,*

later in the advertisement, as Wyld mentions that Sission was 'the *only person* that makes *the theodolite, spirit-level* and *parallelogram* hereafter mention'd'.[3]

Sission was among many manufacturers or sellers of such instrumentation in London in the 1700s. Even Dublin, a far smaller city, had more than a handful of purveyors of scientific instruments.[4] A further example of a collaboration between an instrument maker and surveyor can be found in Benjamin Noble's surveying treatise *Geodæsia Hibernica*, where, like Wyld, Noble informed his readership that every instrument mentioned in his work could be purchased from a Mr E. Spicer, mathematical instrument maker, of Dublin.

As with the land surveying industry, a handful of individuals dominated the trade in scientific instrumentation during the eighteenth and early nineteenth centuries. Of particular note was surveyor/instrument maker Gabriel Stokes (1682–1768).[5] He trained as a surveyor under the watchful eye of the then city surveyor, Joseph Moland, who was also employed by the King's Hospital as a teacher of navigation and mathematics.[6] Stokes appears to have been a talented and highly regarded expert in surveying and precision instrumentation, as, by 1721, he had received a grant of arms with a surveyor's staff as his crest for skill in his profession.[7]

The earliest evidence of Stokes' work in the instrument trade was his repair of a large quadrant as well as supplying new scientific instruments to Trinity College Dublin in 1715.[8] As an endorsement for his bill to the college, Stokes asked the then surveyor general, Thomas Burgh, to support his cause:

> I frequently called at Mr Stokes while he was at work on repairing the quadrant belonging to the college, and I always observ'd he had been particularly careful in amending what was amiss; and it appeared to me when the work was finish'd & the observations made with the instrument afterwards, that he had perfected his work & adjusted the quadrant with skill & exactness: and in my opinion the several articles of the work done by him are moderately rated.[9]

Stokes became the deputy surveyor general in 1748 and was responsible for the development of the certificate of proficiency. During the 1750s, he opened his own office at the 'sign of the dial' in Essex Street, from where he conducted his surveys in and around the city, as well as continuing with his instrumental work.

Stokes also dabbled in engineering. In 1735, he published a document on supplying water to Dublin city, in which he argued that the city could be provided with fresh water without the need for water engines by simply using the natural laws of gravitation.[10] One of Stokes' more unusual pieces of work was his invention of the *pantometron* which was a miniaturized theodolite designed to be easily transported for

preface. **4** *Wilson's Dublin directory.* **5** Andrews, *Plantation acres*, p. 271. **6** L. Whiteside, *A history of the King's Hospital* (Dublin, 1975), p. 16. **7** Andrews, *Plantation acres*, p. 271. **8** Quadrant, Trinity College Dublin (TCD MUN/P/4/20/21). **9** Thomas Burgh, 6 May 1715, quoted in A.D. Morrison-Low and J. Burnett, *Scientific instrument making in Dublin, 1700–1830* (Dublin, 1991), p. 21. **10** Gabriel Stokes, *A scheme for effectually supplying ever part of the city of Dublin with pipe-water* (Dublin, 1735). **11** Robert Gibson, *Practical surveying*

surveying fieldwork.[11] His invention failed to grasp the surveying community's imagination and there are no known records of its use.

William King, possibly an in-law of Stokes, operated his own mathematical instrument workshop in Temple Bar. King was active in the industry until at least 1784, when he produced an octant for a Mr John Jackson.[12]

Three generations of the Lynch family, all named James, were also active Dublin-based instrument makers from the 1760s to the 1840s. The eldest is known from a single bill in Trinity College Dublin, dated 1767, for an air-pump, gauge and receivers. His son was the assistant to the professor of natural philosophy in Trinity and was also a member of the Royal Dublin Society. While certainly not one of the most influential practitioners of eighteenth-century surveying, James Junior was also active and knowledgeable in surveying matters. In 1802, he proposed making a map of Dublin county,[13] and was able to analyze several suggestions sent to the Royal Dublin Society by the American surveyor Richard Freeman on his ideas for improving circumferentors.[14] While disagreeing about the practicalities of the majority of Freeman's theories, Lynch did find a number of ideas appealing:

> I will now take the liberty to mention a curious coincidence of idea between Mr Freeman and myself on this subject [the diurnal variation], having for some time past projected a similar improvement; but I neither executed the instrument, nor published my intentions, Mr Freeman remains unrivalled in his claim as the original inventor.[15]

James Lynch Junior established his own instrument business with his son, which ran until 1846.[16]

As in most skilled professions in Dublin during the eighteenth century, foreign craftsmen made their presence felt. John Margas[17] and Richard Castle,[18] who moved to Dublin during the century, each produced a number of surveying instruments. Other individuals operating in the mathematical instrument trade at the time, and who fortunately signed their instruments, included James Woodside (1733),[19]

(Dublin, 1752), p. 160. **12** Morrison-Low and Burnett, *Scientific instrument making in Dublin, 1700–1830*, p. 22. **13** Ibid., p. 167. **14** James Lynch, *Observations on Mr Freeman's paper* (Dublin, 1806), pp 67–8. **15** Ibid. **16** Morrison-Low and Burnett, *Scientific instrument making in Dublin, 1700–1830*, p. 35. **17** T. Murdoch, *The quiet conquest: the Huguenots, 1685–1985* (London, 1985), p. 234. **18** Castle, *Essay on artificial navigation*, p. 7. **19** National Science Museum of Ireland, St Patrick's College/NUI Maynooth, inventory number 1912–393. **20** Geraldine Fennell, *A list of Irish watch and clock makers* (Dublin, 1963), p. 31. **21** 6 Jan. 1785, *Dublin Morning Post*, 'John Fawcett ... makes and repairs all sorts of clocks and watches ... theodolites, spirit levels, circumferentors'. **22** Whipple Museum of the History of Science, Cambridge, inventory number 698. **23** National Science Museum of Ireland, St Patrick's College/NUI Maynooth, inventory number 0729. **24** Ibid., inventory number 0731.

Alexander Stephens (1747),[20] John Fawcett (1785),[21] George McEvoy (1743),[22] Seacome Mason (1780)[23] and William Walker (1805).[24]

The levels of accuracy achievable in a period survey were directly related to the manufacture of the instrument used. It must be remembered that such instruments were made and assembled by hand, however, and often from materials that were liable to expand or contract depending on the relative atmospheric temperature, or could be easily damaged, especially survey chains, which were prone to being stretched. Modern survey instruments are constructed from synthetic materials, which are far more resilient to changes in temperature and are generally more sturdy. The element of human error introduced through the manufacturing process must also been taken into consideration. Surveyors of this era were well aware that such potential errors could exist within their instrumentation, with one commenting that 'no instrument is perfect, nor can be perfectly well used'.[25] Benjamin Noble estimated that a surveyor using a theodolite or circumferentor could achieve accuracies good to a quarter of a degree tolerance as 'it cannot be supposed that any instrument, finished by the nicest hand, can be mathematically true'.[26] He also made an observant comment on many of the surveying disputes that occurred in Dublin's newspapers of the mid-eighteenth century:

> From what has been said, we may see the absurdity of those who would be for taking the lengths of stations, or their difference of latitudes and departures to half links, or decimals; when perhaps at the same time, they are not within three or four links of the truth.[27]

UNITS OF MEASURE

Once a surveyor had acquired his instruments, he could begin to measure. But this was not the straightforward process that one might assume – measurements varied wildly depending on what system a surveyor used and occasionally what part of the country he found himself in. Like so many aspects of eighteenth-century surveying, there was a distinct lack of homogeneity in measurement units. In 1825, British legislation insisted on the yard as the unit of measurement, and all measurements were to be multiples and fractions of it, with the acre containing 160 perches or 4,840 yards.[28] Such laws were difficult to implement on a loose affiliation of surveyors. Traditional and archaic forms of measurement such as the Irish, English, Cunningham (named after an area in Scotland) and plantation acre remained on Irish maps for decades afterwards.

Discussions and descriptions of units of measurement are found in some of the oldest surveying manuals and treatises. Elizabethan surveyor Valentine Leigh's *The*

---

25 John Grey, *The art of land-measuring explained* (London, 1757), p. ii.   26 Noble, *Geodæsia Hibernica*, p. 78.   27 Ibid., p. 86.   28 5 Geo. IV.c.74 [Eng.] (1825).

most profitable and commendable science of surveying (London, 1577) described such units used in the sixteenth century and their relationship to each other:

> Three barley cones faire and round, taken out of the myddest of the eare, maketh an inche.
> Twelve inches make a foote.
> Three foote make a yard.
> Five yards and a halfe maketh a pearch, which in some countries men call a pole or rod.
> Four pearches make a day worke.
> Tenne daye worke or fourtie pearches maketh a rode or quart of an acre.[29]

Fortunately, by the eighteenth century, using barley cones as a basis of standardized measurement, no matter how 'faire and round' they were, had been replaced. Yet there persisted an assortment of measurement units and scales available to Ireland's surveyors. Irish, English, Cunningham and plantation measures were used in Ireland throughout the eighteenth century. Each was divided into acres, perches and roods, with differences existing between each measure's divisions. The Irish acre, for example, was the equivalent of 6,555 square metres, whereas the Cunningham acre was 5,226 square metres.[30] This problem was not unique to Ireland – in Italy, cartographers could choose from Ancona miles, Bologna miles, Fermo miles, Ferrara miles, Firenze miles, Perugia miles, Ravenna miles and Roman miles.[31] Robert Gibson described some of the more common forms of measurement in his *Treatise of practical surveying*:

> The *English statute perch* is 5½ yards, the two-pole chain is 11 yards, and the four-pole one is 22 yards: hence the length of a link in a statute-chain is 7.92 inches. There are other perches used in different parts of England, as the perch of *woodland-measure*, which is 6 yards; that of *church land-measure*, which is 7 yards (or the same with the *plantation-perch*) and the *forest measure perch*, which is 8 yards. The *Irish* or *plantation perch*, is 7 yards, as before; the two-pole chain is 14; and the four-pole one is *28* yards: hence the length of a link in a plantation chain is 10.08 inches. The *Scotch perch* is 18 feet, or 67 yards, or 6 Scot's ells. In the shire of Cunningham in Scotland, their perch is 18 feet, and this perch is used in some few places in the north part of Ireland, as the statute perch is in some other parts.[32]

29 Valentine Leigh, *The most profitable and commendable science of surveying* (London, 1577), section 4, p. 2. **30** *Unit comparisons* http://www.sizes.com/units/cunningham_acre.htm (accessed 1 May 2012). **31** J.H. Andrews, *Maps in those days* (Dublin, 2009), p. 86. **32** Robert Gibson, *Treatise of practical surveying* (Dublin, 1752), p. 130. **33** Rocque, *City and suburbs of Dublin*.

Occasionally, French units of measurement, called *échelle de toise*, can be found in eighteenth-century Irish mapping.[33] The toise, derived from the Latin *tensa brachia*, was the equivalent of six *pieds* or 72 *pounces*. Its equivalent in British feet was 6ft4in or 1.949m.[34] France itself had various separate units of measure, with one author describing how each French province had its own measurement variation.[35] The royal foot (*Pied du roi*, 1688–1799) was the standard unit of measurement that avoided regional variations and discrepancies.[36]

James Ramsey, Dublin city surveyor during the 1720s, was asked by Dublin Corporation to produce three brass standard yards as a form of standardized measurement for civic use. The three yards were to be directly based on 'the standard yard remaining in the custody of the chamberlain of his majesties exchequer in England'.[37] This task took Ramsey nearly two months to complete, at a cost to the city of ten pounds and seven shillings. Ramsey's role in establishing a standard unit of measurement with potential uses in many different industries suggests that he was no amateur surveyor, but someone within the same league as Benjamin Noble or Robert Gibson, whose writings on standard practice would be published later in the century.

In Ireland, maps were usually printed at a scale of one inch to x number of perches, with several scale bars drawn on the map to assist those who were familiar only with a particular form of linear measurement, that is, English or Irish. Benjamin Noble discussed this variety in measurements in Ireland during his opening statement in *Geodæsia Hibernica*:

> The common standard measure mostly used in Ireland, by which we express the contents or quantity of any piece of ground, is the *acre*, containing four *roods*, each rood forty square *perches*, the perch consisting of seven *yards* in length, the square perch 49 square yards; therefore the acre contains 7,850 square yards, or 160 square perches. In England, their acre contains as many square perches as ours, but their perch is only 5½ yards in length, so that their acre contains only 4,840 square yards. Hence, an Irish acre is to an English acre in the proportion of 7,850 to 4,840, or as 49 to 30¼. Which last are the square of the Irish and English perches.[38]

Such huge differences between the units of measurement could lead to serious confusion if the unit on which a survey was to be based was not decided at the planning stage. The location of a survey could also affect the type of perch used. The English perch was found most often in Cos Cork and Waterford, and the Cunningham perch (eighteen feet nine inches) in Ulster, with the Irish perch

---

34 Kenneth Ferguson, 'Rocque's map and the history of nonconformity in Dublin: a search for meeting houses', *Dublin Historical Record*, 58 (2005), 129–65. **35** George Adams, *Geometrical and graphical essays* (London, 1803), p. 458. **36** James Douglas, *The surveyor's utmost desire fulfilled* (London, 1727), p. 62. **37** 29 Apr. 1720: Gilbert (ed.), *Ancient records*, vii, p. 121. **38** Noble, *Geodæsia Hibernica*, p. 10. **39** Andrews, *Plantation acres*, p. 126.

(approximately twenty-one feet) being appropriated throughout the rest of the country.[39] In 1824, parliament decreed that the whole of Ireland was to be reduced to 'statute acres' and that the Irish acre was to henceforth be referred to as 'late Irish measure'.[40] Even after this officially came into effect, local measurement systems were often still found on maps in addition to the statute acre value. John Longfield, for example, continued to use both statute and plantation systems on his maps.[41] Map scales during this period ran in multiples of twenty perches, that is, 1 inch to 20 perches; 1 inch to 40 perches and so on., the logic being that forty perches were equal to ten chains, and so conversion between chains and links to perches was a simple calculation that could easily be performed in the field.

40 Fitzwilliam estate correspondence, 14 Dec. 1748 (NLI Fitzwilliam papers, mic.P.1020).
41 John Longfield, 'Glasnevin' (n.d.) (NLI Longfield papers, MSS 2789–90(88)). John Longfield, 'Portraine' (n.d.) (NLI Longfield papers, MSS 2789–90(92)). John Longfield, 'Grangegorman' (1829) (NLI Longfield papers MSS 2789–90(95)). John Longfield, 'Lands in Crumlin' (1829) (NLI Longfield papers, MSS 2789–90(98)).

6 'Exactness is required': survey instrumentation

Practicality is the paramount element underlined in eighteenth-century surveying manuals.[1] Then, as now, surveying was a profession built on scientific principles, geometry, mathematics, precision and accuracy. The goal of survey instrumentation was therefore to combine these principles in the most convenient and suitable form. The eighteenth century saw a steady increase in both the level of technological sophistication in instruments and awareness by surveyors of the limitations of such devices. Advances in the fields of optics, metallurgy and instrument manufacturing ensured that levels of accuracy that had remained relatively static in the preceding centuries improved exponentially throughout this period.

Surveyors often had more than one instrument that they could call upon during the course of their work. Each instrument had its own advantages and disadvantages; each could suffer from a variety of instrumentational errors and was the subject of trends in surveying, although Irish surveyors regularly displayed a stubborn preference for older, more established instruments over more modern equivalents with a higher degree of accuracy. To understand the instruments used, and particularly their limitations, is to understand measurement and mapping in this era.

THE SURVEYOR'S CHAIN

The surveyor's chain was the primary means of distance measuring for land surveyors until the development of electronic distance measurement systems in the late twentieth century. Rather like a large steel measuring tape, the chain was used to take direct measurements between two points. It consisted of a series of links and joints with brass handles at each end. Surveyor's chains were used extensively for mapping, and proved both highly adaptive and popular (pl. 1). Measurement with a surveyor's chain was calculated by the number of links in the chain required to reach from one point to another. If the two points were further apart than the length of one chain, as was often the case in rural surveying, distances were recorded as the number of chains and links required to cover the distance.

Surveyors' chains were decimalized to aid in determining distances without having to count every link in a chain close to thirty metres long. One popular variant

---

1 Wyld, *The practical surveyor*; William Leybourn, *The complete surveyor* (London, 1674); Robert Gibson, *Treatise of practical surveying* (Dublin, 1763); Castle, *Essay on artificial navigation*; Callan, *A dissertation*; Noble, *Geodæsia Hibernica*.

to this format was created in the seventeenth century by Edmund Gunter, professor of astronomy at Gresham College, England. The term 'Gunter's chain' is often found in treatises.[2] Decimalization was achieved by attaching small brass markers along the length of the chain, usually at every tenth link. Some surveyors also attached brightly coloured cloths along the length of the chain to help see the decimalized markers in long grass.[3] This adaptation was highly praised by surveying authors, with Benjamin Noble commenting that 'nothing could be more convenient than this decimal division of the chain'.[4]

As with many units of measure during this period, chain lengths varied, and were divided into groups depending on their length, known as poles. Generally, these consisted of two-pole and four-pole chains, being fifty links (33ft) and one hundred links (66ft) respectively.[5] Irish surveyors found that using the English four-pole chain was often more convenient, despite the requirement for measurement conversion, as the Irish plantation four-pole chain was too cumbersome.[6] The brass handles of the chain were often stamped with the length of the chain, to avoid having to unfold it to visually determine its length. In some parts of Ireland, the Rathborn chain was used and some practitioners noted that it was wise for a surveyor to note that his chain was 'fitted to the customary measure of the country where he lives',[7] to avoid confusion.

Surveyors' chains are large and cumbersome instruments and using them in the field was a two-person job. Even opening the chain and putting it away at the end of a survey could prove troublesome:

> Some little art is necessary in folding the chain. Always begin at the middle and fold up two links at a time, one from each side, until the whole are doubled up, when the handles will consequently be outside. Therefore, when the chain is required to be undone in the field, it only requires to be thrown out from the handles, thus: – *hold the handles in the left, and throw the chain out with the right hand.*[8]

The surveyor's assistant, also known as a chainman, would help the surveyor guarantee that the chain was laid in a straight line between the two points being measured and ensure that it was held tight enough to avoid slack altering the distance, but not tight enough that the chain was stretched. The quality and professionalism of the chainman employed for the survey was therefore of great importance to the accuracy of measurements:

2 William Leybourn, *The works of Edmund Gunther* (London, 1662), p. 103; Adam Martindale, *The country-survey-book* (London, 1702), p. 26; J. Waddington, *A description of instruments used by surveyors* (London, 1773), p. 6. **3** Wyld, *The practical surveyor*, p. 5. **4** Noble, *Geodæsia Hibernica*, p. 25. **5** Equating to approximately 66 and 33 feet respectively. **6** Noble, *Geodæsia Hibernica*, p. 25. **7** Martindale, *The country-survey-book*, p. 52. **8** 'A civil engineer', *The present practice of surveying and levelling* (London, 1848), p. 3.

it is necessary to have a person that can be relied on, at the hinder end of the chain, in order to keep the foremost man, in a right line; and a surveyor who has no such person, should chain himself. The inaccuracies of most surveys arise from bad chaining, that is, from straying out of the right line, as well as from other omissions of the hinder chainman: no person, therefore, should be admitted at the hinder end of the chain of whose abilities in, this respect, the surveyor was not previously satisfied and convinced; since the success of the survey, in a great measure, depends on his care and skill.[9]

If the distance was more than one chain length apart, a straight line between the two points (which was the path to be followed by the chain) would be marked out with pegs in the ground. This would guide the survey party during their work and keep them on track.

MEASURING WITH THE CHAIN

Measuring the distance between two points is good for survey measurements, but straight lines are rare in the real world, particularly in rural areas. Chain surveys worked on the principle of offset measurements. If a field was being surveyed, for example, a straight line would be measured between two survey stations, which usually consisted of a small marker or peg hammered into the ground. Using this straight line as a reference, the surveyor would take a second chain and measure to the edge of the field at a right angle to the base chain, which was known as an offset measurement. When the survey was transferred onto paper, the points that made up the edge of the field would consist of two distinct measurements – the length along the base measurement between the two stations and the distance it was offset from this base. Even the most irregular hedgerow could be accurately measured and plotted using this method.

Chain measurements were taken along the surface of the earth, which is rarely flat or level (pl. 2). Measurements therefore had to be transformed from their slope distance to their horizontal distance if the measurement was to be planimetrically correct. This could often prove extremely difficult, especially in the context of the Irish landscape, and the need for transformation between measurements at times caused dispute among surveyors.[10]

Another method to assist with irregular-shaped areas that required measurement was to subdivide them into regular geometric shapes, particularly triangles. This method was highly adaptive and allowed the surveyor to obtain the maximum information possible from minimal measurements. As such, it was highly recommended by surveying authors.[11]

9 Gibson, *Treatise of practical surveying*, p. 131. **10** Ibid., p. 134. **11** Wyld, *The practical surveyor*, p. 63.

Occasionally, surveyors' chains were known to break during transport. A small hand vice was carried by some surveyors to mend their broken chains, although this may have unintentionally altered the length of the chain slightly.[12] Diarist and surveyor Joshua Wight documented the satisfaction he had with his own well manufactured chain:

> [It is an] excellent plantation chain, made by the ingenious Daniel Voster; the wire was well tempered and strong and the rings true, and so well turned that it never broke with me all the while nor seldom a chink in the chain, nor never opened but one in one of the rings.[13]

The stretching and pulling that a chain endured during its daily work was a more regular source of error. In ideal circumstances, an error of a half link in every ten chains could be expected,[14] increasing greatly the more stretched the chain became. There were a number of options available to surveyors working in the field with stretched chains, with two popular methods being to compare the chain's length at the start of the survey against a known measurement staff, or the reduction of the chain length by one or two links to compensate for the stretching it would encounter during the survey:[15]

> I have been informed by an accurate and very intelligent surveyor, that when the chain has been much used, he has generally found it necessary to shorten it every second or third day. Chains made of strong wire are preferred.[16]

The chains utilized on a daily basis by Dublin surveyors were of an adequate accuracy to allow them to complete their work. There were nonetheless occasions on which a chain's accuracy went far beyond the scope of regular surveying. General William Roy had a purpose-built heavy-duty chain for his measurement of the Hounslow-Heath baseline in London during the triangulation survey of Britain in 1784. This chain was far more durable and exact than any chains found in contemporary Irish surveying and was built to produce highly accurate results, yet withstand extensive manual handling, or occasional pranks on his assistants:

> This most excellent chain seems not to have suffered any perceptible extension from the use that has hitherto been made of it. It is so accurately constructed, that when stretched out on the ground, as in common use ... if a person, laying hold of either end with both hands, gives it a flip or jerk, the motion is, in a few seconds, communicated to the other end, in a beautiful

12 Hammond, *The practical surveyor*, p. 66. **13** Joshua Wight's diary, 25 Sept. 1752 (Friends Library, Dublin). **14** Noble, *Geodæsia Hibernica*, p. 79. **15** Wyld, *The practical surveyor*, p. 6; Noble, *Geodæsia Hibernica*, p. 79. **16** Adams, *Geometrical and graphical essays*, p. 190.

vertical serpentine line; when the person holding that handle receives a sudden shock, by the weight of the chain pulling him forcibly.[17]

This special purpose chain helped Roy win the Royal Society of London's Copley medal in 1785.

THE PLAIN TABLE

The plain table, also known as the parallelepipedon,[18] panorganon[19] or geometrical table,[20] is an instrument that has virtually disappeared from modern surveying. Even during the eighteenth century, the plain table was rarely mentioned in Irish surveying treatises.[21] Used to record angular measurements, the instrument consisted of a board fifteen inches long and twelve inches wide that could be separated into three parts for transportation. A central, removable, paper sheet, onto which observations were recorded, was surrounded by a frame divided into inches to assist in scaling the survey. This served also as a form of survey control when replacing the plain table's sheet.[22] A moveable sight was positioned across this paper, allowing the surveyor to take angles of points – thus the draft map would be created during the survey rather than afterwards from notes, as was the norm with most other instruments. Additional instrumentation could be added to assist in orientating the survey, such as a compass (fig. 6.1).[23]

The plain table's physical make-up proved to be its main weakness. It was, in essence, an exposed sheet of paper, and, as such, was highly vulnerable to weather conditions, especially rain:

> The great inconveniency of the plain table is that its paper renders it imprac-ticable in moist weather. Even the dew of the morning and evening is found to swell the paper considerably, and of consequence to stretch and distort the work. To avoid this inconvenience, and render the instrument useful in all weathers; by leaving off the paper, and setting up a pin in the centre, it becomes a theodolite, a semicircle, or a circumferentor, and applicable.[24]

The paper would also have to be replaced if the survey proved to be too large to display on one sheet, in a process called 'shifting the paper'.[25] William Gardiner noted that instrumentational errors were often beyond the capability of a surveyor to adjust:

17 William Roy, *An account of the measurement of a base on Hounslow-Heath* (London, 1785), p. 15. 18 Leybourn, *The complete surveyor*, p. 48. 19 Hammond, *The practical surveyor*, p. 31. 20 Arthur Hopton, *Speculum topographicum* (London, 1611), p. 93. 21 Gibson dedicates only four pages to the plain table in his *Treatise of practical surveying*, pp 162–5. 22 Ibid., p. 162. 23 Ephraim Chambers, *Cyclopaedia* (2 vols, Dublin, 1741), ii, p. 19X. 24 Chambers, *Cyclopaedia*, ii, p. 15T. 25 Gibson, *Treatise of practical surveying*, p. 162; Martindale, *The country-survey-book*, p. 102.

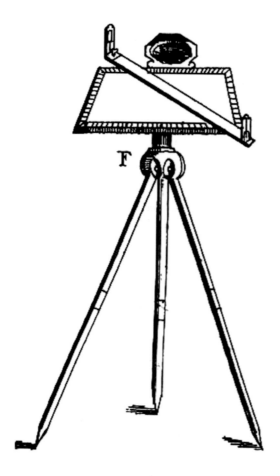

6.1 The plain table (from Ephraim Chambers, *Cyclopaedia* (London, 1741), courtesy of the Governors and Guardians of Marsh's Library © Marsh's Library).

> The plain-table surveyors, when they find their work not to close right, do often close it wrong, not only to save time and labour, but the acknowledging an error to their assistants, which they are not sure they can amend, because in many cases it is not in their power, and may be more often the fault of the instrument than the surveyor; for in uneven land, where the table can't at all the stations be set horizontal, or in any other one plane, it is impossible the work should be true in all parts.[26]

Overall, the plain table appears to have been still popular in the seventeenth century, but was considered outdated by eighteenth-century standards. William Leybourn's *The complete surveyor* (London, 1674) noted how the instrument was suited for measuring small enclosures in urban areas[27] and described the plain table and a similar

---

26 William Gardiner, *Practical surveying improved* (London, 1737), p. 41.   27 Leybourn, *The complete surveyor*, p. 41.

6.2 The surveyor operating a plain table in the field while a putti holds a chain (from William Leybourn, *The complete surveyor* (London, 1674), courtesy of the Governors and Guardians of Marsh's Library © Marsh's Library).

instrument known as a Parallelepipedon as 'the most absolute instruments for a surveyor to use'.[28] Adam Martindale supported Leybourn's preference for the instrument, referring to it as 'the best of all fixed instruments'.[29] Vincent Wing also praised the instrument in his treatise *Geodaetes practicus redivivus* (London, 1699), stating that:

> Amongst the manifold instruments which have hither to been invented, for the exact and speedy plotting and measuring of all kinds of land, there is none so plain and perspicuous in use and practice, as this instrument, and therefore it aptly reciveth the name ... of the plain table.[30]

The plain table's main advantage was its ease of use, especially for amateur or novice surveyors conducting work on small areas of land with minimal detail (fig. 6.2). For the professional, however, the same processes could be reproduced to a higher degree of accuracy and detail with a circumferentor or ideally a theodolite:

> The plain table may still be, if considerably managed, very useful in planning the ground plot of buildings, gardens or a few small parcels of land nearly on a level; but it is unfit in general for the practical surveyor, who ought to have an instrument whereby to plot large tracts of land as well as small, or hilly as well as on a level.[31]

28 Ibid., p. 48. **29** Martindale, *The country-survey-book*, p. 82. **30** Vincent Wing, *Geodaetes practicus redivivus* (London, 1699), p. 128. **31** Gardiner, *Practical surveying improved*, p. 41.

As highly praised as it was in seventeenth-century surveying treatises,[32] its failure to be even mentioned in the majority of eighteenth-century surveying treatises indicates the instrument's slow fall from grace over that time.

THE CIRCUMFERENTOR

The circumferentor was one of the most popular and common survey instruments used by eighteenth-century Irish surveyors. Easy to learn and effective in the field, this instrument became established in Ireland during the seventeenth century and continued to have great influence up until the mid-nineteenth century, when it was slowly replaced by the theodolite.

What made this instrument so popular in Ireland can be traced to its history of use. It was the primary instrument used by Petty's personnel during the Down Survey,[33] and its influence may have spread nationwide as a result. The exact date of when the circumferentor was first used in Ireland is not known, but it seems probable that it was in use since at least the late sixteenth century.[34] The instrument was closely associated with British colonial expansion as it was suited to taking surveys of large areas of land, particularly in forests, where line of sight was limited, and was also very popular in the North American colonies, as in Ireland.[35] With Irish land being stuck in the cycle of confiscation, distribution, settlement and then re-distribution after the various military campaigns fought on the island; the circumferentor would have found regular use in both military and civilian roles. Its ease of maintenance was another advantage over similar instruments, however this did not mean that it could be neglected or ignored:

> I say 'tis for want of land surveyors procuring good proof instruments, & keeping them in good order, that they fall into so many blunders & make such difference in their returns to the confusion of themselves & creating trouble for others.[36]

The circumferentor may also have been cheaper to purchase compared to the technologically more sophisticated theodolite, which may further explain its Irish popularity. The circumferentor measured angles – more precisely magnetic bearings. An angle is the measurement between two random points; a bearing is the angle between one random point and a known reference. A magnetic bearing used the

32 Leybourn, *The complete surveyor*, p. 48; Vincent Wing, *Geodaetes practicus redivicus* (London, 1699), p. 128. **33** Andrews, *Plantation acres*, p. 302. **34** Hopton, *Speculum topographicum*, p. 129. The instrument is also known as *La boussole* in period French surveying treatises: Louis Poussant, *Traité de topographie* (Paris, 1807), p. 154. **35** '…which is much in use in America, and in some other foreign countries, for surveying woods and forests': Waddington, *A description of instruments used by surveyors*, p. 5. **36** Diary of Joshua Wight, 25 Sept. 1752 (Friends Library, Dublin).

magnetic north pole as its reference, thus acting like a large compass. This capability
proved highly advantageous in Ireland. Circumferentors could work in areas that
were not visible to each other, such as widely separated fields or dense woodland,[37]
yet all measurements would be orientated in the same direction – north.

The instrument consisted of a round compass face with an elevated magnetically
charged pin that lay horizontal and gave the direction of north (fig. 6.3). The main
compass points – north, south, east, west – were often indicated on the compass face
with arrows or similar designs.[38] The compass was enclosed within a circular box,
either made of brass or, in earlier instruments, wood,[39] and the compass face was
covered with a glass top to avoid the magnetic pin being disturbed by the wind.[40]
The rim of the box was divided into 360 degrees, with each degree subdivided into
60 minutes, which allowed the surveyor to take his angular measurements. To use the
instrument during a survey, the rotational arms of the circumferentor were aligned
with the point the surveyor wished to measure. The bearing between magnetic north
and the direction in which the arms were pointing was then recorded from the
angular values along the rim of the box.[41] The instrument was mounted on a wooden
tripod, and fixed to a tripod by a ball-and-socket joint.[42]

Despite its popularity in Ireland, the circumferentor had several distinct faults. Its
rotational arms were fixed in a horizontal plane, which meant that it could not
observe survey points above or below it.[43] This would not have been a major issue
on flat land, but given the hilly and mountainous terrain that covers much of Ireland;
a surveyor would have to set up time and time again to achieve a good horizontal
view of points of detail or survey stations. As the circumferentor was in essence a
large compass, its ability to measure could be affected by magnetic anomalies. Large
deposits of metal in the earth's surface could alter the direction of the magnetic
needle, making readings incorrect. Surveyors at the time were aware of this problem,
and it concerned them that their measurements may be rendered incorrect through
no fault of their own:

> [the circumferentor] is very liable to attraction by minerals that hid from us,
> & unseen, especially on or near the mountains, which I have found by many
> years experience that my needles have faltered two degrees in some places.[44]

This may also have reduced its accuracy in an urban environment such as Dublin,
where metal was more common. One surveyor at the time suggested that carrying

37 Leybourn, *The complete surveyor*, p. 44. **38** Circumferentor dial by Johannes Lewis
(Dublin, 1688); circumferentor dial by Seacome Mason (Dublin, 1780–*c.*1804); circumferentor by Walker and Son (Dublin, *c.*1805–*c.*1818): all held by the National Science
Museum. **39** John Grey, *The art of land-measuring explained, in five parts* (London, 1757), p.
273. **40** Ibid., p. 33. **41** Gibson, *Treatise of practical surveying*, p. 148. **42** Wyld, *The
practical surveyor*, p. 55. **43** Callan, *A dissertation*, p. 32. **44** Diary of Joshua Wight, 25 Sept.
1752 (Friends Library, Dublin).

6.3a/b Circumferentors. Top – *c.*1770, by Edward Spicer, Plunket Street, Dublin, recommend by Benjamin Nobel in *Geodæsia Hibernica* (Dublin, 1768); bottom – 1688, by Johannes Lewis of Dublin, photograph by Finnian Ó Cionnaith, courtesy of the National Science Museum of Ireland).

a second reserve magnetic pin may be the only method of ensuring measurements did not go astray:

> if, after all, the needle does not play freely, place in the box another pin, or use another needle, or do both, and these necessaries a surveyor ought to have in his pocket while he is in the field.[45]

The main weakness with the circumferentor lay in a phenomenon present in the earth's magnetic field – magnetic variation. This stems from the movement of the magnetic north and south poles. While the effect was generally understood by eighteenth-century surveyors, they were unable to counteract it and its cause remained a mystery to them. The level of understanding that Irish surveyors had of this issue was discussed in great detail at the time (see below, ch. 7).

The circumferentor was capable of dealing with the majority of tasks required of eighteenth-century Irish land surveyors. Its vulnerability to error and its technical limitations, however, meant that it failed to maintain its position as the pinnacle of survey instrumentation and was slowly replaced by the theodolite throughout the eighteenth and nineteenth centuries. This technological gap was highlighted by English surveyor William Gardiner in 1737:

> In surveying commons, roads or wastelands, where only the shape of the boundens and the length of the lines are required nearly, but not with accuracy either in them or the quantity, the circumferentor may do well enough for the angles ... but it is by no means a fit instrument for taking a plan, where exactness is required; because we can't be certain of its giving any particular angle ... I have frequently found my needle varying more than five degrees [compared to a theodolite measurement].[46]

Despite its faults, the circumferentor's legacy lies in the thousands of maps of both rural and urban Ireland from the eighteenth century. Its impact on Irish mapping is undeniable, but its technological restrictions and its limited scope for further development meant that its connection with Irish surveying was finite.

THE THEODOLITE

The theodolite represented the cutting edge of eighteenth-century surveying (fig. 6.4). Despite the many characteristics it shared with the circumferentor, it proved to be a far more accurate and more capable survey instrument. The theodolite is an angular measuring device that is still widely used by modern surveyors, albeit now

---

45 Wyld, *The practical surveyor*, p. 60. **46** William Gardiner, *Practical surveying improved* (London, 1737), p. 49.

6.4 A theodolite constructed by London instrument maker Thomas Heath (photograph by Finnian Ó Cionnaith, courtesy of the National Science Museum of Ireland).

with over two centuries of technical advancements. It was used to record angles, not magnetic bearings. As with the circumferentor, it had a graduated horizontal circle, of about twelve inches, for measuring angles about that plane. It also contained a vertical circle perpendicular to this, which allowed it to record points above and below the horizon – an extremely useful adaptation for taking slope measurements. These two sets of angles, vertical and horizontal, coupled with a magnifying tele-scope, made the theodolite perfectly suited to high-precision trigonometric surveys, city surveys and working in large open areas. Unlike the circumferentor, it was unaf-fected by the magnetic properties of the earth and it also avoided problems caused by weather, which hampered the plain table.

In its basic form, the theodolite did not include a magnetic compass, meaning that it had an arbitrary reference system. Such references could include distant church steeples, or later trig(onometric) stations on top of hills, to ensure that its surveys were positionally correct. By using such reference stations, theodolite surveys could be conducted in separate areas out of sight of each other, connected by accurate trigonometry measurements and calculations. A large theodolite was used by Ramsden during the 1780s to connect the triangulation network of England and France together – perhaps one of the greatest surveying projects of the entire eigh-teenth century.[47] This also meant that the instrument was perfectly suited to working on surveys of large areas, such as counties. The theodolite was also suited to high-

47 Edwin Danson, *Weighing the world* (Oxford, 2006), p. 215.

6.5 The circumferentor's face and theodolite's dials in a combined instrument (photograph by Finnian Ó Cionnaith, courtesy of the National Science Museum of Ireland).

accuracy survey traverses and station networks for smaller surveys. It was highly praised by authors, 'being the most absolute instrument yet invented for surveying land'.[48]

Some theodolites were combined with a circumferentor to allow them to produce bearing measurements as well as angular ones (fig. 6.5; pl. 3). The presence of such hybrid instruments during the eighteenth century demonstrates that there was a distinct transition period within the evolution of the theodolite:

> This double observation is of great use to the surveyor; fore hereby he may either plot by the angle or the bearing, or by both, as he shall find most convenient; and also, may prove his observations before he moves the instrument.[49]

The history of the instrument in Ireland is difficult to determine. Richard Castle claimed to have brought the first example into the country in the 1730s,[50] and Rocque included a small image of himself working with such an instrument in his

48 Ibid., p. 35.   **49** Hammond, *The practical surveyor*, p. 19.   **50** Castle, *Essay on artificial navigation*, p. 7.

1756 map of Dublin. An instrument known as a 'theodelius' was in use in England in the early seventeenth century, however, so the possibility of its application in Ireland before the eighteenth century must also be acknowledged.[51]

Period surveying authors Gibson,[52] Callan[53] and Wyld[54] were aware of the instrument's advantages over both the plain table and the circumferentor. Wyld[55] and Gibson praised the instrument's adaptability to the difficult terrain and conditions that were often encountered by Irish surveyors: 'this instrument may be used in windy and rainy weather, as well as in mountains and hilly grounds'.[56] Callan noted that the instrument bore many traits similar to the semi-circle and circumferentor, but that 'he that knows how to use the theodolite, cannot fail to know how to use any instrument of the like nature'.[57] Surveyor general of Ireland Thomas Burgh was particularly enthusiastic about theodolites constructed by Dubliner Gabriel Stokes during the 1720s.[58]

The theodolite faced a difficult time in Ireland. The circumferentor had become engrained in the Irish surveying industry and the marketing of theodolites was slow. The instrument tends to be found in the work of the professional and engineering surveyor, which may be linked to its price, with the theodolite being mechanically far more complex than the circumferentor. It was, however, a more accurate and stable measurement platform and, while its initial popularity with Irish surveyors was limited, its obvious superiority ensured its long-term success.

The eighteenth century saw the introduction of the theodolite into the wider surveying community. While it may not have had the same impact on everyday work as did the circumferentor, it marked another milestone in the progress of such work towards the greater accuracy and standardization that followed in the nineteenth century.

51 Hopton, *Speculum topographicum*, p. 136. **52** Gibson, *Treatise of practical surveying*, p. 160. **53** Callan, *A dissertation*, p. 30. **54** Wyld, *The practical surveyor*, p. 66. **55** Ibid., p. 34. **56** Gibson, *Treatise of practical surveying*, p. 160. **57** Callan, *A dissertation*, p. 30. **58** Thomas Burgh, *A method to determine areas of right-lined figures universally* (Dublin, 1724), p. 13.

7 'This unaccountable attractive virtue': the problem of magnetic variation

The eighteenth century saw some of the most important and far-reaching connections between surveying and science of the early modern era. France and Britain underwent pioneering triangulation surveys that were the most accurate and advanced mapping projects ever conducted in either country. Neville Maskelyn conducted his famous Schiehallion experiment in Scotland in 1772 to determine the earth's density, which depended greatly on surveying techniques and technology. European explorers travelled the world's oceans, mapping unknown and distant continents. The mysteries of the earth and its lands were slowly but inexorably removed.

Dublin's surveyors failed to match such lofty cartographic goals, however they were not entirely removed from scientific discussion or experimentation. One issue that directly affected the city's surveyors during this period was the phenomenon of magnetic variation. In 1786, a controversial publication by a Dublin mathematician, Thomas Harding, based in Meath Street, set in motion a series of articles and discussions that were highly relevant to the way in which Irish land surveyors operated. These discussions, as was typical, were conducted in a far from gentlemanly manner, with insults and insinuations being levelled by all concerned. Despite the venom contained in their words, the participants highlighted the level of understanding that Irish surveyors and scientists had on the important issue of magnetic variation. To understand magnetic variation is to understand one of the core issues of eighteenth-century surveying, not just in Dublin or Ireland, but globally.

During this time, the nearest an Irish surveyor could get to a reference system by which maps could be compared and combined were reasonably accurate latitude and longitude values. These were not always the most practical measurements, given the unreliable Irish weather and the time involved in taking the readings. Thus circumferentor bearings, all taken from the same reference point (magnetic north) were a quick, easy and cheap method of aligning scattered surveys or large estate surveys. Magnetic readings were also the primary method to navigate at sea and were thus vital to international commerce. But this method was also inherently flawed. Magnetic north does not always equal true north. Variations in the earth's magnetic field caused by the movement of the magnetic poles, known as *magnetic variation*, caused magnetic measurements to change year-to-year and had the potential to introduce errors into high precision surveys.[1]

The reason for magnetic variation remained a mystery until the discovery of the

---

1 Waddington, *A description of instruments used by surveyors*, p. 7.

magnetic north pole in 1837. Some of the earliest known observations of the phenomenon were by Christopher Columbus in 1498, during his third voyage to the Caribbean, and by Sebastian Cabot, son of John Cabot, during his attempt to discover the fabled North-west Passage for Henry VII of England.[2] Harding was not the only author on the subject, however. Edward Halley (1633),[3] William Whiston (1750)[4] and Joseph Delande (1762)[5] each published their theories on the causes of this variation with theories that tried in vain to explain the mysterious phenomenon: 'this variation is much greater in summer than in winter, and is always irregular during the Aurora Borealis'.[6] Another author supported this theory, but instead noted the time of day rather than season: 'the general cause of the [variation] arises from the sun's heat in the forenoon and afternoon [heating the earth's ferrous metals]'.[7] This issue even found its way into one of the great works of fiction of the early nineteenth century. In Mary Shelley's *Frankenstein*, the narrator's original mission was to try and locate the source of magnetic variation in the arctic:

> I may there discover the wondrous power which attracts the needle; and may regulate a thousand celestial observations, that require only this voyage to render their seeming eccentricities consistent forever.[8]

Shelley's use of the word 'eccentricities' is key to understanding this problem. Unlike true north, magnetic north varies depending on the observer's position on the earth and the year in which the reading was taken (fig. 7.1). For example, if a surveyor set up a circumferentor and established that magnetic north varied from true north by 2° west, he would find that after a year this difference may have increased or decreased. To complicate matters, the reading of magnetic north also varies depending on the observer's position on the earth thus readings taken in London, Paris and Dublin at the exact same time would not necessarily be the same. For surveyors, this could be of utmost importance. They regularly referred to old maps when conducting new surveys. Magnetic variation between the old and new survey may make it impossible to compare the two separate maps or result in incorrect measurements being given as true. At first glance, this may seem to be only a slight inconvenience, but when one considers the serious financial and legal consequence of incorrect maps being entered in property disputes or tenant/landlord quarrels, the significance of magnetic variation becomes apparent.

2 Charles Hutton, *A philosophical and mathematical dictionary* (London, 1815), p. 556. **3** Edmond Halley, *Theories of the variation of the magnetic compass* (London, 1683). **4** William Whiston, *New laws of magnetism* (London, 1750). **5** Joseph Delalande, *Exposition du calcul astronomique* (Paris, 1762). **6** John Hood, *Tables of difference of latitude and departure for navigators and land surveyors* (Dublin, 1772), p. 5. **7** Mr Carton, quoted in Hutton, *A philosophical and mathematical dictionary*, p. 555. **8** Mary Shelley, *Frankenstein* (London, 1818), p. 1.

7.1 A north arrow demonstrating magnetic variation (from John Rocque, *Exact survey of the city and suburbs of Dublin* (Dublin, 1756), by permission of the Royal Irish Academy © RIA).

THOMAS HARDING VERSUS 'MAGNETICUS IN ANGELO', 1786

The 1786 publication by Harding, unflatteringly referred to as 'rather extraordinary' by a nineteenth-century author,[9] summarized his findings of investigations into magnetic variation. During the month of May that year, he had taken nineteen separate readings of magnetic north and found that it lay on average 26°21' west of true north. By comparing his results to those of years past, Harding concluded that the westward movement of magnetic variation was a regular and calculable occurrence:

> This unaccountable attractive virtue (whether resident in the atmosphere or in the earth is equally uncertain) has engaged the attention of many since the invention of the mariner's compass, but in no particular so much as its wonderful change of position, which appears to be as uniform as any other motion of the solar system.[10]

9 Hutton, *A philosophical and mathematical dictionary*, p. 553. **10** *Hibernian Journal*, 29 May

Harding concluded by stating that he was unsure if this westward trend would ever stop and that the magnetic north and south poles could reverse polarity and positions, which at the time was unheard of by scientists, but is now a known occurrence.[11] Harding reached a figure of a regular westward movement of thirteen minutes per annum. If changes in variation were indeed regular and calculable, then effects on Ireland's land surveyors would be felt immediately. A catalogue of the level of magnetic variation for any given year, both future and past, could be produced, resulting in a beneficial resource for the country's surveyors to correct circumferentor measurements. It also had the potential of reopening many legal boundary disputes, in which such a catalogue could be used as evidence of incorrect mapping. But was Harding correct? Was his scientific method sound and were his conclusions apt?

Almost a month later, a response was printed in the *Hibernian Journal* regarding Harding's work, and it was not a positive one. Harding's detractor, writing under the pseudonym *Magneticus in Angelo*, publically dismissed each of Harding's findings, particularly the one claiming that the variation changed at a calculable rate each year. Despite Magneticus' recognition of Harding's mathematical abilities, he also made sure to belittle him, by claiming that the value of magnetic variation is something that 'every common seaman and surveyor knows also how to find'.[12]

Harding failed to respond to (or simply ignored) Magneticus in Angelo's initial reply, so it was again printed in the *Volunteer's Journal*. This second publication was enough to cause Harding to break his silence. Calling Magneticus 'an obscure writer', Harding defended his claim that knowledge of the variation of the needle was essential to surveying and stated that Magneticus obviously was not familiar with the science of surveying. Noting that Magneticus failed to supply any figures to support his dismissal of Harding's work, Harding challenged him to back up his claims with evidence:

> I therefore call upon him for the proof of his objections: if he advances an iota of anything like reasons, I shall corroborate what I have said by abundant authorities; if he withholds them from the public, I shall take no further notice of an illiberal anonymous writer, who only substitutes assertion for demonstration and abuse for argument.[13]

Magneticus, not to be dismissed, responded by listing readings taken from several mathematicians and astronomers, including Burrows (1580), Gunter (1622) and Graham (1722), quoting their figures of magnetic variation and stating that these demonstrated that the change in this variation was not regular or predictable. He

1786. **11** Earth Changes: Magnetic Field Reversal, pesn.com/2005/02/27/6900064_ Magnet_Pole_Shift (accessed 1 May 2012). This has been proven to have occurred on several occasions, shown by changing polarity of rocks extracted from the mid-Atlantic ridge rift system. Such samples have significantly expanded knowledge of sea floor spreading and helped explain continental drift theory. **12** *Hibernian Journal*, 29 May 1786. **13** Ibid., 30 Aug. 1786.

continued by implying that Harding's knowledge of simple mathematics was either missing or he must have had an uncommon knowledge of it. He asserted that Harding mistook what he said about variation not being important to surveying, but rather the knowledge of obtaining the variation and applying it was more important than actually understanding how it occurred.[14]

The mathematical gloves were off. Harding penned his next defence the following week, stating in great detail the results of his work. He gave the positions of the sun at the various times he performed his calculations, which was necessary to see how far magnetic and true north differed. He also determined that, of the nineteen readings he took to calculate the magnetic variation, the greatest differentiation from the mean was in the region of sixteen minutes, and this was followed by the details of his calculation that gave him the magnetic variation 26°20' for May 1786. Harding followed the explanation of his calculations by quoting the results of those scientists previously mentioned by Magneticus to defend his findings. By this stage of the newspaper battle, Harding appears to have grown tired of repeatedly defending his work and testified that he had supported his findings to the fullest and was walking away from the argument:

> Hereafter, Magneticus may snarl on, while he can get a corner in a newspaper to creep into; I, for my part, shall not endeavour to unkennel the cur. Like his variation, he may shift as he pleases, and bungle on in his usual uncertainty. I am determined to be uniform in one point, which is, that he shall never extort another *syllable* from me on the subject. Every word here is my own, which is a sufficient display of the comparative abilities of Magneticus in Angelo. Thomas Harding, Meath Street, Sept. 5 1786.[15]

Scientific discussion and personal insults had merged into one entity, as Magneticus delivered his response to Harding's insults with equal force and venom:

> On observing Mr Harding appearing before the public with an air of sufficiency, putting off his nostrum vapours of false science, which floated for some time past in the whimsical atmosphere of his brain, but are now happily dispersed without contaminating the understandings of the incautious with its noxious tendency. ... In his last address to the public, he concludes thus 'every worked here is my own'; but I can prove, if called upon, that he had the assistance of a certain mathematician, whereas I had not the smallest from any.[16]

But, between the insults and insinuations, Magneticus introduced a number of interesting ideas. He explored the possibility that magnetic variation was not the same when measured at two different points on the earth and that Harding's use of read-

---

14 Ibid.   **15** Ibid., 8 Sept. 1786.   **16** Ibid., 13 Sept. 1786.

ings from both Dublin and London was an inherently flawed methodology. He also referred to the work conducted by a M. Le Monnier, who in his memoirs affirmed that the magnetic variation in Paris was stationary for several years before his time and that it had repeated this stationary pattern in 1773. Cracks were beginning to appear in Harding's work, and while his argument with Magneticus had ended, there were others in Dublin more than willing to take up the challenge of attacking Harding's findings.

THOMAS HARDING VERSUS 'A LINEN DRAPER', 1787

The next salvo directed towards Harding came almost a year later in August 1787 from another critic, under the pseudonym of 'A linen draper'. Draper's argument began much as Magneticus left off – that Harding's work was only relevant in calculating the present magnetic variation and that any attempts to predict future variations would be impossible because the variation was random rather than regular as stated by Harding. To support his argument, Draper gave several examples of magnetic variation from London, Dublin and Paris in various years, and demonstrated that variation between these three cities was not regular and even but 7' per annum in London between 1580 and 1622, 16' per annum in Dublin between 1733 and 1751, and 6' in Paris between 1640 and 1666. From these clear examples, it is obvious that magnetic variation did not change at the same rate for every location, and Draper continued by stating that Harding either 'wilfully or ignorantly endeavoured to mislead the public'.[17]

Possibly trying to maintain some dignity after the Magneticus debate, Harding failed to respond to Draper's public challenge. On 8 September 1787, Draper again published his opinion on Harding's work, this time being far more forthright in his concern about the degree of truth behind it. Referring to Harding as a 'modern Merlin', Draper's personal opinion of Harding was made clear:

> There is a certain description of people we sometimes meet with, who are so wedded to their own opinion, however erroneous, that they will risque everything in sport of it; and it is very observable that the more chimerical this opinion is, the more inflexible such persons are in defend it – of this class your correspondent Mr Harding seems to be one.[18]

To demonstrate the errors behind taking magnetic variation readings from the same location but from dates decades apart, Draper gave the following example:

> Suppose I engage to perform a journey of 500 miles *uniformly* in 5 weeks: here if I travel 100 miles per week (neither more nor less) it is evident I fulfil my

17 Ibid. **18** *Freeman's Journal*, 8 Sept. 1787.

engagement, for this is a *uniform* motion; but if I travel 10 miles the first week, 20 the second, 30 the third, and so on, here it is equally evident that though I may perform the journey within the time, still it is not by a *uniform motion*, but a very desultory one, for no two days journey are alike; yet this is Mr Harding's idea of uniformity! – This is precisely his mode of proving his position.[19]

The logic behind Draper's argument was scientifically sound. If Harding had taken magnetic variation readings over a series of years from the same location and could show that the change in variation was uniform over this time, then Harding's theory would have been correct. But he failed to do this. Instead, he chose a narrow sample of results on which to base his findings. Modern research has shown that the speed of magnetic variation is not uniform, but can increase or decrease in any given year, thus proving that Harding was wrong.[20] There is also evidence that Draper had some knowledge of surveying, as he quotes Robert Gibson's treatise on surveying: 'if he [Harding] knows a better authority than Gibson, let him cite it'.[21] Such constant attacks on his work were too much for Harding, and he finally broke his silence in mid-September 1787, when he published a retort in the *Dublin Journal*, in which he insinuated that Draper was of poor moral standing, was 'a scoundrel, a pilferer &c.', and had simply used Magneticus' ideas as his own. These accusations were repeated in an article in the *Volunteer Evening Post* at around the same time, and Draper responded in kind. The anger behind Draper's words in a submission to the *Freeman's Journal* is almost palpable, as insults like 'incorrigible block head' and accusations that Harding was prone to 'vomit forth his crude, frothy ideas in the face of the public' resonate throughout. Draper challenged Harding to a meeting to conduct a number of measurements on variation themselves, all under the supervision of a set of judges appointed by the two men. Draper insisted that at least half of these judges be made up of fellow linen drapers and that a knight from Ballyfermot Castle also be appointed to review their work. Harding could appoint the remainder of the judges if he chose to defend his theories and accept the challenge.[22]

Harding failed to respond to the challenge. By October 1787, Draper was accusing Harding of being the laughing stock of European mathematics and pointed out that no land surveyor had rallied to his cause. Harding had published an open address to the surveyors of Ireland in the *Volunteer Evening Post*, saying that by retaking two of his readings, a somewhat scientifically inadequate approach, he had proven his theory correct. Draper again dismissed these findings and, like Callan in his fight with Bell, suggested that his opponent was suffering from mental delusions and that 'we must only prevail on his friends to make him a present of a strait waistcoat, and procure him apartments in Swift's [mental] hospital'.[23]

---

19 Ibid. **20** Magnetic north pole drifting fast, www.news.bbc.co.uk/1/hi/sci/tech/4520982.stm. (accessed 1 May 2012). **21** *Freeman's Journal*, 8 Sept. 1787. **22** Ibid., 20 Sept. 1787. **23** Ibid., 9 Oct. 1787.

At this point, a third and unlikely player entered the melee – John Heylin, a land surveyor from Mount Wilson near Edenderry, Co. Offaly. Heylin was a firm supporter of Harding's work and it was possibly after reading Harding's address to Ireland's surveyors that he decided to voice his opinion in the press:

> I cannot decline the opportunity which now offers, of testifying, in this public manner, my grateful sense of the advantages I received from your observations on the variation of the compass or magnetic needle. Having in the course of the last month taken a re-survey of a tract of land surveyed in the year 1724, during the interval the greater part of the ancient mearings were totally defaced – the map was perfectly safe – and the variation at that time (as appeared by the map was 13 degrees 15 minutes westerly. After having taken a fresh bearing of such of the stationary lines of the old survey as were not defaced, and comparing them with the bearings taken in 1724, it appeared clearly that the bearings taken at that time were less than present by 12¼ to 12½ degrees each yearly. This decrease, rightly applied (being nearly equal to the increase of the variation), I found to answer every necessary end and purpose – the lost or defaced mearings were perfectly restored – 9A 2R 27P regained and the true content of the land ascertained with the greatest certainty.[24]

Heylin made a mistake in stating that the change was 12½ degrees a year, meaning minutes instead, but he did prove one of the advantages to surveying of knowing magnetic variation. By being able to compare his measurable bearings with the change in magnetic north since the time of the original survey, Heylin was able to deduce the location of the missing boundaries of the property. Using magnetic north as a common reference system in this case helped solve a serious surveying problem, but Heylin's defence failed to meet Harding's expectations. Heylin was correct in stating that there had been a change in magnetic north between the two surveys, but again jumped to conclusions that this change had been uniform over time. Again, the sample data was simply too limited to prove that Harding was correct in his reasoning.

Harding's critics were closing in. Not only had Magneticus in Angelo and the linen draper gone against Harding in the newspapers, but so had a Mr Walsh of Waterford and Mr B. of Chatham Street, Dublin – a group that Harding was now referring to as 'this thundering legion'.[25] Possibly trying to help end the battle on a somewhat positive note, Draper extended a hand to Harding saying 'yet if he can behave himself for five minutes, and knows any person with whom he has interest sufficient to borrow a *clean shirt*, he has the linen draper's permission to make on the party'.[26] So, who was correct in their theories – Thomas Harding or the thunderous legion?

24 Ibid., 11 Oct. 1787. 25 Ibid., 16 Oct. 1787. 26 Ibid.

It seems that Harding's theories, though interesting, were wrong. While it was practical to have a catalogue of the magnetic variation for different parts of the country to compare past and present surveys, as demonstrated by Heylin's case study, there was simply no way at that time to determine that the variation changed at regular and calculable intervals and that future values could be calculated. Even in the twenty-first century, the position of the magnetic north pole is something of a hit-and-miss science, albeit with a higher chance of being close to the true value than Harding's estimations. Surveying, by its definition, cannot rely on approximate figures. Surveys must be produced to the highest standards of precision and accuracy, so eighteenth-century estimations of future magnetic variation values would not have been adequate for surveyors' use.

Harding's initial publication certainly added to the science of surveying and navigation, but probably not in the manner he had initially envisaged or hoped. Through his suppositions and theories, he provided a unique forum through which the level of understanding of magnetic variation in Dublin at the time was laid bare. This insight into a serious land surveying and cartographic phenomenon is of indisputable value to anyone interested in historic mapping and provides further perspective into the complex and occasionally controversial world in which Dublin's surveyors operated.

8 Miscellaneous surveying instruments

The instruments previously mentioned, while being the most common and widely used by land surveyors in eighteenth-century Dublin, did not represent their entire arsenal. There also existed a plethora of smaller, less common or more unusual instruments that met with various degrees of popularity during this period. It is important to review these alternative instruments as, while they did not regularly fall into the core of surveying practice, they were often of great use to specialized surveys.

THE LEVEL

When reviewing eighteenth-century maps, it is sometimes notable that there is a distinct lack of height data. Modern mapping is often inundated with height data, usually in the form of contour lines, which are regularly reinforced by colour patterns that mimic real-world vegetation. This results in many eighteenth-century maps appearing to be empty, with large sections clear of any markings or notes. One reason may be the lack of use of the level in surveying in Ireland at this time.

In view of the central role it plays in the modern surveying and construction industries, it is surprising that the level is rarely mentioned in eighteenth-century surveying texts. Peter Callan and Richard Castle were two Ireland-based authors who discussed the instrument as part of their writing surveys.

The level consisted of a telescopic sight with two transparent tubes, which were almost entirely filled with water or alcohol, leaving room for a small air pocket (fig. 8.1). The instrument was attached to a wooden tripod and was made level by the manipulations of small screws linking it to the tripod. Levelling measurements were not taken from the instrument itself, but rather by reading the decimalized markings on a wooden levelling rod held vertically by the surveyor's assistant. Callan claimed to have been able to take levelling readings from a gigantic distance of five hundred yards,[1] although this seems extreme as, over that distance, the earth's curvature would come into effect. Castle recommended a maximum distance between the instrument and levelling rod of no more than four chains or about ninety metres. Levelling was primarily seen as a part of engineering surveying and played a particularly important role in canal construction: 'there must be the greatest care taken in levelling right the ground which the canals are to be cut, a mistake in this point being in a manner irrepassable'.[2] Very little is mentioned about the level in estate or urban surveying outside of its engineering role.

---

1 Callan, *A dissertation*, p. 42.   2 Castle, *Essay on artificial navigation*, p. 7.

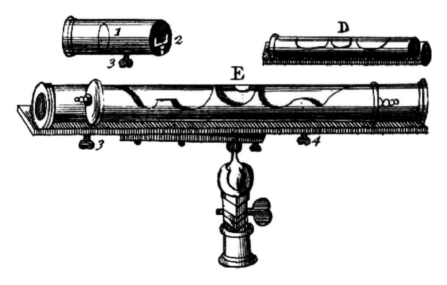

8.1 A basic surveying level (from Ephraim Chambers, *Cyclopaedia* (London, 1741), courtesy of the Governors and Guardians of Marsh's Library © Marsh's Library).

THE SEMICIRCLE

The semicircle was often used during the earlier decades of the eighteenth century. It was simply a half-circumferentor without the magnetic element. Its horizontal circle was divided into 180° rather than 360°, and was recommended for use in open areas, much like a theodolite and circumferentor (fig. 8.2).[3] The semicircle seems to have been a rare instrument during the eighteenth century, and this is reflected in the surveying treatises of the time. Gibson was the only Irish author to mention this instrument, albeit in less than a page of his work.[4] The semicircle was also known as a graphameter.[5]

THE PANTOMETRON

The pantometron was a theodolite offshoot that appeared during the mid-eighteenth century. The instrument, developed by Dubliner Gabriel Stokes, appears to have been a miniature theodolite, being only six or seven inches in diameter.[6] Stokes' invention, despite its compact size, failed to make an impact on the Irish surveying industry, and it is mentioned only once in eighteenth-century Irish surveying literature.

3 Leybourn, *The complete surveyor*, p. 441. **4** Gibson, *Treatise of practical surveying*, p. 161. **5** Chambers, *Cyclopaedia*, ii, p. 18R. **6** Gibson, *Treatise of practical surveying*, p. 160.

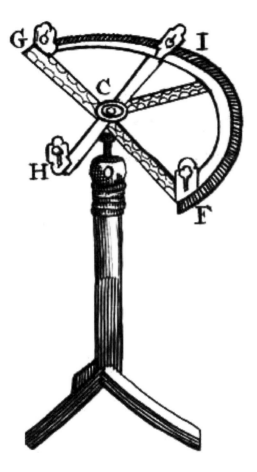

8.2 The semicircle (from
Ephraim Chambers,
Cyclopaedia (London, 1741),
courtesy of the Governors
and Guardians of Marsh's
Library © Marsh's Library).

TRIPODS

Tripods were commonly used throughout the eighteenth century to attach instruments to a secure and stable platform, as demonstrated by images of surveyors operating in the field.[7] Despite their common occurrence, however, none of the surveying treatises consulted, either Irish or foreign, described the apparatus in any detail, let alone gave recommendations from manufacturers for material from which they could be constructed. From images of period tripods, one can conclude that the legs were wooden, probably with a pointed metal tip at the end of each leg and a metal connection point for a surveying instrument at the top of the tripod.

7 John Rocque, 'A survey of Tullagorey' (Kildare, 1756), reproduced in Horner, 'Cartouches and vignettes on the Kildare estate maps of John Rocque', p. 58; Wyld, *The practical surveyor*, preface; James and Edmond Costello, 'A map of the land of Killamy' (1768), reproduced in Longfield, 'A Co. Sligo estate map of 1768', pp 57–70. Dupain de Montesson, *L'art de lever des plan* (Paris, 1763).

THE PROTRACTOR

The protractor was the instrument of choice when transferring surveying readings from field books to paper (fig. 8.3).[8] By supplementing the protractor's angular measurements for those of the instrument used in the field (that is, from a theodolite or circumferentor), the surveyor could plot his survey in the same fashion. Protractors were made of brass, ivory or horn and were about four or five inches in diameter.[9] Choice between the full circle or semi-circle protractor was left up to the user, as both instruments fulfilled the same function.

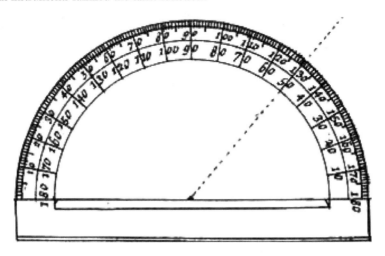

8.3 The protractor (from Ephraim Chambers, *Cyclopaedia* (London, 1741), courtesy of the Governors and Guardians of Marsh's Library © Marsh's Library).

THE FIELD BOOK

The field book was used to record data during a survey before the development of internal surveying software during the late twentieth century.[10] Despite its relative simplicity, the field book was an extremely important item, as stressed by Edward Laurence in his 1717 surveying treatise:

> You must always have in readiness in the field, a little book, in which fairly to insert your angles and lines; which book you may divide by lines into columns as you shall think convenient in your practice.[11]

8 Leybourn, *The complete surveyor*, p. 56; Edward Laurence, *The young surveyor's guide* (London, 1717), p. 113; Hammond, *The practical surveyor*, p. 30.   **9** Noble, *Geodæsia Hibernica*, p. 35.   **10** Wyld, *The practical surveyor*, p. 46; Leybourn, *The complete surveyor*, p. 59; Noble, *Geodæsia Hibernica*, p. 40; Gibson, *Treatise of practical surveying*, p. 272; Laurence, *The surveyor's guide*, p. 111.   **11** Laurence, *The surveyor's guide*, p. 111.

No. stat. Off-sets, &c.[1]	Chaing. and bearing	Observations	No. stat. Off-sets, &c.	Chaing. and bearing	Observations
A	269½[2] SE[3] 89½[4]		E	77¾ NW 77¾	Through a bog. A ford. Crosses the bounds.[5]
In. 0.15 0.15 0.00 In. 0.20[6]	0.00 15.00 17.00 20.00	*Begins at a ford.*	Off. 0.10 0.00 0.00 0.20 0.00 In. 0.40	0.00 35.10 60.00 62.00 63.00 66.00	
B	251¼ SE 71¼		F	30¾ NW 30¾	*A small river. The bounds mearing L—d M—tg—t's estate, in U— g—d.*
In. 0.20 0.15 0.15 0.05[7]	0.00 4.00 26.00 41.00	*Mearing Squire H—y's estate.*	In. 0.00 1.40 Off. 0.40 4.00 0.30 1.00	0.00 7.00 8.20 8.20 1-.20 23.00 36.25	
C	252¾ SE 72¾		G	345¼ NE 5¾	
In. 0.10 0.00 Off. 0.30 2.20 2.00 0.15 0.00	0.00 7.00 15.20 15.20 21.00 33.00 36.40	*Crosses the bounds.*	Off. 1.40 0.10 1.30	0.00 7.10 18.48	
D	162¼ SW 17¾	*A wall mears rest of 'Squire B—r's.*			
	41.40				

[1] Survey station.
[2] Bearing.
[3] Direction.
[4] Chainage to next station.
[5] Survey detail – each listed individually.
[6] Number of chains from station 1 to offset measurement point.
[7] Offsets taken – *In.* indicating inside the survey. *Off.* indicating outside the area contained by the survey. Some surveyors used additional *left* and *right* columns showing the direction of the offset. Measurements given in decimal chains: e.g. 2.00 = 2 chains.

8.4 Example field book entry (from Benjamin Noble, *Geodæsia Hibernica*, p. 40; annotated by Finnian Ó Cionnaith).

Surveyors' field books were small, hard-cover notepads, roughly equivalent in size to a modern A5 page (148.5 by 210mm).[12] Period field books were not produced specifically for surveying; they were ordinary blank page books divided into columns and rows by the surveyor. The only time a surveyor did not require a field book was when working with the plain table, as the survey observations were drawn directly on sheets of paper.[13] Figure 8.4 demonstrates a typical field book layout, with survey observations included. Layouts varied with each surveyor, as did their comment structure regarding survey detail, yet all contained the same basic information: survey station number/name; bearing or angle to next station; chainage to next station; and distance from offset measurements to survey detail. The station occupied by the surveyor, and the offsets from the main chain were listed in the first column. The distance along the chain line from which offsets were taken was listed in the second column, and comments and observations in the third. It should be noted that the recording of field notes varied from individual to individual,[14] and the example below is generic.

THE QUADRANT

The application of a common geometric coordinate system – latitude and longitude – was rare in smaller eighteenth-century Dublin surveys. It was, however, deemed of great importance in many maps at a county, provincial, national, Continental and global level. The theodolite could be used to establish latitude from astronomical bodies, such as the sun or North Star,[15] but another instrument available to eighteenth-century surveyors was the quadrant. This simple device allowed surveyors to establish their latitude by combining a series of measurements indicating the level of elevation from the horizon of an astronomical body, usually the sun, from the horizon in the morning and comparing the time at which the sun reached the same elevation in the evening.[16] By comparing these measurements to a series of loga-rithmic tables, a surveyor could determine his latitude. Once latitude was established, it was possible to apply corrective calculations to surveys of large areas, in order to compensate for the effect of the earth's curvature, thus correcting the cartographic projection. Distance to various parts of the earth's surface could then be calculated.[17] The simple Davis quadrant, and its more elaborate derivative, the Elton quadrant,[18] were popular in the early eighteenth century, with Campbell's quadrant being widely used in the latter part of the century.[19] Quadrants could also be used to reduce slope measurements to their true horizontal values.[20]

(NLI Mountrath papers, MS 2793).   **13** Batty Langley, *Practical geometry* (London, 1726), p. 8.   **14** 'Scarcely any two surveyors set down their field notes exactly in the same manner': A. Nesbit, *Treatise on practical surveying* (York, 1824), p. 36.   **15** Wyld, *The practical surveyor*, p. 176.   **16** Ibid., p. 177.   **17** Robertson, *A treatise of mathematical instruments*, p. 89.   **18** John Elton, 'The description of a new quadrant for taking altitudes without a horizon, either at sea or land', *Philosophical Transactions of the Royal Society*, 37:423 (1731–2), 273–5. **19** J.A. Bennett, *Divided circle* (London, 1988), p. 136.   **20** Wyld, *The practical surveyor*, p. 77.

THE PERAMBULATOR

A specialized distance measurement instrument operated by surveyors during the eighteenth century was the perambulator,[21] also known as the pedometer, way-wiser[22] and odometer (fig. 8.5). This instrument consisted of a wheel mounted onto a handle and was pushed in front of the surveyor. Each revolution of the wheel measured a specific distance (such as a yard), and a small protrusion in the wheel made a clicking noise every time the wheel completed one full revolution, thus allowing the surveyor to 'count' the distance between two points without using a chain. Additionally, a small box about ten inches in width on the shaft of the wheel contained three separate circles to record large distances – one rotation of the smallest circle being the equivalent of one chain, the second circle's rotation being one mile and the third being fifty miles. This adaptation had several advantages:

> The tiresome repetition of stooping with the chain or pole will be avoided. The expense of one or both chain-men will be saved. The length of a day's journey may be measured without keeping any account, till the end.[23]

The perambulator was best suited to low-accuracy surveys, such as road distances, because rough terrain could cause the instrument to give inaccurate results due to wheel slippage. It did, however, provide an easy-to-use replacement for survey chains when the accuracy obtained from chains was not required:

> The wheel, with its indices showing the distance, and its box and needle with sights showing the bearing or position in respect to the meridian, is an instrument speedy and sufficiently exact; provided we reject the breadth of the road and only regard the bearing and length.[24]

Gibson recommended its use for road surveys. The readings thus obtained could easily be converted into measurement values in common use at the time:

> Roads are usually measured by a wheel for that purpose, to which there is fixed a machine, at the end whereof there is a spring, which is struck by a peg in the wheel, once in every rotation; by this means the number of rotations is known. If such a wheel were 3 feet 4 inches in diameter, one rotation would be 10 feet, which is half a plantation perch; and because 320 perches make a mile, therefore 640 rotations will be a mile also: and the machinery is so contrived, that by means of a hand, which is carried round by the work, it

---

21 Waddington, *A description of instruments used by surveyors*, p. 6; Thomas Breaks, *A complete system of land surveying* (Newcastle-upon-Tyne, 1771), p. 285. **22** Adams, *Geometrical and graphical essays*, p. 197. **23** Hammond, *The practical surveyor*, p. 159. **24** Ibid., p. 12.

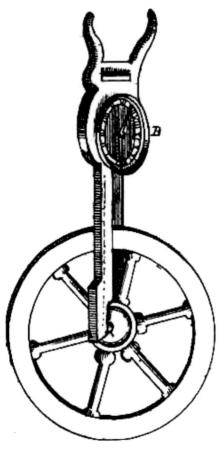

8.5 The perambulator (from Ephraim Chambers, *Cyclopaedia* (London, 1741), courtesy of the Governors and Guardians of Marsh's Library © Marsh's Library).

points out the miles, quarters and perches, or sometimes the miles, furlongs and perches.[25]

The instrument's method of use did, however, introduce a degree of error to results:

> It gives a measure somewhat too long by entering into hollows, and going over small hills. This is certainly the case; the meaning wheel is not an infallible mode of ascertaining the horizontal distance between any two places; but then it may with propriety be asked whether any other method is less fallible.[26]

One surveyor also acknowledged the perambulator's potential flaws when compared to chain measurement:

---

25 Gibson, *Treatise of practical surveying*, p. 134.   **26** Adams, *Geometrical and graphical essays*, p. 197.

Give me leave to ask the question, which of them is nearest to the truth? For I esteem it a matter of difficulty to gain the true and exact horizontal distance between any two places, by measuring up the surface of the earth, let the same be performed with the utmost care; for though the chain be free from some objections, which the other instrument [the perambulator] is liable to, yet what person can pretend to lead a chain in that horizontal position, which is required to make a true distance?[27]

Despite its simplicity and obvious practicality, the perambulator was rarely mentioned in Irish surveying treatises.

INSTRUMENT STORAGE

Instrument transportation was another practical concern for surveyors. These instruments were the sole means for a surveyor to perform his work, so if they were damaged or broken while travelling to the survey site this would have serious ramifications. Peter Callan complained that inexperienced or unprofessional surveyors carried their instruments in a loose and scattered fashion, which caused the sights, centre pins and other elements of the instruments to become warped and battered. Callan deduced that this was often the cause of poor surveying in Ireland, as damaged instruments are inaccurate instruments. To solve this serious problem, Callan suggested the following:

Let a pair of saddle-bags be made, each twenty inches in depth and twelve inches in breadth, with straps and loops for a hanging lock, and a long wooden case, with convenient clefts and concavities, to slide in, and fix all the afore-described sights, indexes, scales and sliding compasses; a leather case with a wooden bottom for the box of the circumferentor, a tin case for the protractor, and a long leather case for a roll of paper; all which, together with the ball and sockets, screw-pins, staves, chain and pins, pencils and colours, can be safely kept and carried in the said saddle-bags; and for the conveniency of travelling, a few changes of linen, with shoes and stockings, can also be carried in the said bags.[28]

LEAD PENCILS

Often overlooked, the common lead pencil was of vital importance to any survey during this period. The pencil held many advantages over contemporary pens and quills when recording data in surveying field books, as inkwells would have proved

---

27 Breaks, *A complete system of land surveying*, p. 286. **28** Callan, *A dissertation*, p. 39.

difficult to use in the field and the ink was liable to run if exposed to damp weather conditions. The quality of the lead mattered greatly to the surveyor:

> Black lead is produced in many countries, but the best yet discovered is found in the north of England: it is dug out of the ground in lumps, and sawed into scantlings proper for use: the kinds most proper to use on paper must be of an uniform texture, which is discoverable by paring a piece to a point with a penknife; for if it cuts smooth and free from hard flinty particles, and will bear a fine point, it may be pronounced good. There are three sorts of good black lead; the soft, the middling, and the hard: the soft is fittest for taking of rough sketches, the middling for drawing of landskips [landscapes] and ornaments, the hard for drawing of lines in mathematical figures, fortifications, architecture, &c.[29]

Instructions for surveyors were also clear on how to assemble and maintain their pencils in the field:

> The best way of fitting black lead for use is first to saw it into long slips about the size of a crow-quill, and then fix it in a case of soft wood, generally cedar, of about the size of a goose-quill, or larger; and this case or wood is cut away with the lead as it is used.[30]

Ink from quill pens was of little use, as survey field books could become damaged by rain or moist conditions, thus making writing difficult or impossible. One English surveyor advised on how best the measurements in the field books could be preserved in such a situation:

> An industrious surveyor will not leave the field for a small mizzling rain; and altho' he cannot then write in his book with ink, yet his observations may be entered with a black lead pencil, and these wrote over with ink when he return to his abode.[31]

For surveyors, penmanship counted. One early nineteenth-century surveyor highlighted the importance a surveyor should place on legibility and properly formed letters and numbers: 'whoever would excel in the art of planning, should use his utmost endeavours to become a complete and elegant penman'.[32] Surveyor's clothing could also play an important role in measurement observation as well as keeping the surveyor dry and warm. Due to the lack of communication equipment, Gibson suggested that the surveyor direct his chainman in the correct direction by the use of his hat:

---

29 Robertson, *A treatise of mathematical instruments*, p. 6.   **30** Ibid.   **31** Hammond, *The practical surveyor*, p. 67.   **32** Nesbit, *Treatise on practical land surveying*, p. 251.

Looking through the sights which govern the direction, and waft your hat to one or to the other side, as a token to the person you sent forward to stand more to the right or to the left, and continue to give the signal 'till you have him in the direction of the sights, and then put on your hat as a signal to him that he is in the true direction.[33]

The wealth and variety of instrumentation, both mainstream and specialized, available in eighteenth-century Dublin, meant that surveyors often had more than one option for suitable equipment, and the choice of instrument often indicated the surveyor's proficiency.

33 Gibson, *Treatise of practical surveying*, p. 288.

1 A surveyor's chain (photograph by Finnian Ó Cionnaith, courtesy of the National Science Museum of Ireland).

2 Surveyor conducting chain measurements (from John Rocque, 'A survey of Tullagorey' (1756) TCD MS4278, courtesy of the Board of Trinity College Dublin).

3 A surveyor, probably Rocque, operating a combined theodolite/circumferentor. The arms extending from the instrument are the circumferentor's sights (from John Rocque, 'A survey of Tullagorey' (1756) TCD MS 4278, courtesy of the Board of Trinity College Dublin).

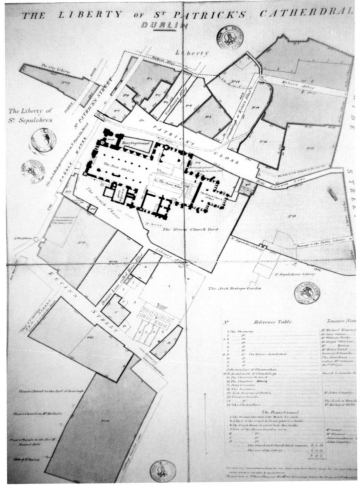

4 Colour used to highlight separate properties around St Patrick's Cathedral (from Roger Kendrick, 'Map of the Liberty of St Patrick's Cathedral, Dublin' (1754), courtesy of the Governors and Guardians of Marsh's Library © Marsh's Library).

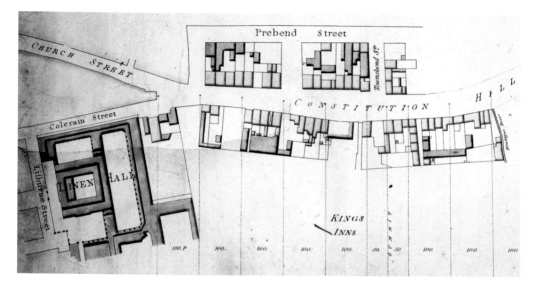

5 Building use along Constitution Hill distinguished by colour (from Thomas Sherrard, 'Church Street, Constitution Hill and Phibsboro Road' (1790), WSC/Maps/263, courtesy of Dublin City Library & Archive).

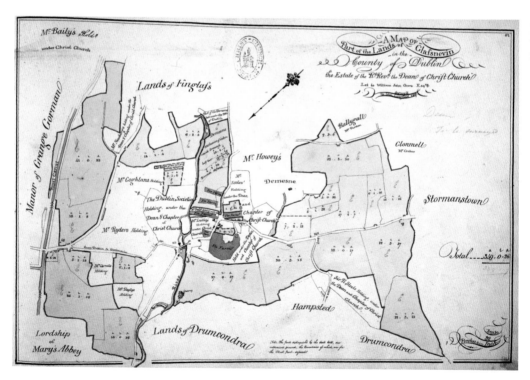

6 Glasnevin shown with realistic colouring (from John Longfield, 'Glasnevin' (1807), NLI MSS 2798–90(62), courtesy of the National Library of Ireland © NLI).

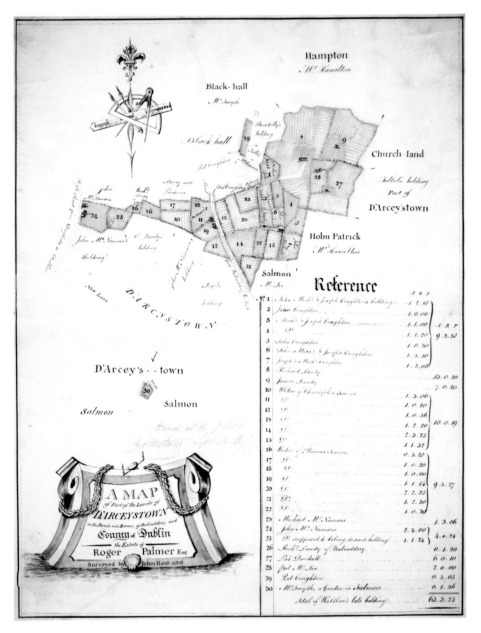

7 A real-world colour scheme used in a map of D'Arc[e]ystown by John Roe (1806) (NLI MS 21.F.141(32), courtesy of the National Library of Ireland © NLI).

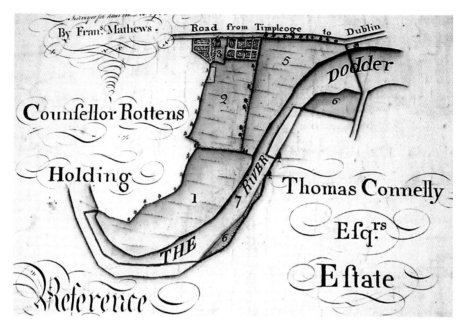

8 A portion of Templeogue (from Francis Mathews, 'Map of lands in Templeogue' (1783), courtesy of the Representative Church Body ©).

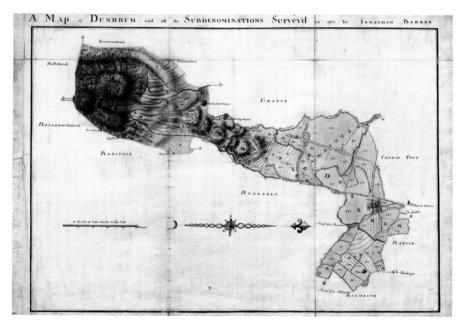

9 Jonathan Barker, 'Map of Dundrum and all its sub-denominations' (1762) (courtesy of the National Archives of Ireland (NAI), Pembroke Estate papers, 2011/2/2/4).

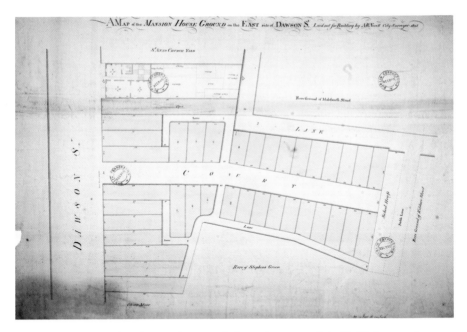

10 Proposed plans from Arthur Neville for replacement of the Dublin's mayoral residence, the mansion house, with a row of houses (1805) (courtesy of Dublin City Library & Archive).

11 *View from Capel Street, looking over Essex Bridge, Dublin* by James Malton, *c.*1797. Parliament Street is visible in the background leading to the Royal Exchange (courtesy of the National Library of Ireland © NLI).

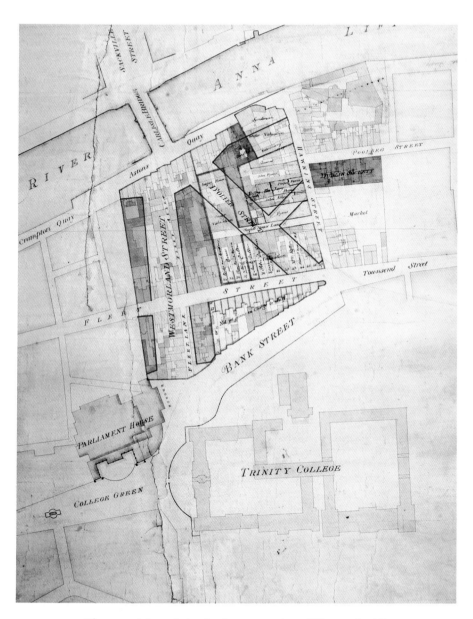

12 The commissioners' plan for the construction of Westmoreland Street and D'Olier Street (*c.*1800) (courtesy of Dublin City Library & Archive).

13 *Trinity College, College Green, Dublin*, by James Malton (1796). Ink and watercolour on paper (53 x 77.4cm) (NGI 2184; photograph courtesy of the National Gallery of Ireland ©).

14 George Chinnery, *General Charles Vallancey* (*c.*1799). Oil on canvas (123 x 97cm (detail)) (courtesy of the Royal Irish Academy © RIA).

Part III
The art

9 'With all the accuracy in my power': map compilation and copying

Maps rarely went straight from survey to finished product. An intermediate draft map was often produced to facilitate the complicated and somewhat messy process of drawing up field notes. Dublin's surveyors often had the option of either producing a map from entirely new data or combining original survey data with existing mapping. This step in a map's production was often unseen by the public or the client, but provide a unique perspective into the rationale used by professional surveyors.

The differences between copying and compilation are many, but frequently subtle. Compilers would often reference their sources, either field surveys by themselves or existing mapping that they had combined with new geographical data sources, newly available charts or written narratives, to create a new and distinct map. Many compilers would only base their work on previous maps known to be a first-hand record of field surveying, thus regularly making a compiled map more accurate than its cartographic cousin, the copied map. Copied maps often exist as a family – an original progenitor map based on fieldwork, then generational copies, over decades or centuries, with their own alterations, mistakes and evolved designs.

MAP COMPILATION

During fieldwork, the surveyor was advised to produce a rough sketch of the survey site before he left it, to avoid having to travel back to correct simple mistakes.[1] This was a sensible precaution, given that the fastest a surveyor could travel in the eighteenth century was the speed of a horse. It would be time consuming to have to return simply to take one missed but important distance or bearing. The paper used for compiling surveys was either parallel lined papers[2] – useful when there was a possibility that the paper might be warped by damp conditions – or strong cartridge paper, several sheets of which could be glued to a cloth or canvas backing if the survey was so large that it could not fit on a single sheet.[3]

The surveyor or draughtsman would consult the measurements recorded in the field book, and try to position their initial markings in a manner that allowed the entire survey to fit onto one sheet. By using the parallel lines of the paper to represent north, the draughtsman would establish the bearings of the survey stations

---

1 Callan, *A dissertation*, p. 35. **2** Note: parallel line paper was used only when compiling survey data, not for recording it in the field. **3** Gibson, *Treatise of practical surveying*, p. 283.

recorded in the field with a protractor and then use a scale ruler to draw a straight line between these stations, representing the chain line.[4] Draughtsmen would mark each measured line's location with a pin, thus removing any errors introduced in the marking of the map with pencil or ink dots. Such pin marks can still occasionally be found on manuscript maps or draft copies.

The image of the survey would slowly take shape as the field notes were meticulously plotted. A common trait of cadastral surveys throughout the eighteenth century was the identification of land adjoining the survey area by the neighbouring owners' last names. This information was recorded in the comments section of the surveyor's field book and it highlighted the importance of accurate field notes, primarily as property demarcation disputes were a very common source of employment for surveyors, as noted by several period authors.[5]

COPYING MAPS

Was a completely new survey and map always called for? Why spend time and money producing a new map when altering an existing one or adding to it would be most effective? Map duplication and revision was common within the surveying community, not only in Dublin but internationally, throughout the eighteenth century. Both manuscript maps, particularly in relation to estate surveys, and large city and town plans printed with copper plate, were copied, both legally and illegally, during this period.

Duplication – or revision – removed the need for complete and extensive resurveys. The various estate holders within Dublin during the eighteenth century routinely kept surveys of their lands on record for future use,[6] and it was on these originals that later generations of surveyors based their updated and revised maps. The relatively small and close-knit surveying community at this time facilitated the acquisition of previous surveys, whether from their own master's notes or from a colleague, with any previous surveyor's work being regularly cited on the reproduction.[7] Even the eminent John Speed once stated that he had 'put my sickle into other

---

4 Wyld, *The practical surveyor*, p. 141.   5 Ibid.; Leybourn, *The complete surveyor*, p. 59; Noble, *Geodæsia Hibernica*, p. 40; Gibson, *Treatise of practical surveying*, p. 272.   6 Roger Kendrick, *Maps of the liberty of St Patrick's Cathedral* (Dublin, 1741–1825); Various, 'Manuscript maps of the Hatch estate' (1727–1871) (NLI MS 21F11); John Longfield, 'Book of maps of estate of Christ Church' (1812) (NLI MSS 2789–90); Various, 'Manuscript maps of the Domville Estate in Dublin City, Dublin county and Meath' (1655–1816) (NLI MS 11,937).   7 John Longfield, 'Holding on Arran Quay', copy of Byron (1790) (copied 1812) (NLI Christ Church papers, MSS 2789–90(1)); John Longfield, 'Lands in Deansgrange', copy of Frizzell (1791) (copied 1820) (NLI Christ Church papers, MSS 2789–90(25)); John Longfield, 'Skinners Row', copy of Thomas Reading (1762) (copied 1814) (NLI Christ Church papers, MSS 2789–90(31)).

men's corn'.[8] The system was not without its critics, however, as one cartographer stated: 'exact geographic knowledge cannot be obtained by sitting at home'.[9]

THE DOWN SURVEY, 1655

One of the main cartographic sources available to Dublin surveyors in the pre-Ordnance Survey era was the 1655/6 Down Survey of Ireland by Sir William Petty. The survey was conducted in the wake of Cromwell's Irish campaign and consisted of a large number of barony and parish maps. It was kept in the surveyor general's office in Dublin Castle and could be consulted and maps copied for a fee of 6s. 8d. Unfortunately, a fire in 1711 damaged a large number of the maps, which meant that a surveyor could often be disappointed when trying to find a relevant map:

> Before leaving Dublin, to commence the territorial survey of Clare, I was anxious to examine to what extent they possessed documents of the county, in the Record Tower, Dublin Castle, where Sir William Petty's maps are kept. I found only three baronies of the county of Clare. I was anxious to take outlines of them, in order to compare with the surveys that were to be executed. I found the price high, and declined.[10]

The survey itself was highly regarded in both legal and cartographic circles, being described as 'great use to gentlemen; though the Down Surveys only are those allowed by the laws of the land to be final and decisive'.[11] Regardless of the esteem in which it was held, its physical storage was not ideal:

> I found that survey in, I thought, a very perilous state in point of location, and a very impaired state in point of preservation. It was situated, I believe, on the upper stories of a very old building, and very liable to accident by fire; some parts of it, as well I recollect, bore the marks of having already suffered by fire ... [it was vulnerable to the] slower but equally sure process of destruction which it was undergoing, by the mode in which those who had occasion to consult it were allowed both to handle the sheets themselves, and to make tracings or drafts from it.[12]

8 John Speed, *Theatre of the empire of Great Britain* (London, 1611), p. iii.   **9** Braddock Meade, *The construction of maps and globes* (London, 1717), p. 58.   **10** Evidence of William Bald, *Report from select committee on survey and valuation of Ireland*, p. 62 [445], H.C. 1824, viii.79.   **11** Gibson, *Treatise of practical surveying*, p. 285.   **12** Evidence of John Wilson Croker, *Report from select committee on survey and valuation of Ireland*, p. 34 [445], H.C. 1824, viii.79.

Despite the efforts of Charles Vallancey to duplicate many of the missing maps from
a dubiously acquired French copy, there existed no fully complete map reference for
the entire island of Ireland before the 1820s.[13]

OLDER SURVEYS

Eighteenth-century surveyors understood the benefits of and problems relating to
consulting older mapping and that the survival of mapping and real-world property
markers was often a matter of chance:

> To the antiquarian of the 25th century, I hope it will be found useful should
> a single copy of it have the singular good fortune to be preserved till that
> period, as affording them an opportunity, by consulting the angular measure-
> ment, of determining the position of many places in the country with a
> tolerable degree of accuracy, of which the devouring hand of time may not,
> perhaps, have left the least vestige remaining.[14]

Combining older maps with new survey data presented a particular problem that
could render a whole survey null and void – scale. It was imperative that if a surveyor
was combining two surveys both should be to the same scale or altered so that they
were equal. An instrument known as a pantographia was used to reduce maps from
one scale to another through a simple method of ratio conversion. Wyld described
the instrument thus:

> A plot may be reduced with the utmost exactness to any given ratio, in respect
> of the former, either in proportion, as the length of the sides of the soul plot
> shall be to the fair one, or else as the area of the one to the area of the other;
> and another thing may be said of this instrument, that curves are as well
> reduced thereby as right-lines; which by any other instrument is exceeding
> difficult, if not impossible to be done.[15]

The advantage of being able to accurately copy an original map, without damaging
it, was noted by several surveying authors throughout the eighteenth century.[16]

After an enlarged or reduced rough copy had been produced, another copy was
made on thin paper covered lightly with oil so as to make it transparent. This trans-

---

13 Charles Vallancey to Leopold de Biretiue, Paris, 14 Mar. 1789 (NLI MS 1614). **14** John
Lindley, *Memoir of a map of the county of Surrey* (London, 1793), quoted in *Historian's guide to
early British maps: Royal Historical Society* (18 vols, London, 1994), ix, p. 463. **15** Wyld, *The
practical surveyor*, p. 110. **16** Hammond, *The practical surveyor*, p. 173; Leybourn, *The complete
surveyor*, p. 60; Benjamin Martin, *The new art of surveying by the Goniometer* (London, 1771), p.
17.

parent copy could then be overlaid onto the new map made by the surveyor, and common points could be identified, thus establishing the true property boundaries.[17]

The nature of geographical information[18] means that it changes regularly and randomly. Maps can rapidly become out-dated, particularly in urban areas, where the construction of buildings and changes in infrastructure are ongoing processes. John Longfield's 1816 map of the grounds of the King's Inns on Constitution Hill, Phibsborough, was grossly out of date by the 1830s, due to the demolition of a row of houses along the Phibsborough Road. As such, William Longfield, John's son and successor, was able to trace the unaffected sections from his father's original map, and the new survey work for William's map was restricted to the small area affected.[19] This method of partial tracing and partial copying was also employed by John Longfield[20] and John Brownrigg,[21] while direct traces, inclusive of the original survey's non-geographic decorations, also appear to have been a common practice.[22]

John Rocque's map publication business in London prior to his arrival in Ireland in the 1750s specialized in cartographic duplication. A list of Rocque's published and advertised works indicates that a staple of his business was the copying of maps originally produced abroad, as was common in eighteenth-century Europe. There is no evidence that Rocque surveyed Berlin in 1747, Halifax, Nova Scotia and Constantinople in 1750, Minorca in 1753 or Lima in 1755,[23] yet maps of these far-flung and distant lands and cities were all advertised by Rocque, suggesting that they were copies.[24] Maps could easily be copied from an original parchment onto copper plate, edited, updated and republished far more cheaply and quickly than conducting an original survey from scratch. The importation of maps from other countries was an expensive process and many map producers found it economically advantageous to trade home-grown maps with colleagues in other countries for a 'juste prix',[25] as commented by French map-seller Roch-Joseph Julien in 1763, while trading French maps for English ones. London map-seller William Fadden and his Dutch colleagues went so far as to smuggle maps to each other in order to avoid customs fees: 'The captain has asked that you would please have one of your servants pick up the roll [of maps] in order to avoid declaring it to customs'.[26] During the 1740s, Rocque

---

17 Gibson, *Treatise of practical surveying*, p. 287. **18** Naturally occurring geographical features or man-made structures present in the real world represented in a cartographic context. **19** William Longfield, 'Constitution Hill' (1835) (NLI Christ Church papers, MS 2789(52)). **20** John Longfield, 'Rathmore, Naas' (1824) (NLI Christ Church papers, MS 2789(82)); John Longfield, 'Plot of land covered by the high court' (1818) (NLI Christ Church papers, MS 2789(60)). **21** John Brownrigg, 'Chancery Street and Great Ship Street' (1800) (NLI Longfield papers, MS 21F87(103)). **22** John Longfield, 'Cook Street' (1805) (NLI Longfield papers, MS 21F88(125)); Brownrigg and Co., 'Glasnevin' (1800) (NLI Longfield papers, MS 2789(28)). **23** At this time, Rocque was operating in Ireland. **24** Varley, 'John Rocque: engraver, surveyor, cartographer and map-seller', pp 83–91. **25** R.J. Julien, *Nouveau catalogue de cartes géographiques et topographiques* (Paris, 1763), p. 4, quoted in Mary Sponberg-Pedley, *Commerce of cartography* (Chicago, 2005), p. 76. **26** Covens and Mortier to Faden, 18 Sept. 1778, quoted in Mary Sponberg-Pedley, *Map trade* (Chicago, 2000), p. 95.

produced dozens of maps of cities and countries throughout Europe and the Americas, indicating that he had many contacts in the cartographic community, both in England and further afield.

ILLEGAL REPRODUCTION

Map copying could also be conducted outside of established professional channels, with illegal copies of well-known and top-selling maps appearing on the market. Charles Brooking's *A map of the city and suburbs of Dublin* (London, 1728) was copied more than once – with two versions being produced in 1728, an illegally copied version in 1729 and a reprint *c.*1740 with minor alterations.[27] Brooking's official publisher was a man named Bowles, who produced the first edition of Brooking's map from his workplace in Mercers Hall, Cheapside, London,[28] in 1728, and another edition from Black Horse, Cornhill, London. Andrews points out that the main differences between the Mercers Hall and the Black Horse editions were minor changes to Brooking's prospect of the city and the inclusion of lots along the North Wall similar to those laid out prior to Brooking's work in 1717.[29] In early 1729, a non-Bowles edition of Brooking's work appeared on the Dublin cartographic market, in a two- and three-sheet format and at a far cheaper price:

> Just imported from London, a new and correct map of the city of Dublin, either in two or three sheet, coloured: The price of the 3 sheets, 3*s*. 6*d*., and the 1 of 2, at 2*s*., 2*d*. unframed. Sold by Hanna Madocks at the Red Lyon in New Row, near Thomas Street, and by Thomas Benson at Shakespear's Head in Castle Street.[30]

The appearance of this illegal copy did not go unnoticed by the sellers of the original map:

> About six months ago was publish'd a map of the city of Dublin, from the actual survey of C. Brooking, sold at 5 shill. English; and whereas there has lately been sent over a spurious, imperfect, and piratical copy of the said map, sold at an under price. The proprietor of the original map done from Brooking's survey finds himself obliged (notwithstanding the considerable expense he has been at in prosecuting said map in the best manner, and the great loss he is like to sustain thereby) to fall the price to an English Half Crown; which it is hoped will give no offence to any of these gentlemen who

---

27 Includes new compass rose, the lots along East Wall and views of St Patrick's and Christ Church cathedrals. **28** *London Daily Journal*, 19 Dec. 1728. **29** J.H. Andrews, 'Mean piratical practices, the case of Charles Brooking', *IGSB*, 23:3/4 (1980), 33–41. **30** *Dublin Weekly Journal*, 15 Feb. 1729.

encourag'd the work. NB: It is not to be doubted but that the publick will shew their abhorrence of these mean piratical practices, by discouraging the spurious copy; at least every one before they buy it will compare it with the original, which has Brooking's the surveyor's name, and Bowles the proprietor. All others are imperfect and spurious. The said original map is now sold by most booksellers in Dublin, at an English half crown.[31]

In England prior to 1735, publishers who wished to protect their right of sale of a printed or engraved graphic work, rather than its content, had to apply for privilege from parliament or the king.[32] Brooking's work was produced in England. Therefore, to protect the work, Bowles or Brooking must have applied to the English parliament for privilege. In contemporary France, the engraver or publisher had to supply one copy of a map to the office of the Librairie,[33] two to the royal library, another to the Cabinet du Louvre, another to the keeper of seals, one more to the censor and three to the Communauté de la Librairie.[34] In both countries, such privileges only protected works within the country and not when those works were abroad. The legal loopholes thus created opportunities for those who wished to provide a cheaper alternative to the original product, as in Brooking's case. Those affected by such 'piratical practices' often felt the need to highlight their unfortunate position:

> Since maps have begun to be multiplied and entered into pecuniary commerce, one has seen many ignoramuses who, by greed for profit, have mixed themselves up in doing what they don't understand, and some sellers of images who have wanted to make geography a subsidiary of print making … The profession of geography has become a real den of thieves … The plagiarists try not to copy line for line … making it a tricky business to discern who is the robber and who the robbed.[35]

English publisher Samuel Buckley added:

> That the man may not, after an expense of much money and many years application and study, be liable to lose the profits he might justly promise to himself and family from his labours, and to have only the honour at last of having made a very good copy for a Dutch bookseller to raise a fortune by, tax-free, quickly and surely, at no more trouble than that of reprinting it.[36]

31 *Dublin Gazette*, 15 Mar. 1729. **32** David Hunter, 'Copyright protection for engravings and maps in eighteenth-century Britain', *Library*, 9:2 (1987), 28–47. **33** Sponberg-Pedley describes the *Librairie* as a central office in Paris that supervised and controlled the book and print trade. The bureau was headed by a court-appointed director whose agents looked out especially for anti-establishment, pornographic and other unseemly prints: Sponberg-Pedley, *Commerce of cartography*, p. 103. **34** 'Book sellers' guild', Sponberg-Pedley, *Commerce of cartography*, p. 105. **35** Broc, *Plagiat cartographique*, quoted in Sponberg-Pedley, *Commerce of Cartography*, p. 105. **36** Samuel Buckley, 'A short statement of the public encouragement

ACCURACY OF COPIED MAPS

Repeated tracing of older maps can undermine the quality of the work being traced through propagation of error. Each individual who copied a map had the potential to introduce his own errors and mistakes, which would then be considered correct. Eighteenth-century surveyors appear to have regularly copied from surveys that were decades old, sometimes even dating back to the early seventeenth century. John Brownrigg's map of Glasnevin (1800)[37] was copied from a Thomas Cave map produced sometime in the early eighteenth century, which in turn had been copied from a survey conducted by Richard Francis in 1640. While it is difficult to ascertain how much of Brownrigg's data came from the original Francis map, Brownrigg did not specifically state that the map was a combination of survey and traced work, only that it had been copied from both Cave and Francis, potentially making some of the map data well over a century old.

While there is no evidence of discrepancies in the Brownrigg/Cave/Francis map, there is proof elsewhere that maps of the same area produced by various surveyors at different times resulted in fluctuating measurements, making the selection of what map to use, and from what surveyor, an important issue in copying and revision. In January 1698, Abraham Carter surveyed an area of land in Roganstown, near Swords, Co. Dublin, which belonged to the estate of Christ Church Cathedral. This same map was copied in 1714 by Moland, whose product was copied in 1743 by Thomas Cave, who, like Moland and Carter before him, had his map copied in 1814 by John Longfield.[38] The map was produced to a scale of twenty perches to an inch and the area of the land in question was calculated to be 31 acres, 3 roods exactly. While there is no direct documentary evidence, the accuracy of this area figure must have come under question as, in the same year as the 1814 copy was made, Longfield was asked to resurvey the exact same land.[39] Longfield's 1814 survey calculated the area as 32 acres, 2 roods and 7 perches. Delving back into the records of the Christ Church Estate, Longfield found and copied yet another map of the same lands in Roganstown, surveyed by Samuel Byron in 1794,[40] which yielded a third set of figures, 32 acres, 1 rood and 8 perches. Given the relative closeness of the 1794 and 1814 surveys and the small errors that would have been introduced to these surveys by the period instrumentation, it is highly probable that the figure of 32 acres calculated separately by Longfield and Byron was correct, rather than the figure of 31 acres obtained from the Carter/Moland/Cave/Longfield copy.

Surveyors were ever ready to point out errors in previous surveys to their

given to printing and bookselling in France, Holland, Germany and at London' in S. Parks (ed.), *English publishing, the struggle for copyright, and the freedom of the press, 1666–1774* (New York, 1975). **37** Brownrigg and Co., 'Glasnevin' (1800) (NLI Christ Church papers, MS 2789(28)). **38** John Longfield, 'Roganstown' (1814) (NLI Christ Church papers, MS 2789(34)). **39** John Longfield, 'Roganstown' (1814) (NLI Christ Church papers, MS 2789(37)). **40** John Longfield, 'Roganstown' (1815) (NLI Christ Church papers, MS 2789(36)).

employers, as it helped explain discrepancies. In 1805, Sherrard and Brassington attached a note to a survey they conducted in Brunswick Street, during which they had consulted a previous survey:

> It appears by the old map that there is a deficiency of about 7ft in depth on the east side of this holding. We account for it that in rebuilding the corner house it has been set back so much for the purpose of widening and improving the street.[41]

A similar note regarding discrepancies in maps was written by Longfield while examining previous surveys of an area in Lucan, Co. Dublin:

> The result which I expected by an examination of the ancient maps of Ash Park, have (in my opinion) been realized, and therefore the *whole* of W. Hyland's stores & Matt Hiln, together with Kirwan's holdings, as proposed for by those persons, are the sole property of dean & chapter of Christ Church, *and not partly so*, as described by Mr Reading's map & survey of 1751–2. The authority upon which I have made this conclusion is Abraham Carter's map of 1704 annex'd to the cancel'd lease of Ash Park and which I said to agree with the map of Sir Rich. Steel's estate, which bounds the south side of Ash Park. Since the survey of 1704, there has been a small increase of propend on the north side of Lucan Lane, now called Garden Lane, and I have discovered a clerical error in the length of the estate boundary marked 141½ feet, which, allowing for the shrinking of parchment, I think should measure on the map 232½. This error of 101 feet I find was so copied by Tho. Cave in his map of 1729, and I am of opinion that those errors or wrong information was the cause of Thos. Reading's mistake in the Southern Boundary as described in his map of 1751–2.

The propagation of error had also been missed by Dublin city surveyor, Samuel Byron, when he was asked to copy the Ash Park map in the 1780s:

> In 1781, Samuel Byron made accessory of Ash Park, on the authority of Reading's map of 1751–2, and he also copied its inaccuracies, which from want of interior measurements, he was unable to detect, and it is probable some of the whole was not let in *one demise*. I should have fallen into the same errors. However, on reviewing the separate holdings on the south side of Garden Lane, it occurred to me that the line of boundary marked in the maps of 1751 & 1781 could not be correct, and I trust the discovery is made in sufficient truce for the benefit of the estate. I have in present to the direction of

41 Sherrard and Brassington, 'Brunswick Street' (1805) (NLI Christ Church papers, MSS 2789–90).

the committee viewed & valued the separate holdings in Ash Park and I
recommend the proposals of Mr Hyland, Eustace and Kirwan to [be]
accepted by the chapter.[42]

Longfield's suspicions and analysis of his predecessors' maps was not only useful, but,
as one cartographer advised decades earlier, very necessary when examining copied
maps:

> 'Tis no excuse for one to say he copy'd his from another's maps; because he
> never aught to copy that which he has not first examin'd, and found agreeable
> with the best discoveries. The truth is, everyone that can copy or engrave a
> map, sets up for a geographer, and having done that, thinks the property is
> transfere'd and accordingly calls himself the author![43]

In addition, he also advised:

> But no maps are not always exact copys of others, there are some which seem
> to be patch'd up with a piece out of one and a piece out of another, without
> any judgement or care: for the map maker often thinks himself obliged to
> make alterations from others, that something new may appear in what he
> publisheth, to this end, the situation of places is transposed, the course of rivers
> turn'd, the bounds of countys, provinces and coasts extended, or contracted in
> a very strange manner.[44]

Questions on the reliability of copied geographic information were obviously valid
during the eighteenth and early nineteenth centuries. As such, the most highly
regarded reference source for geographic data in Ireland during this time, the Down
Survey, sought to maintain its reputation for accuracy and its privileged legal status.
Irish surveyors regularly consulted and copied the Down Survey[45] and, in order to
protect the status of the maps, the deputy surveyor general would attach a note to
such maps, stating that surveyors had consulted an official source of information.
These brief notes contained enough information to enable the client to confirm that
the surveyor's work and the Down Survey maps consulted came from the same area
and that the maps the surveyor was copying were legitimate:

> This trace, for so much, agreeth with the map of the Down Survey taken from
> the Parish of Santry in the County of Dublin, remaining on record in the
> office of His Majesties surveyor general of lands in Dublin Castle.[46]

---

42 NLI Christ Church papers, MS 861(265).   **43** John Green (alias Braddock Meade), *The
construction of maps and globes in two parts* (London, 1717), p. 134.   **44** Ibid., p. 135.   **45** John
Longfield, 'Lands in Killenaule, Tipperary' (1817) (NLI MS 2789(59)); *Report from select
committee on survey and valuation of Ireland*, pp 34, 129, 134, 313 [445], H.C. 1824, viii.79;
Gibson, *Treatise of practical surveying*, p. 286.   **46** Note by Richard Holmes, deputy surveyor

Such notes are rare within Irish estate maps, yet they occasionally appear in map collections.[47]

Even rarer are surveyors' comparisons of their own work to that of the Down Survey. Michael Kenny, a Dublin-based surveyor in the late eighteenth century, enclosed one such comparison in a note to the Domville family regarding a map of their lands in Glasnevin, as well as a description of his state of health:

> Above, you have the map of that field. I surveyed it with all the accuracy in my power, and make it 4A 3R 2P, cast it up various ways, and found able to answer the same, what I made of it, in the general survey, I can't tell, as I have no paper related to your estate, thus in one line from A to B that the gripe was uncertain much defrauded but on enquiring strictly, find it was your gripe therefore brought it in. I have been very unwell this fortnight past and not much better since.[48]

The copying, tracing and revision of maps was an important, time-saving and economically viable way of reproducing and updating of surveys. Such advantages appear to have encouraged the preservation of maps, particularly manuscript estate maps, which allows modern researchers to compare and contrast separate surveys and identify the advantages and errors associated with the recycling of geographic information.

general of lands: anon., 'Santry' (1766) (NLI Domville papers, MS 11,937(11)). **47** Anon., 'Corbally, Co. Dublin' (1766) (NLI Domville papers, MS 11,937(48)); James Molly, 'Santry' (1764) (NLI Domville papers, MS 11,937(50)); anon., 'Rathleigh, County Meath' (n.d.) (NLI Domville papers, MS 11,937(54)). **48** Note by Michael Kenny, 'Glasnevin' (1804) (NLI Domville papers, MS 11,937(20)).

10 'To convey a correct and statistical representation': printing, manuscripts and consumer demands

Maps are the legacy left to us by past generations of surveyors. Their financial value rarely comes close to the true historic and cultural worth contained within each map's border. These surviving maps can be divided into two distinct groups – prints and manuscripts – each with its own particular merits and drawbacks. As a result, the decision as to whether a map in eighteenth-century Dublin should remain in hand-drawn manuscript form, or be engraved or etched into copper for mass print production, was dependent on several important and mostly financial factors.

FINANCIAL VIABILITY

In the modern world, printing a map for personal use involves little more than the click of a mouse button. This effortless process, now taken for granted, was substantially more complicated and costly in the eighteenth century. Printed maps were painstakingly engraved onto copper plate by skilled artists. This was an expensive and time consuming process, and therefore required a suitably large audience to be cost effective. Rocque, for instance, had a large monetary reserve derived from customer subscriptions before his map of Dublin had been created, providing the finances needed for engraving and printing.[1] It is precisely because of these financial and technical hurdles that the majority of maps from the eighteenth century currently in the nation's various museums and libraries remained in manuscript form.

A notable practical advantage of copper-plate printing, particularly over older wood-block printing methods, lay in the fact that copper plate was more adaptable and could easily be edited. Map producers had the ability to recycle older copper plates by editing or adding new features to the plate. One of the most obvious examples of this occurred in 1773, when Bernard Scalé ran a reprint of Rocque's 1756 Dublin city map. Changes in Dublin's streets were engraved directly onto the original plates, which, unusually for Scalé, produced somewhat crude results (fig.10.1).[2] The small city plans that accompanied William Wilson's Dublin street directories throughout the later eighteenth century are another example of this geographic recycling process. These maps reproduced the same cartographic information year

1 *Dublin Journal*, 31 Aug. 1754.   2 Bernard Scalé, *A survey of the city, harbour, bay and environs of Dublin* (Dublin, 1773).

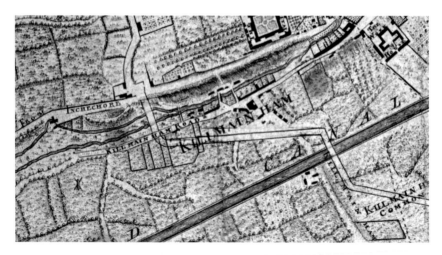

10.1 Engraving of the newly built South Circular Road and Grand Canal on top of old map detail (from Bernard Scalé, *A survey of the city, harbour, bay and environs of Dublin* (Dublin, 1773). Courtesy of the Board of Trinity College Dublin).

after year, with only the changes made to the city since the map's last publication being added.[3]

Despite the obvious economic savings that reusing copper plates had on map production, it also had its drawbacks. In the 1779 issue of Wilson's map, Eccles Street, off Dorset Street, was engraved outside the map border, as it did not fit inside the original map's boundaries – a very serious lapse, from both engraving and map-making perspectives. Such distracting mistakes could lower a map's overall status and, as eighteenth-century French cartographer Nicolas Le Clerc stated, 'the punishment for bad maps is that no one buys them'.[4]

Wilson himself also stated that copper-plate printing, while it had many advantages, was expensive, had a limited production life and required considerable effort to produce a final map:

> The old [copper] plate of the city of Dublin, heretofore given in the Dublin Directory, being quite worn out, the editor found it impossible to convey a correct and statistical representation of the city in its present enlarged and improved state, so as to bind up with the work, has therefore with no small labour and very considerable expense, completed the above elegant plan, which is now offered to the public at little more than half its value, in order

3 See *Wilson's Dublin directory*, maps 1762, 1779, 1795, 1810. **4** Nicolas Le Clerc, *l'Imprimerie de Clousier, imprimeur de Roi* (Paris, 1786), p. 64, quoted by Sponberg Pedley, *The commerce of cartography*, p. 43. **5** *Wilson's Dublin directory* (1799), preface.

to accommodate merchants and others, who may wish to frame the same for their respective counting houses.[5]

The time and money spent on copper-plate printing required justification in monetary terms, for both the surveyor and the engraver. Although many successful maps were produced through copper-plate printing, some inevitably failed. Roger Kendrick's proposed map of Dublin is a typical example of this. Having been partially surveyed and laid out, the map was never published, which must have cost Kendrick a significant amount of time and money. The decision to print from copper plate was a risky business and was not guaranteed to meet with financial success.

COPPER-PLATE PRINTING

The era of copper-plate printing lasted from the mid-fifteenth to the mid-nineteenth century. The earliest known graphic print by this method is a series in the *Passion of the Christ* printed in 1446 in Berlin.[6] Copper-plate printing gradually replaced woodcut printing, which was a popular method of mass-producing maps for a commercial market during the seventeenth century. Copper plate made it possible to show greater detail than woodblock, and could survive the printing process longer. It therefore allowed printers to produce more ornate maps in greater quantities than had been possible. The industrialization of mapping had begun.

The older wood-block method of map production required that for larger maps, the engraved or chiselled surface had to be a combination of several wooden pieces, thus creating the possibility of gaps appearing in the joins. This would be transferred onto the final print, resulting in unsightly and unwanted lines. Copper plate, however, could be produced in larger sizes than wood block. The physical properties of the copper itself also allowed for finer and neater lines to be made than the relatively straight and rough lines associated with wood-block engraving. Aaron Arrowsmith, who produced a map of Ireland in 1811, was a keen user of large sheets of copper: 'thus avoiding the numerous junctions, which too often injure the appearance of good maps, when printed on many sheets'.[7] Copper plate was easier to alter if mistakes were found during the revision of engraved work.[8] In addition, it had a longer printing life, reducing the final cost of a single copy and allowing for a better penetration of the product into the commercial market. Its use was not common in the Irish surveying industry, with simple property maps such as those of the WSC, city surveyor, estate and cadastral maps being produced nearly exclusively in manuscript format throughout the eighteenth century.

6 British Museum, *A guide to the processes and schools of engraving* (London, 1914), p. 20.
7 Arron Arrowsmith, *Memoir relative to the construction of the map of Scotland* (London, 1809), p. 31.   **8** William Faithorne, *The art of graving and etching* (2nd ed., London, 1702), p. 41.

ETCHING AND ENGRAVING

Printing from metal plates is an 'intaglio' process (a printmaking techniques in which the image is incised into a surface), in contrast to the relief process of wood-block printing. Intaglio printing from metal plates was accomplished through line engraving, dry point, etching, mezzotint[9] or similar methods of incising lines in a plate. The plate used for printing could be any relatively soft metal, including gold, silver or zinc, but for the production of maps, copper was the preferred metal, and line engraving was the most commonly used intaglio method.[10]

Copper's main variation, aside from weight and size, was its colouring, and it was regularly classified for sale along these lines. Brass, although similar to copper, was considered too brittle.[11] Red copper was best for its adherence to the cutting stroke of the engraver's tool, the burin. Yellow or brassy copper was regarded as being too hard for engraving, as its high zinc content made it difficult to engrave and could easily result in the burin breaking.[12]

There were two common methods to transfer the initial map design from a manuscript onto copper. The first involved the coating of the copper plate in wax, onto which the map would be drawn in reverse.[13] The second method was proposed by French geographer Abraham Bosse in the seventeenth century.[14] It involved the use of transparent paper onto which the map was copied. A form of carbon paper was then used to transfer the tracing directly onto the copper plate. After the map had been transferred onto the plate, etching and engraving of map detail could take place. Etching, the less common of the two techniques found in eighteenth-century Dublin, required the scarring of the plate with acid to produce a shading effect,[15] and this was utilized to add terrain or decorative effects more than main cartographic detail. Engraving was the most common technique in use in map printing. A burin – the primary tool used for engraving – was employed to indent and scar the copper plate, by running it along the cartographic detail of the transferred map. The produced indent would hold ink when the copper plate was finally pressed to print the map on paper. Engraving was the preferred method of map production, as the depth of the indent in the copper plate was generally greater, making it more robust for printing and enabling more prints of a map to be produced from one copper than a plate that had been etched.

The burin consisted of a sharpened metal blade with a wooden handle for ease of use.[16] It came in a variety of shapes and sizes, depending on the style and the width/depth of the indent that the engraver wished to make on the copper plate. Text was not engraved due to its complexity and the time it took to engrave each letter in a detailed map. Instead, lettered punches were utilized. Due to the purely

---

9 A dry point method to produce tonal difference in an image. **10** David Woodward, *Five centuries of map printing* (Chicago, 1975), p. 52. **11** Faithorne, *The art of graving and etching*, p. 4. **12** Ibid. **13** Woodward, *Five centuries of map printing*, p. 53. **14** Abraham Bosse, *Traicté des manières de graver* (Paris, 1645). **15** Faithorne, *The art of graving and etching*, p. 11. **16** Ibid., p. 43.

manual nature of eighteenth-century copper-plate engraving, mistakes could easily occur. Unlike the older wood-block method, mistakes in copper-plate engraving were relatively easy to correct. A tool called a burnisher, which was an abrasive hand brush, would remove scratches and shallow indentations on the copper plate.

While these two methods of adding detail to the plate were the most popular during the eighteenth century, several experiments were conducted by French and German engravers using other tools. One of French geographer Alexander Dalrymple's engravers would use a stone to scuff the copper plate, thus producing a shading effect. Despite the ingenuity of this technique, however, Dalrymple himself admitted that 'it is more elegant than convenient'.[17]

Despite the relatively high numbers of printers compared to surveyors operating in Dublin during the period, not all were involved with copper-plate printing or map production. Some classified themselves as simply printers, booksellers and printers, or map and print sellers. Printers in Dublin existed in loose partnerships or companies relatively free of legislative restrictions, until the Stamp Act,[18] which required printers to print their names and addresses on their published works. Print shop staff, depending on the shop's size, usually consisted of several journeymen and one or two apprentices. Apprentice printers worked for seven years, learning the trade before graduating as journeymen, and their experiences of such an education could vary widely. Dublin-born Thomas Gent suffered physical abuse under his tutor, Stephen Powell, before fleeing to England in 1706. Gent eventually became a printer in York in the 1730s.[19] Other runaway apprentices include 15-year-olds John Price and George Slack, whose master, Robert Hudson, warned the public not to harbour them after they left 'without the least provocation'.[20]

A valuable record of Dublin's copper-plate printers and engravers can be found in the various newspapers in circulation in eighteenth-century Dublin. Many printers and engravers advertised their intention to publish maps made by the top surveyors of the period, with the purpose of increasing awareness and to encourage sales. William Allen, print seller, advertised his connection with D.A. Beaufort's *Map of Ireland* (Dublin, 1792),[21] as well as A.R. Neville's *Map of the county of Wicklow* (Dublin, 1795).[22] Surveyors would also use a combination of separate engravers and printers to publish their maps. Jacob Neville hired engraver George Byrne of Smock Alley[23] to engrave his *Map of County Wicklow* (Dublin, 1760), and had the resulting copper-plate printed by Thomas Silkock of Nicholas Street[24] in the same year.

Surveyors themselves could also double as engravers. Perhaps the most renowned of these surveyor/engravers operating in Dublin during this time was John Rocque, assisted by his subordinates. Rocque's 1756 map of the city was etched, engraved and

---

17 Quoted in Andrew Cook, 'Alexander Dalrymple's *A collection of plans of ports in the East Indies* (1774–5): a preliminary examination', *Imago Mundi*, 33 (1981), 51–8. **18** 34 Geo. 3 [Ire.] (1794), c.3. **19** Thomas Gent, *Life of Mr Thomas Gent, printer of York* (London, 1832), p. 2. **20** *Dublin Chronicle*, 3 Oct. 1789. **21** *Dublin Evening Post*, 5 Apr. 1792. **22** Ibid., 13 June 1795. **23** *Public Gazette*, 6 Dec. 1760. **24** Ibid.

printed in Dublin. He also referred to his engravers/survey assistants in the *Dublin Journal*:

> Said John Rocque, in gratitude for the many favours he hath received in this kingdom, thinks it a duty incumbent on him to engrave the above maps in Dublin, and is therefore provided with proper artists for that purpose, being the same persons who assisted him in this surveys.[25]

Rocque began his engraving practice in the 1740s in London, where he lost one printing shop in Piccadilly to fire, and later opened a second one on the Strand.[26] Following his return to London in the 1760s, and his subsequent death, his engraving business passed to his widow, Mary Ann Rocque. She was still operating a successful business in 1766, in which year military engineer John Montresor engaged Mary Ann's engraving shop to produce his maps of Nova Scotia, Canada, Boston Harbour and New York.[27]

John Rocque utilized a variety of engravers and printers for his works, which may in reality reflect the demand for his maps rather than a specific trend within his own work practices. For his map of *Dublin and its environs* (Dublin, 1756), he employed Andrew Dury as his engraver.[28] George Byrne engraved his *Map of Kilkenny* (Dublin, 1758), J.J. Perret his *Map of Thurles* (Dublin, 1757),[29] and John Dixon the title piece of his *Map of Dublin county* (Dublin, 1760).[30] Scalé followed a similar trend, by varying his engravers and printers – Patrick Halpin engraved the *Geometrical elevation of the Parliament House* (Dublin, 1767), J.J. Perret engraved the *Plan of Dublin city, suburbs and environs* (Dublin, 1773),[31] and Richard Bushell was involved in selling Scalé's *Plan of Trinity College* (Dublin, 1761).[32] Others involved in the engraving, printing and selling of maps in eighteenth-century Dublin and who advertised their business include James Barlow,[33] George Cowan[34] and John Duff.[35]

The close connection that many engravers and printers had with surveying demonstrates that map printing from copper plate did occur in Dublin during the eighteenth century. However, there is little direct evidence of these engravers and copper-plate printers regularly printing maps aside from the large town plans. Several Irish surveyors had their maps engraved abroad, thus widening the potential numbers of engravers available for work in Irish-related mapping.[36] For example, William

---

25 *Dublin Journal*, Sept. 1754. **26** Sponberg Pedley, *The commerce of cartography*, p. 100. **27** Scull, *The Montresor journals*, p. 392, quoted in J.B. Harley, Barbara Petchenik and Lawrence Towner, *Mapping the American revolutionary war* (Chicago, 1978), p. 85. **28** Rocque, *An exact survey*. Dury signed his name on sheet four of this map. **29** Pollard, *Dictionary of members of the Dublin book trade, 1550–1800*, p. 457. **30** *Exshaw's magazine*, Apr. 1760, p. 182. **31** Ibid. **32** *Public Gazette*, 7 Nov. 1767. **33** Pollard, *Dictionary of members of the Dublin book trade, 1550–1800*, p. 21. Barlow's name appears on a 'Map of Hudson Bay' published in 1749. **34** *Hibernian Journal*, 6 Dec. 1774: 'new maps by late J. Rocque and B. Scalé'. **35** Pollard's *Dictionary of members of the Dublin book trade, 1550–1800* advertised the *Plan of Kilkenny* (p. 170). Duff also printed Charles Vallancey's *Collectanea de Rebus Hibernicus* in 1781. **36** William Bald – Paris, Alexander Nimmo – London, *Report from select committee on survey*

Petty's *Ireland* (1675) was engraved in Amsterdam,[37] while Bernard Scalé chose to have his *Hibernian atlas* (1776) engraved and printed in London.

COLOURING

Colouring is a feature of modern cartographic works that has become not only common, but expected. In contrast, most maps produced in Dublin during the eighteenth century were uncoloured. The application of colour can be separated into several distinct categories, which generally relate to the use for which the map was intended. Manuscript maps were primarily coloured by the surveyors themselves, whereas printed maps were often sold uncoloured, as separate colours could not be applied during the printing process.

   The first category consists of maps on which colour was used as a means of highlighting boundaries or administrative areas, such as city wards or counties – this includes both printed and manuscript maps. Rocque's map of the *Kingdom of Ireland* published in 1760 involved four different colours to highlight the borders of the four provinces of Ireland in a simple yet highly effective way. Dublin city surveyor A.R. Neville replicated the same colouring scheme in 1800 to highlight a section of city property on the south side of College Green to establish three separate properties let to Sir William Fownes in the mid-seventeenth century, as did Thomas Reading and Peter Callan in their work for the Hatch Estate during the 1740s.[38] This well-established method tended to be best and most effectively applied to cadastral maps, on which individual properties could be easily distinguished.

   A second group of surveyors employed watercolours more extensively to highlight and classify areas rather than boundaries alone. Much like the first group, colouring retained a practical rather than decorative function for this method. Plate 4 shows a section of a map produced by then city surveyor Roger Kendrick in 1754, highlighting landownership and leases in and around St Patrick's Cathedral, Dublin. The watercolour allowed the map detail to remain visible, despite being within a coloured area. Such watercolours would have been applied by hand after the map had been printed, either by Kendrick himself or by a member of staff in the print shop. Many examples of the work of Thomas Sherrard and Jonathan Barker belong to this category. A prime instance of Sherrard's uses of this colouring scheme was his eight-foot-long 1790 map of Church Street/Phibsborough Road/Botanic Road, with the main buildings highlighted and classified by colour – red for residences and businesses, and grey for outhouses such as sheds and stables (pl. 5).[39] Thomas Owen, surveyor to the Paving Board, was requested in 1785 to include a simple scheme colour for thematic mapping:

and valuation of Ireland, pp 58–93 [445], H.C. 1824, viii.79.   **37** R.A. Skelton, *County atlases of the British Isles* (London, 1970), p. 106.   **38** Maps of Thomas Reading and Peter Callan, 1727–1871 (NLI Hatch Estate maps, MS 21F107), maps 4 & 5.   **39** Thomas Sherrard, 'Church Street, Constitution Hill and Phibsboro Road' (1790) (DCA WSC/Maps/263).

> With the streets marked with different colours, distinguishing those which are
> to be kept in repair, those done with broad stone pavement &c. &c., also maps
> with the streets that are light with the new globes; which were ordered to be
> distributed to each director & commissioner.[40]

The final group utilized a more opaque colour that fulfilled the dual role of distinguishing separate map features and giving the map a more decorative finish (pls 6–8).
Maps in this group often bear a resemblance to reality, with fields and woodlands
portrayed much like a landscape painting – albeit one in which the view is from
above the area. Such works are often the most visually striking and attractive maps
produced during this period. One practitioner was Francis Mathews, who used this
method in 1783 for a survey of lands in Templeogue, where natural shades of browns
and greens were effectively used to represent the area in a realistic manner. Mathews'
use of colour not only highlighted separate sections of land, but also demonstrated
land usage by distinguishing meadows from ploughed fields, and added to the artistic
quality of the overall map. Maps of this type were rare in eighteenth-century Ireland
due to the time, expense and talent involved, however they can be found in disproportionately higher numbers for estate surveys rather than cadastral or printed maps.

The English surveying author Samuel Wyld was a proponent of this third decorative style of colouring. He attempted to formalize the relationship between colours
and the various features found in maps:

> Lay on the colours in manner following, being first ground, and bound with
> gum-water very thin and bodiless: arable for corn, you may wash with pale
> straw-colour, made of yellow oker and white-lead; for meadows, take pink
> and verdigrease in a light green; pasture in a deep green of pink, azure, and
> smalts; fenns, a deep green; as also heaths of yellow and indigo; trees, a sadder
> green, of white-lead and verdigrease; for mud-walls and ways, mix white-lead
> and rust of iron, or with okers brown of Spain ... for seas, a greenish sky
> colour, of indico, azure, smalts, white lead and verdigrease.[41]

One primary reason for the lack of highly coloured printed maps during this period
is that using copper-plate printing for colour did not become technically feasible
until the nineteenth century.[42] Prior to this, colour was added by hand, either by the
surveyor and his assistants or by the purchaser of the map after printing. Several treatises were produced in the seventeenth and eighteenth centuries describing methods
of colouring maps, as the process was seen as an acceptable and genteel pastime. John
Smith's *The art of painting in oil* (London, 1701) states that map colouring would
appeal to those

---

40 Minutes of Paving Board, 10 Jan. 1785 (DCA PB/Mins/14, p. 25). **41** Wyld, *The
practical surveyor*, p. 114. **42** Woodward, *Five centuries of map printing*, p. 53.

that are inclined in ingenuity, to set forth the way and manner of doing this work, it being an excellent recreation for those gentry, and others, who delight in the knowledge of maps; who by being coloured, and the several divisions distinguished one from the other by colours of different kinds, do give a better idea of the countries they describe, than they can possibly do uncoloured.[43]

Wyld added that the colouring of maps was not necessarily the realm of the land surveyor: 'this colouring and adorning of plots, is rather the painter's work than the surveyor's: yet if he has time to spare, and patience to finish the work, it may prove a pretty diversion'.[44] There were those who took a more disdainful view of map colouring, however, such as the French engineer Hubert Gautier, who felt that 'one can learn the complete essence of it in three or four lessons. Women and nuns can easily occupy themselves with this sort of activity'.[45]

For manuscript colouring, allum-water was applied to the map as the initial preparation, in order to prevent paint from being fully absorbed by the parchment or paper. Taking the materials needed to create different colours, grinding them into a fine powder and adding a small amount of water, produced different colours. Several treatises described methods to produce basic map colours and how these colours could be altered to produce different shades.[46] The paint was applied with a brush and the outline of the colour was highlighted firstly with a black lead pencil and then with a pen, using the same colour paint as that on the map.[47]

English printer William Faithorne attempted to develop a method that removed the need to colour maps by hand, by using more than one identical copper plate, each having incised on it only those parts to be printed in a single colour. When the original black and white print had been produced, the print was realigned and the coloured sections were each superimposed onto the print in turn.[48] This method has not yet been observed in any examples of eighteenth-century Dublin map printing.

---

43 John Smith, *The art of painting in oil* (London, 1701), quoted in David Woodward, *Art and cartography* (Chicago, 1987), p. 134. 44 Wyld, *The practical surveyor*, p. 115. 45 Hubert Gautier, *Art du laver, ou nouvelle manière de peindre su le papier* (Lyon, 1687), quoted in Sponberg Pedley, *The commerce of cartography*, p. 69. 46 Leybourn, *The complete surveyor*, p. 307. 47 Laurence, *The surveyor's guide*, p. 225. 48 Faithorne, *The art of graving and etching*, p. 69.

11 'Please the fancy of the draftsman': decorative features in Dublin period mapping

Maps are more than pure geographic data. They are in many ways a form of communication as informative as any book or as detailed as the spoken word. They are not dependant on the language spoken by the reader nor, on the most basic level, do they need specialized training to interpret. Subtle information about a map's purpose or the reason for its creation can be included in the form of decorative features – primarily cartouches, vignettes or decorative titles. This chapter examines a number of decorative features commonly found in Dublin mapping from this era, how such features can be used to assess the surveyor's skill and how, under pressure from a demanding audience, map ornamentation progressed and evolved to meet the latest cartographic fashions.

CARTOUCHES

The cartouche[1] provided the eighteenth-century map maker with an opportunity to display his creative artistic talents. The presence of such non-geographic features[2] separated the amateur surveyor from the professional; with high-quality cartouches and vignettes separating the artistic surveyor from the professional. Cartouches, vignettes and title boxes are non-geographic, decorative or ornate features containing a map's title, its dedication, its author's name and occasionally its scale bar. In Ireland, such features ranged from the simple shapes of the late seventeenth and early eighteenth centuries,[3] to the ornate baroque[4] and later rococo[5] extravagance of the eighteenth century, to the modest, yet decorative, works of Dublin's early nineteenth-century surveys.[6]

1 Ornate tablet or shield bearing an inscription, monogram or heraldic arms framed in elaborate scrolls, shell-shaped volutes or similar designs: Jane Turner (ed.), *The dictionary of art* (34 vols, New York, 1996), v, p. 899.   2 This term relates to features that are part of a map's framework but were not measured as part of the survey; for example, north arrows, scale bars, cartouches, vignettes etc.   3 For example, Joseph Moland, 'Map of Lusk' (1716), reproduced in Refaussé and Clark, *A catalogue of the maps*, p. 59, pl. 8.   4 'The principle European style in visual arts … often extended to the whole period 1600–1750 without qualifying restrictions … to mean a florid and elaborate style in art, architecture, music or literature': Turner (ed.), *Dictionary of art*, iii, p. 261.   5 'A decorative style … the character of its formal idiom is marked by asymmetry and naturalism, displaying in particular fascination with shell-like and watery forms': Jane Turner (ed.), *Dictionary of art*, xxvi, p. 491.   6 Thomas

The evolution of cartouche and title box design throughout the eighteenth century reflects contemporary artistic trends. Several surveyors active during this period were educated at the Royal Dublin Society's schools of drawing, architecture and ornamental design, and this education is reflected in their work. Dublin surveyors Thomas Sherrard and Richard Brassington and Samuel Byron, for example, were educated at the same school as artist Bland Gallant, who was known for his work as an engraver servicing the silver trade.[7] The connection between map design, symbolism and fashions in eighteenth-century art was commented on by William Allen in 1789:

> The advantages which assure the community … the study of design [is] not confined to the superior ranks of life; they are defined through a variety of ingenious branches of manufacture, in which a taste of knowledge of drawing is indispensably necessary, for their attaining perfection.[8]

Cartouches allowed more information to be conveyed to the map reader than simply the name of the area mapped, who produced it and in what year. The cartouche can hint at the social background of a map or even the political climate within which it was created, without the need for large sections of text, as noted by the modern writer Christian Jacob:

> Writing interferes with the drawing, and only through a complex process of visual adaptation can the one order be dissociated from the other. Writing and drawing conform to two different forms of graphic logic.[9]

The early nineteenth-century English surveyor, A. Nesbit, had the following advice as to what non-geographic decoration may be included in mapping:

> Any compartment or device may be chosen to fill up the vacant corners of a plan, such as the compass, scrolls of paper, wreaths or festoons of leaves and flowers, branches or springs of oak, palm trees, weeping-willows, myrtle, laurel, olive &c. &c. Also shields, coats of arms, columns supporting vases or urns, mathematical instruments, cattle, sheep or whatever else may please the fancy of the draftsman.[10]

Period Irish cartouches and title boxes can be divided into three distinct groups. Firstly, the basic shape – that is, a square, a rectangle, a triangle, an oval – in which is contained the map's title, its author, the date of survey etc. These title boxes are very

Sherrard, *A survey of part of the city of Dublin showing several improvements intended by the Commissioners of Wide Streets* (Dublin, 1801).   **7** John Turpin, *A school of art in Dublin since the eighteenth century* (Dublin, 1995), p. 49.   **8** Ibid., p. 6.   **9** Christian Jacob, *The sovereign map* (Chicago, 2006), p. 215.   **10** Nesbit, *Treatise on practical land surveying*.

simple, with minimal, if any, decoration, and are commonly found among estate maps[11] and other day-to-day cadastral surveys[12] not meant for mass duplication or publication. They are found throughout the entire period covered by this study (1690–1810).

Rococo and baroque style cartouches make up the second category. Baroque is an artistic style primarily associated with the seventeenth century but continuing well into the eighteenth, while rococo emerged during the eighteenth century. A particular master of baroque was Gabriel Stokes,[13] while Rocque[14] and Scalé are both associated with rococo.[15] Such cartouches contain examples of landscape painting, surveying equipment and surveyors at work, putti, heraldry and images of local industry and agriculture. These features are found mainly in prestige pieces or adorning city and town plans.

The third group is noted for its use of minimalist curved and swirled lines in and around the title of the map without any box or containment of such text (fig. 11.1). While mainly being associated with Irish cartography from the beginning of the nineteenth century, one of the earliest examples of this style can be traced back to the 1780s.[16] Although lacking the artistic range of the baroque and rococo examples, or the definition of a title box format, this rounded and discrete format was both elegant and simple and its presence is a useful method in estimating the age of a map missing either a date or a surveyor's signature.

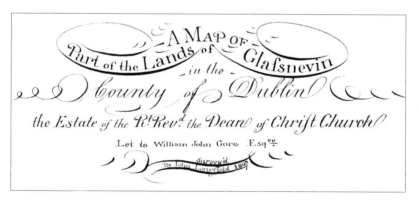

11.1 A minimalist design and curved lines of an early nineteenth-century map title (from John Longfield, 'Glasnevin' (1807), NLI MSS 2798–90(62), courtesy of the National Library of Ireland © NLI).

11 Michael Kenny, 'Map of Glasnevin' (1804) (NLI Domville papers, MS 11,937(21)). **12** Sherrard and Brownrigg, 'Fishamble Street' (1805) (NLI Longfield papers, MS 21F88 (153)). **13** Gabriel Stokes, 'Map of Tallaght' (1718), reproduced in Refaussé and Clark, *A catalogue of the maps*, p. 63, pl. 10. **14** John Rocque, *Kildare* (Kildare, 1758). **15** Bernard Scalé, *Dublin city and suburbs* (Dublin, 1773); Bernard Scalé, 'A survey of the demesne of Dundalk' (1777), reproduced in O'Sullivan, *Dundalk* (Irish Historic Towns Atlas, no. 16, Dublin, 2006), map 11. **16** Francis Mathews, 'Map of lands in Templeogue' (1783), reproduced in Refaussé and Clark, *A catalogue of the maps*, pl. 46.

TITLE BARS

Basic shape title boxes were the simplest, fastest and cheapest method of displaying surveyor and map information. There were a number of possible reasons for the selection of this style. Low prestige maps required less investment on the cartographer's side, so less time and effort would be spent on map decoration. Such basic shape title boxes were very common in seventeenth- and eighteenth-century maps of Dublin. John Speed's 1610 map of the city presents this style in its simplest form, with the word 'Dubline' in a box. Forty years later, the work of Robert Newcomen showed the beginnings of a more decorative style, yet the titles for his map of Tallaght (1654) and Rathcoole (1654) were still very much of this basic shape. This simple style was relatively widespread in cadastral manuscript maps throughout the eighteenth century. As these were for a practical purpose and not designed to be mass produced, relatively little attention was paid to elaborate map decoration.

This simple title box, while being common in maps from the first half of the eighteenth century, can also be found in manuscript cadastral maps into the first decade of the nineteenth century.[17] The surveying firm Sherrard, Brassington and Green produced some of the most ornamental and elaborate examples of Irish map decorations seen since the era of John Rocque.[18] Yet, for many of their lower prestige cadastral maps,[19] they used a simple box format title. John Brownrigg, Roger Kendrick and Thomas Cave, all known to have produced elaborate cartouches,[20] also reverted to a more understated cartouche design for their cadastral maps.[21]

BAROQUE AND ROCOCO

Some of the most high profile maps produced in Ireland during the eighteenth century are those considered, then as now, to be prestige pieces (figs 11.2, 11.3). These maps, usually estate, city or town plans, were commissioned for commercial purposes or by wealthy clients and were embellished with elaborate cartouches which regu-

---

17 Michael Kenny, 'Map of Glasnevin' (1804) (NLI Domville papers, MS 11,937(21)). **18** Sherrard, Brassington and Greene, 'A map of Balbutcher, Ballymun' (1808) (NLI Domville papers, MS 11,937(61)), is an excellent example of a detailed, watercolour cartouche produced by Sherrard during his long surveying career. **19** Sherrard and Brownrigg, 'Fishamble Street' (1805) (NLI Longfield papers, MS 21F88 (153)). **20** Thomas Cave, 'Map of Belinstown and Loughmartin' (1728), reproduced in Refaussé and Clark, *A catalogue of the maps*, p. 68, pl. 16. Roger Kendrick, 'Map of lands in the parish of Tallaght' (1752), reproduced in Refaussé and Clark, *A catalogue of the maps*, p. 74, pl. 19. **21** Thomas Cave, 'Map of Loughlinstown' (1716) (NLI Domville papers, MS 11,937(10)); Roger Kendrick, 'Map of Bridesglen' (1757) (NLI Domville papers, MS 11,937(57)); John Brownrigg, 'Merrion Row' (1791) (NLI Longfield papers, MS 21F89(189)); John Brownrigg, 'Harcourt Street' (1793) (NLI Longfield papers, MS 21F89(159)); John Brownrigg, 'Hawkins Street' (1790) (NLI Longfield papers, MS 21F89(165)).

11.2 Rocque's map decoration often surpassed the design level of native Irish surveyors (cartouche, John Rocque, *County Dublin* (Dublin, 1760), courtesy of the Board of Trinity College Dublin).

larly reflected the heraldry or industry of the town or individual. Many of these decorative cartouches were drawn in the baroque and the later rococo style – fashionable decorative trends emphasizing dramatic, often strained effect and typified by bold, curving forms and elaborate ornamentation. The artistic quality to which many of Ireland's cartouches were produced during the eighteenth century varies immensely.

The way in which non-geographic features were planned and changed can be seen in a rare copy William Petty's *Hiberniae delineatio* (London, 1685), presented to Ireland's surveyor general sometime in the mid- to late seventeenth century, and preserved in Dublin's Marsh's Library.[22] This draft allows an insight into changes that Petty envisaged before his final print as well as possible features he chose to exclude. Putti made regular appearances throughout *Hiberniae delineatio*. Petty's scale bar on his map of Queen's County, for instance, contains three winged putti holding a

22 William Petty, *Hiberniae delineatio* (1685) (Marsh, H4.1.1).

11.3 Rocque's apprentice, Bernard Scalé, continued his master's style
(cartouche, Bernard Scalé, *A plan of Trinity College Dublin* (Dublin, 1761),
courtesy of the Board of Trinity College Dublin).

surveyor's chain, while the map of Kildare included one putto drawn in ink, and
another lightly drawn in pencil for possible inclusion in the final print (fig. 11.4). The
use of putti with surveying instruments was a common decorative device in maps
both in Petty's time[23] and later.[24] Drafts were important when producing maps. They
represented an essential element of quality control – one example being a map of
Connaught by Petty missing all three Aran Islands as well as Achill Island.[25]

Baroque and rococo cartouches can be recognized by their contents. The dedication or map title tends to be surrounded by curving shells,[26] curtains[27] or natural
features such as flowers.[28] Putti are a regular feature,[29] as are heraldic symbols, either
of cities[30] or of the patrons of the map.[31] Rococo differs from baroque in several
subtle ways, mainly being less symmetrical and lighter in theme. Often the differen-

23 Leybourn, *The complete surveyor*, p. 43.   **24** Robert Gibson, 'Map of Kimmage' (1749)
(NLI Domville papers, MS 11,937(3)).   **25** Petty, *Hiberniae delineatio* (1685) (Marsh H4.1.1),
Connaught.   **26** Rocque, *Kilkenny*.   **27** John Ewing, *City of Londonderry* (Derry/
Londonderry, 1747).   **28** Rocque, *Kildare*.   **29** Petty, *Hiberniae delineatio*; Rocque, *An exact
survey*; Thomas Cave, 'Map of Belinstown and Loughmartin' (1728), reproduced in Refaussé
and Clark, *A catalogue of the maps*, p. 68, pl. 16.   **30** John Ewing, *City of Londonderry* (1747),
reproduced in Avril Thomas, *Derry* (Irish Historic Towns Atlas, no. 15, Dublin, 2006), map
15. William Wilson, *Dublin* (Dublin, 1810).   **31** Scalé, *Dublin city and suburbs*; idem, 'A survey
of the demesne of Dundalk' (1777), reproduced in O'Sullivan, *Dundalk* (Irish Historic Towns
Atlas, no. 16), map 11.

11.4 A partial drawn putti (r) in Sir William Petty's *Hiberniae delineato* (1685) (courtesy of the Governors and Guardians of Marsh's Library © Marsh's Library).

tiation between rococo and baroque cartouches can be difficult. Baroque themes can be found throughout eighteenth-century mapping, whereas rococo, often with transitional baroque elements, are found in mid- to late eighteenth-century examples.

With the growing popularity of baroque decoration both in mainland Europe and in Britain, it is no surprise to find this fashion in eighteenth-century Dublin mapping. A highly skilled and well implemented early eighteenth-century baroque cartouche can be found in Gabriel Stokes' *Map of Tallaght* (1718), which, despite its immense detail, seems out of place when compared to the map's sparse cartographic detail – one boundary line and four minute houses. Richard Frizzell is known to have used a stamp for repeated use of the same ornate cartouche (fig. 11.5).[32]

Change came hard to some sections of Dublin's surveying community. Thomas Reading, for example, tried to alter his style to keep abreast of fashion, but demonstrated a reluctance to move from established norms. In 1764, Reading produced a map of the area around Christ Church Cathedral (fig. 11.6).[33] The geographic detail was well laid out and easily read, with the intricate internal structure of the cathedral included. Reading's cartouche featured rococo motifs such as shells and flora. Its text was clear and legible. However, Reading's scale bar and reference table would not

32 Richard Frizzell, 'Map of Clondalkin' (1781) (NLI Domville papers, MS 11,937(38)); Richard Frizzell, 'Map of Ballyfermot' (1781) (NLI Domville papers, MS 11,937(60)). **33** Thomas Reading, 'Map of the Liberty of Christ Church' (1764), reproduced in Clarke, *Dublin part 1, to 1610* (Irish Historic Towns Atlas, no. 11), map 8.

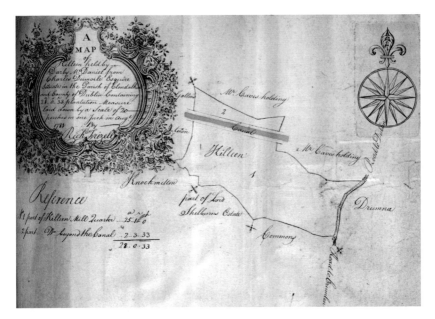

11.5 A rare stamp cartouche used in surveyor Richard Frizzell's 'Map of Clondalkin' (1781) (courtesy of the National Library of Ireland © NLI).

have looked out of place in early seventeenth-century maps, with heavy, dark and simplistic borders surrounding small and difficult-to-read text. The overall effect of such a mismatched and disjointed style is to take focus away from the well-executed cartouche and good cartographic features, and to draw attention to the out-of-place reference table, which clashed with both the cartouche and the map detail. Reading appeared to be attempting to follow popular cartographic fashion, yet seemed to be reluctant to leave behind certain aspects of cartography that he was either trained in or had grown accustomed to. Such mixed styles provide a very useful insight into the evolution of Irish cartography during the first half of the eighteenth century and the changes in cartographic fashion.

One of the most influential individuals in cartographic fashion in Ireland was also perhaps the most skilled surveyor of the eighteenth century – John Rocque. What Rocque brought to Ireland during his stay in the 1750s, aside from his unique level of standardization and detail in geographic features, was a new style of cartouche that combined traditional features with innovative elements of classicism and symbolism previously unseen in Irish cartography. Rocque's *Exact survey of Dublin* (Dublin, 1756) combined the map title and dedication (fig. 11.7). The centre of the image was dominated by a shell arch, under which flowed a river, which (from the three castles of Dublin) the reader would understand to be the Liffey. Beside the Dublin coat of arms lay a woman, who may represent Anna Liffey,[34] Hibernia, charity or a mixture of all

34 The personification of the River Liffey, which possibly originated in the anglicization of the Irish name for the river, *Abhainn na Life.*

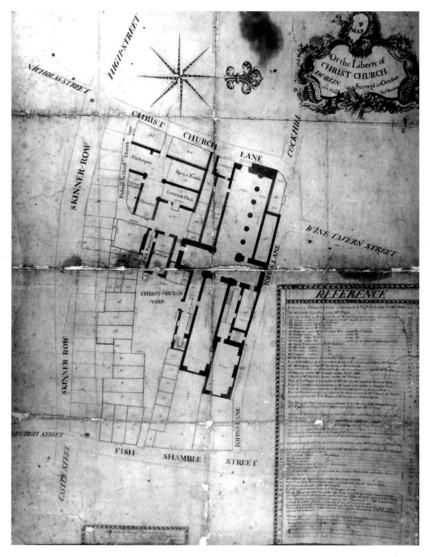

11.6 A mixture of map decorative styles by Thomas Reading, 'Map of the Liberty of Christ Church' (1764) (© Representative Church Body).

three, breast-feeding putti. The presence of a royal sceptre and the Irish houses of parliament to the left of the cartouche symbolized Dublin's importance as the political and administrative centre of Ireland, while to the right of the cartouche Britannia distributes books to two putti while holding a shield on which is displayed the symbol of Ireland, a twelve-stringed harp. Britannia and the royal sceptre underlined the strong connection between Dublin and England during this period. Dublin is a port city, and Rocque represented its maritime connection with ships' masts in the

11.7 Rocque's cartouche from the *Exact survey of Dublin* (Dublin, 1756)
(courtesy of the Royal Irish Academy © RIA).

cartouche's background, and an anchor and rope lying on top of several packages
ready for shipment.

Rocque was not the only surveyor to include human figures in his non-
geographic decoration during the mid-eighteenth century, but he did so far more
regularly and to a higher artistic standard than contemporary Irish surveyors,[35] in a
style being closely connected to French cartographic fashion.[36] Yet Rocque did not
limit himself to pure urban surveying during his time in Ireland. In 1756–60, he was
employed by James, the twentieth earl of Kildare, to create maps of his various estates
in Co. Kildare. Several of the cartouches and vignettes,[37] while not equal to the
grandeur of Rocque's masterpiece London cartouche, were among the most sophisticated of any eighteenth-century Irish manuscript map. These maps, totalling over
160, were drawn at large scale, usually sixteen perches to the inch, plantation measure,
and, in conjunction with the accompanying reference tables, give information on
physical conditions, acreage and land use of each field, type of field boundary and
type of buildings present.[38] Rocque again utilized his traditional baroque shell design
and natural elements, such as trees, to enclose his drawings.[39] Putti feature promi-

35 Michael Kenny, 'Book of maps of the estate of Charles Domville' (1778) (NLI Domville
papers, MS 11,936); James and Edmond Costello, *A map of lands in Killamy* (Sligo, 1768);
James Williamson, 'A book of maps of the estate of John Hamilton O'Hara' (1884) (NLI
O'Hara papers, MS 14A24).   36 J.B. Nolin, *Le globe* (Paris, 1707); Robert de Vaugondy,
Mappemonde ou description du globe terrestre (Paris, 1752); G. Delisle, *Carte du Canada* (Paris,
1703); George-Louis Le Rouge, *Atlas Amériquain septentrional* (Paris, 1778).   37 'Ornamental
or pictorial illustrations ... used to refer to an illustration not enclosed in a border or
squared off at the edges but shading away': Jane Turner (ed.), *Dictionary of art*, xxxii, p. 50.
38 Horner, 'Cartouches and vignettes on the Kildare estate maps of John Rocque', p. 58.
39 John Rocque, 'A survey of Tullagorey' (1756), in Horner, 'Cartouches and vignettes on

nently; however, their activities were more agricultural than expressing urban achievement. Rocque also included vignettes of country scenes,[40] farms[41] and large manor houses in his Kildare work.[42] Such elements were passed on to future generations of his students and were still routinely accompanying maps in the early nineteenth century.[43]

The work of Rocque's assistant during his period in Ireland, Bernard Scalé, is also worthy of note. Scalé's particular cartographic trademark was his antique effects. Through the simple use of shading, Scalé created the illusion of depth and, with minimal effort, was able to significantly improve the artistic quality of the map's non-geographic detail.

The rococo styles of Rocque and Scalé were not unique to Irish mapping. Rocque is known to have produced several rococo designs during his early career as an engraver, in similar style to French designer Juste Aurèle Meissonnier. Others known to have practised such designs during this time in London include engraver William Hogarth and artist John Pine.[44] While in Ireland, Rocque employed several Irish artists to work on the decoration of his maps, including John Dixon, Hugh Douglas Hamilton and Patrick Halpin. These artists produced a style described at the time as 'in point of taste, elegance of design and masterly execution [...], allowed by the connoisseurs not to be inferior to any in Europe'.[45]

Rocque's and Scalé's works were part of this wider Dublin classicism, which was popular among the aristocracy, many of whom were collectors of Italian Renaissance art.[46] Many a nobleman who employed surveyors was also a patron of other arts,[47] and it was often in his interest to be familiar with the latest artistic fashions.

INTO THE NINETEENTH CENTURY

By the end of the eighteenth century, a new, simpler, approach in cartouche design had begun to emerge. This new style, which appeared from the 1770s onwards and,

the Kildare estate maps of John Rocque'; John Rocque, 'A survey of Shanrah, Kildare' (1756). **40** John Rocque, 'A view of Kildare town' (Kildare, 1757); idem, 'A survey of the manor of Maynooth' (1757) in Horner, 'Cartouches and vignettes on the Kildare estate maps of John Rocque', p. 58. **41** John Rocque, 'A survey of Ballegrenie' (1757), in Horner, 'Cartouches and vignettes on the Kildare estate maps of John Rocque'. **42** John Rocque, 'A survey of Duneny' (1757) in Horner, 'Cartouches and vignettes on the Kildare estate maps of John Rocque'. **43** Sherrard, Brassington and Greene, 'Survey of Balbutcher' (1781) (NLI Longfield papers, MS 11,937(61)). **44** Hodge, 'A study of the rococo decoration'. **45** *Dublin Journal*, 11 Oct. 1757. **46** Frederick Hervey, bishop of Derry in the 1740s, was known to possess several paintings by Raphael in his art collection: Nicola Figgis, *Irish artists in Rome in the eighteenth century* (London, 2001), p. 18. **47** The Beresford family, one of whom was a member of the Wide Streets Commission during the 1790s, employed artist Willem van der Hagen (d. 1745) to decorate the family house at Curraghmore: Figgis, *Irish artists in Rome*, p. 42. James Mannin, director of the Dublin Society's school of ornament, was a subscriber to Rocque's 1756 map of Dublin.

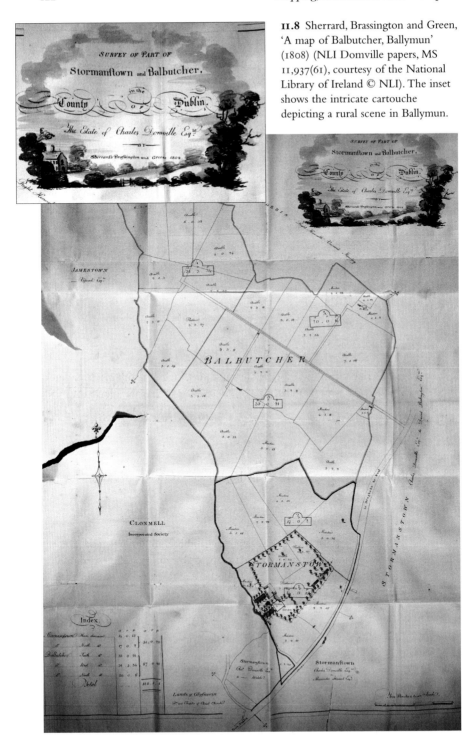

11.8 Sherrard, Brassington and Green, 'A map of Balbutcher, Ballymun' (1808) (NLI Domville papers, MS 11,937(61), courtesy of the National Library of Ireland © NLI). The inset shows the intricate cartouche depicting a rural scene in Ballymun.

with its graceful and neat swirling lines or rural images, lacked the visual impact seen in previous generations of surveyors' maps (fig. 11.8).Yet it reflected the importance of the geographic compared to the non-geographic data displayed on a map. This new method also required less time, investment and skill from the cartographer's perspective, and gradually grew in importance at the end of the eighteenth century and into the early nineteenth. Followers of this design included Bernard Scalé,[48] Thomas Sherrard,[49] John Longfield[50] and A.R. Neville.[51]

Irish cartouche design progressed markedly throughout the eighteenth century. From the heavy lined, basic and at times crude cartouches of the turn of the century, it was influenced by European fashion through the work of John Rocque as the century progressed. Cartouches and title designs often acted as trade or business cards for a surveyor, advertising the range and level of his skills. While Irish cartouche design can be classified (as seen in this chapter), this is not a rigid classification. It must also be noted that many maps, especially manuscript estate maps, were produced without cartouches, and the simple designs were still popular, if less dominant, by the end of the century.[52]

THE PRESENCE OF BUILDINGS IN MAPS

Despite the attention that cartouches and vignettes may draw when being viewed on a map, they were not the only decorative features present. For many maps, the presence of buildings or structures added one or two elements – either a local landmark to help orientate the reader or a decorative effect. Benjamin Noble advised that substantial or distinctive buildings should always be recorded during a survey:

> After this, or a similar manner, an actual survey of a county or province may be made; taking your stations along the different roads; and the various objects as castles, churches, or country seats, may be taken in, as you chain along, by taking the bearing of each object at two different places on the chaining.[53]

Jonathan Barker, for example, used several megalithic monuments and ancient standing stones as boundary points in a 1762 map of Dundrum and its surrounding areas.[54] These are displayed in profile, while the other buildings on the map remained

48 Bernard Scalé, *County Cavan* (Dublin, 1776).   **49** Thomas Sherrard, *A survey of part of the city of Dublin showing several improvements intended by the Commissioners of Wide Streets* (Dublin, 1801).   **50** John Longfield, 'Several holdings in Mercer Street' (1800) (NLI Longfield papers, MS 11,937(185)). John Longfield, 'Skinners Row' (1808) (NLI Longfield papers, MS 2789(115)).   **51** A.R. Neville, 'Land off Kevin Street belonging to St Patrick's' (1811) (NLI St Patrick's estate papers, MS 11,937(194)).   **52** John Brownrigg, 'Merrion Row' (1791) (NLI Longfield papers, MS 21F89(189)); John Brownrigg, 'Harcourt Street' (1793) (NLI Longfield papers, MS 21F89(159)); John Brownrigg, 'Hawkins Street' (1790) (NLI Longfield papers, MS 21F89(165)).   **53** Noble, *Geodæsia Hibernica*, p. 50.   **54** Jonathan

in planimetric format. John Roe included a small profile drawing of a ruined castle in an 1801 map of the lands around Newcastle village,[55] Samuel Byron included 'an ancient cairn' in a map of Kilcullen in 1794,[56] John Brownrigg included an old high cross near Loughlinstown[57] and a 'great military double ditch',[58] while John Longfield included a tower described as 'a turret'[59] in addition to an old castle in Brennanstown.[60] James Mooley used a similar technique when he included a large 'thorn tree' as a local reference point in a survey of Santry in 1764.[61] These written descriptions allow a rough assessment of the condition of such historical features in the eighteenth century, which is of particular interest if such buildings do not survive to the modern age.

Historical features, such as castles, round towers or churches, represented a form of local referencing that was visible for miles. Indeed, even in modern Dublin, Christ Church and St Patrick's cathedrals remain two of the tallest structures within the city centre. There was always a risk that such notable buildings would be featured too prominently in a map, however, particularly in terms of their size. One author advised that:

> The ground-plot of buildings ought in all cases to be expressed by the same scale that the rest of the plot was laid down by, and to be taken notice of in the table of references; but never go about to draw the representation of a house or barn in the midst of the plot, so big as will cover an acre or two of land.[62]

Homes of landlords and 'country seats' were also regularly displayed in profile in eighteenth-century Irish mapping. These can be found most frequently in estate maps. Wyld stated that:

> If [one] would express a gentleman's seat or manor-house, 'tis best done in some corner of the draught, or in the plan by itself, annexed to that of the estate to which it belongs. And the house must be drawn in perspective ... and if the gardens, walks and avenues to the house are expressed, it must be in the same manner; and where there are trees, they must be shadowed on the light side.[63]

Barker, 'A map of Dundrum and all its subdivisions' (1762) (NAI Pembroke papers, 2011/2/2/4). **55** John Roe, 'Lands of Newcastle: part of the estate of Michael Aylmer' (1801) (NLI Cloncurry papers MS 16(G)50(7)). **56** Samuel Byron, 'Kilcullen, Co. Kildare' (1794) (NLI Christ Church papers, MSS 2789–90 (35)). **57** John Brownrigg, 'Loughlinstown' (1798) (NLI Christ Church papers, MS 2789(11)). **58** Ibid. (MS 2789(10)). **59** John Longfield, 'Back Lane' (1815) (NLI Christ Church papers, MSS 2789–90(40)). **60** John Longfield, 'Lands in Brennanstown' (1822) (NLI Christ Church papers, MSS 2789–90(71)). **61** James Mooley, 'Santry' (1764) (NLI Domville papers, MS 11,937). **62** Wyld, *The practical surveyor*, p. 113. **63** Ibid.

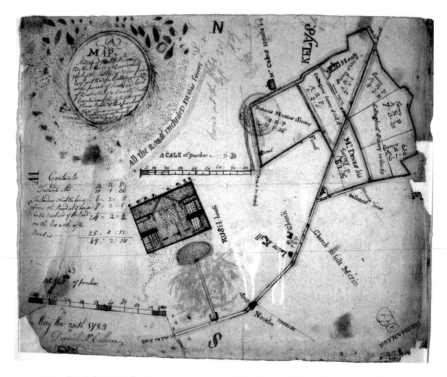

11.9 Daniel McCollon's poor attempt at including buildings in a map of Rush Demesne (1785) (NLI Hatch papers, MS 21.F.141(21), courtesy of the National Library of Ireland © NLI).

Fine examples of profile views of houses in estate maps can be found in the works of Rocque,[64] Longfield[65] and Barker.[66]

Flattering the patron of a map by including a profile of his house made good business sense. Such inclusions may have been requested, or expected, by the landlord himself, although no proof exists of this. The majority of representations of a landlord's house were carried out to a reasonable degree of artistic quality, with Rocque, as usual, producing some of the finest examples. Not all were finished to the same high standards, however. A map drawn by Daniel McCollon in 1785 of Rush Demesne (fig. 11.9)[67] stands out as a particularly poor instance, as the estate house and several surrounding cottages were presented in profile in a style that can only be described as amateurish, with little or no regard to orientation. They were drawn in heavy ink in a careless manner. The inclusion of profile buildings could often be extended to multiple parties, principally when such maps were printed and had required subscriptions as funding. Taylor and Skinner's *Maps of the roads of Ireland*

64 John Rocque, 'A survey of Duneny, Co. Kildare' (1757). **65** John Longfield, 'Kilcullen, Co. Kildare' (1809) (NLI Christ Church papers, MS 2789(125)). **66** Jonathan Barker, 'A map of Owenstown' (1762) (NAI Pembroke papers, 2011/2/2). **67** Daniel McCollon, 'Rush Demesne' (1785) (NLI Hatch papers, MS 21F141(21)).

11.10 Samuel Byron's excellent representation of Trinity College (1790)
(TCD MS Mun/mc/9, courtesy of the Board of Trinity College Dublin).

(Dublin, 1777) offered subscribers such an option, and the environs of each route in
the atlas are littered with small profile drawings of houses of subscribers, the family
name inscribed below.

Profiles of important buildings were not widespread in eighteenth-century Irish
maps. Several surveyors attempted to present such buildings with depth, thus creating
a three-dimensional effect. Samuel Byron was particularly skilled at this method, as
demonstrated by a superbly detailed plan of Trinity College (fig. 11.10).[68] John Roe
presented the manor house of Rush Demesne in such a way, and with a reasonable

68 Samuel Byron, 'Trinity College' (1790) (TCD MS MUN/MC/9).

II.II Bernard Scalé's façade survey of Dublin's parliament buildings on
College Green (1767) (courtesy of the National Library of Ireland © NLI).

degree of success, as the separate wings of the building as well as detail, such as
windows, were visible.[69] Scalé employed a similar technique in a plan of Tallow, Co.
Waterford, in 1774.

Aside from the homes of those financing a map, important civic buildings were
often included.[70] Such buildings were usually presented in profile in the margins of
the map rather than within the actual map itself. Charles Brooking's 1728 map of
Dublin included along the border of the map Dublin Castle, the Poorhouse, St
Werburgh's Church and other important public buildings within the city.[71] Rocque
included a similar feature along the top of his 1756 map of the city and its surroundings, showing Kildare House, the Royal Barracks and Kilmainham Hospital.

Scalé produced a series of plans of Parliament House on College Green[72] around
1767 (fig. 11.11). While it is likely that the four architectural plans are by another
author (as Scalé never ventured into architecture), the fifth plan, showing a complete
façade survey of the building, is acknowledged to be Scalé's own work.

Discussions on façade surveys were rare within period surveying publications.
Two authors – Samuel Wyld and John Hammond – dedicated space, however small,
to this technique. Both suggested that the theodolite was the preferred instrument[73]

69 John Roe, 'The demesne of Rush' (1806) (NLI St Patrick's Cathedral papers, MS
21F141(13)). **70** O'Dwyer, 'Building empires'. **71** Charles Brooking, *A map of the city and
suburbs of Dublin* (London, 1728). **72** Christine Casey, *Dublin* (New haven & London,
2005), p. 380. **73** Hammond, *The practical surveyor*, p. 152.

and that an intersection method was the appropriate technique, that is, measuring the angle and elevation of a particular point (for example, the corner of a door) from two or more separate locations and then joining the lines of observation when drawing the map. Accuracy was of utmost importance as

> objects ought to be delineated thereon according to their dimensions and different situations, in such a manner that the said representation may produce the same effects on our eyes as the objects were of [*sic*] they are the pictures.[74]

The surveyor would record the location of details such as doors, windows and corners of the building from a distance and then move to a second location at a known distance from the original survey location and at the same distance from the building, re-recording the same points. This would provide two sets of angles, both horizontal and vertical, that should meet when drawn, thus giving the location of a recorded point.

Such complicated façade surveys could be quite time consuming, and to reduce the time involved, Wyld suggested the following short-cut:

> Observe that if the building be regular, there will need but few points to be given; for, where you have the height and breath [*sic*] of one window given, with its distance from the next, the whole row may thereby be drawn, being all of the same dimensions, but objects more irregular must be drawn by observing so many points therein, as shall be necessary: but practise in this case is the best guide.[75]

Given the complex nature of the parliament building, it is safe to assume that Scalé's survey took considerable time.

74 Wyld, *The practical surveyor*, p. 165.   **75** Ibid., p. 169.

12 'Much nearer the truth than imagined': geographic referencing and area calculation

Maps are not simply a reproduction of the ground on which a survey took place. Visual ascetics aside, surveyors required an inherent level of practicality to their maps. To the landlord or tenant, a map could demonstrate the extent of a property; to the aficionado, it could substitute as a piece of art or decorative hanging; however, for the surveyor it was primarily a source from which functional information could be obtained. Geographic referencing refers to any measurements, figures or symbols, for example north arrows, evidence of magnetic variation measurement, scale bars, survey control lines or latitude and longitudinal coordinates, that allow the position of a particular survey area to be established within a local, regional or global frame of reference. These elements, coupled with determination of area, are of utmost importance to mapping that originated from land surveys, and their execution often directly portrays the professional skill of the surveyor responsible.

NORTH ARROWS

North arrows and compass roses or markers often played a dual practical and decorative role within period mapping (fig. 12.1). They were among the most common forms of decorative geographic referencing in Irish eighteenth-century mapping and, while some were well executed, ornate, neat and appropriately proportioned,[1] the majority were rough, basic and often, as J.H. Andrews has noted, 'ludicrously large as well as distractingly colourful'.[2]

One unusual feature of geographic orientation in the eighteenth-century was that maps were not universally orientated with the north point facing the top of the page, as is now customary in cartography. Despite Samuel Wyld's insistence that 'the north part of the plot is always supposed to be placed upwards, and the east to be on the right hand',[3] not all maps were thus orientated. One well-known example of this is Charles Brooking's 1728 map of Dublin, which is orientated south/north rather than north/south. While theoretically there is nothing inappropriate about this, considering that the custom of having maps orientated north/south is arbitrary, it does stray from the norm. In this case, there is a logical explanation, as the corresponding view of the city on the top of the map looks southwards over the city, and so the map and the city view are orientated in the same direction.

---

1 Of particular note are Thomas Cave, 'Rath, Navan' (1748) (NLI Domville papers MS 11,937); Thomas Sherrard, *Athlone* (Dublin, 1784), reproduced in Harman Murtagh, *Athlone* (Irish Historic Towns Atlas, no. 6, Dublin, 1994), map 7(a).   **2** Andrews, *Plantation acres*, p. 153.   **3** Wyld, *The practical surveyor*, p. 112.

12.1 Human hand for a map's north arrow (from Michael Kenny, 'Francis Street' (1770), NLI Domville papers, MS 11,937(32), courtesy of the National Library of Ireland © NLI).

Brooking was not the only surveyor to orientate his map in a less traditional manner. Bernard Scalé's map of Essex Street in 1777,[4] produced with the assistance of two apprentices, Thomas Sherrard and John Brownrigg, follows a similar logic. Scalé's north arrow is neat, clear and slightly off vertical. The reason for this is that Scalé had to orientate his survey so that it would fit the paper size chosen for this map, while not reducing its scale. Robert Gibson was another surveyor who focused on visual correctness rather than north alignment for a map of Kimmage in 1749,[5] as did Jonathan Barker for his 1762 map of Dundrum.[6]

Scalé's north arrow design was above the standard for an Irish eighteenth-century surveyor. His arrows were ornate and detailed, depicting scenes of country life or human figures presented in a style more complex and imaginative than that of other Irish surveyors. Of particular note is Scalé's *Hibernian atlas*, published in 1776, which consisted of maps of each province and county in Ireland. These illustrate the range of arrows that Scalé was able to produce, with strong agricultural themes. He was highly creative in their execution.

The *Hibernian atlas* is not the only example of Scalé's artistic style, as several of his maps[7] contain equally artistic and creative north arrows. The real creative strength of Scalé's arrows is that they added to his map's cartographic style rather than competing with it by distracting the reader's attention, as was common with maps by other surveyors of the era.

Scalé's apprentices learned such techniques from their master, and of particular note is the work of Thomas Sherrard, whose maps often demonstrate his master's influence.[8] Sherrard, however, did not add extensively to the style developed in Ireland by Rocque and Scalé, and such high-quality north arrows are very rare in Sherrard's work over his long career. There is evidence of other Irish surveyors with less artistic ability trying to replicate this style. A copy of a Thomas Logan map made by an unknown author includes what could be considered an attempt to copy Scalé's north arrow styling; however, a small man drawn with the arrow appears to have been impaled by the arrow, from the groin upwards (fig. 12.2).[9]

4 Scalé, Sherrard and Brownrigg, 'Essex Street' (1777) (NLI Cloncurry papers, MS 16G16(15)). **5** Robert Gibson, 'Mundon near Kimmage' (1749) (NLI Domville papers, MS 11,937). **6** Jonathan Baker, 'A map of Dundrum and all its subdivisions' (1762) (NAI Pembroke papers, 2011/2/2/4). **7** For example, Bernard Scalé, 'Maynooth' (1773), reproduced in Arnold Horner, *Maynooth* (Irish Historic Towns Atlas, no. 7, Dublin, 1995), map 6. **8** Sherrard, 'Athlone', reproduced in Murtagh, *Athlone*, map 7(a). **9** Thomas

12.2 A man impaled on a north arrow when map decoration went astray for an unknown surveyor (from copy of Thomas Logan, 'Lord Palmerston's estate, Donnybrook' (copy 1795), NLI Longfield papers, MS 21.F.88(133), courtesy of the National Library of Ireland © NLI).

THE COMPASS ROSE

One of the most common styles of north arrow design in eighteenth-century Irish mapping is the circular or star compass, with north indicated by a fleur-de-lis (fig. 12.3). Given the limited amount that could be done with such a simple feature, there is a surprisingly varied degree of quality in this simple compass design. The work of Thomas Cave merits particular note, for the high level of detail, clarity, restrained colouring and proportional size of its compass points.[10]

At the other end of the artistic spectrum is the work of Peter Duff,[11] whose compasses and north arrows were crude, unusually outsized, dominating large portions of the map's surface, and brightly coloured, particularly with yellow, which distracts the reader's attention from the map's geographic data. Such design features, taken into account along with Duff's trademark use of equally large and brightly coloured callipers on his scale bars,[12] meant that excessively large portions of his maps were unnecessarily dedicated to such geographic reference markers (fig. 12.4). An even more enthusiastic use of north arrows is found in the work of Roger Kendrick, who on one occasion produced two north arrows on the same map, facing in opposite directions (fig. 12.5).[13] Stylistically, the majority of Irish north arrows and compass points fall between those of Cave and Duff. Several surveyors[14] produced the same style north arrows throughout their professional careers, and strayed little if at all from the same basic designs.

Common traits, such as a fleur-de-lis marking the position of north, a single or double circular ring around the compass, lack of human figures or floral decoration,

Logan, 'Lord Palmerston's estate, Donnybrook' (copied 1795) (NLI Longfield papers, MS 21F88(133)). **10** Thomas Cave, 'Loughlinstown' (1716) (NLI Domville papers, MS 11,937(10)); Thomas Cave, 'Great Rath, Navan' (1748) (NLI Domville papers, MS 11,937(34)); Thomas Cave, 'Waterside, County Meath' (n.d.) (NLI Domville papers, MS 11,937(43)); Thomas Cave, 'Loughlinstown' (1746) (NLI MS 11,937(53)). **11** Peter Duff, 'Ballymun' (1713) (NLI Domville papers, MS 11,937(14)). **12** Ibid.; Peter Duff, 'County Meath' (1713) (NLI Domville papers, MS 11,937(6)); Peter Duff, 'Raleigh, County Meath' (1713) (NLI Domville papers, MS 11,937(42)); Peter Duff, 'Tallow, County Meath' (1718) (NLI Domville papers, MS 11,937(46)). **13** Roger Kendrick, 'Upper Coombe' (1741) (Maps of the liberty of St Patrick's Cathedral (1741), Marsh's Library). **14** John Longfield, 'Lands in Simonscourt' (1814) (NLI Christ Church papers, MSS 2789–90(70)); John Brownrigg, 'Fishamble Street' (1779) (NLI Longfield papers MS 21F87(150)); Roger Kendrick, 'Maps of the liberty of St Patrick's Cathedral' (1741), Marsh's Library.

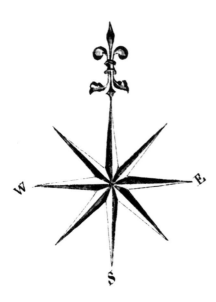

12.3 Compass rose from Robert Gibson's map of Kimmage (1749) (NLI Domville papers, MS 11,937(3), courtesy of the National Library of Ireland © NLI).

the simple use of shading and colour, and the lack of words or letters to indicate the different positions of the compass, are found throughout eighteenth-century Irish cartography. Compasses were produced at such regularity that at least one surveyor[15] used a wood-block stamp of a compass for his maps.

DIFFERATIONS FROM THE NORM

The standard north arrow and compass point were not the only features available to Irish surveyors during this period. Of sporadic occurrence is the use of a human hand with a pointed finger, usually extended to an arrow to demonstrate north. Michael Kenny, a Dublin-based surveyor during the 1780s, specialized in the use of the human hand north point, and it appeared in many of his manuscript maps.[16] Other users of this style of point include John Rocque[17] and William Cox.[18]

Another method of displaying the orientation of a map was through the use of letters. This method, usually found in simple urban cadastral maps with limited decoration, involved the positioning of the letters N, S, E and W at the corresponding side

---

15 James Orr, 'Map book of the estate of Edward Brice, Co. Down' (1751) (NLI Brice papers, MS 19848). There is a possibility that Brownrigg used a stamp for his north arrows in some of his manuscript maps as well: John Brownrigg, 'Beresford Street' (1790) (NLI Longfield papers, MS 21F86). **16** Michael Kenny, 'Francis Street' (1770) (NLI Domville papers, MS 11,937(32)); Michael Kenny, 'Ballyfermot' (n.d.) (NLI Domville papers, MS 11,937(29)); Michael Kenny, 'Ballyfermot' (1777) (NLI Domville papers, MS 11,937(37)). **17** John Rocque, *Dublin and its environs.* **18** William Cox, *Map of part of the demesne of Tallaght* (Dublin, 1767).

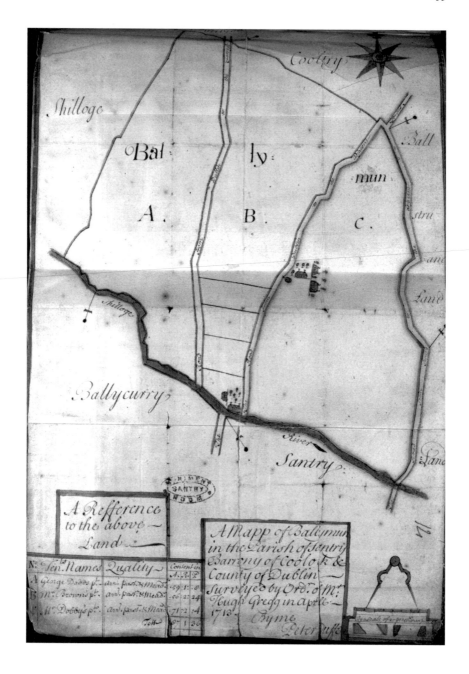

12.4 Large map decorations were a trademark for surveyor Peter Duff (from Peter Duff, 'Ballymun' (1713), NLI Domville papers, MS 11,937(14), courtesy of the National Library of Ireland © NLI).

134

12.5 Two north arrows facing in opposite directions in Roger Kendrick's map of Upper Coombe (1741) (courtesy of the Governors and Guardians of Marsh's Library © Marsh's Library).

of the map border, indicating the four cardinal points of the compass. This method was in use throughout the eighteenth century. A map of Lusk[19] produced by Joseph Moland in 1716 is one of the earliest known examples. During the latter part of the eighteenth and the early nineteenth century, Brownrigg[20] and Longfield[21] also regularly used this style of orientation, most often in their simple, less ornate cadastral maps.

By the early nineteenth century, the artistic north arrows and decorative compass points in Irish mapping began to be replaced with simpler arrows[22] indicating north and south. Coupled with the decline in complexity of cartouches during the same period, this indicates a trend towards standardization of non-geographic map decorations and a drastic reduction in artistic detail and individual diversity.

North arrows provide an insight into not only how a map was prepared, but also the surveyor's understanding of problems inherent in surveying – magnetic variation, for instance. The impact that this phenomenon had in surveying eighteenth-century Dublin can be understood through an analysis of their maps. Overall, the vast majority of maps produced during this period make no reference to magnetic variation, and of the few that do, only a handful make an effort to document the degree to which this variation affected the difference between true and magnetic north. North arrows indicating magnetic variation prioritize true north, with magnetic north being drawn across the true north arrow indicating the angular difference, in a dashed or less visually dominant style, such as a single line.

During the time of the Down Survey (1655–6), the variation between magnetic and true north was negligible, yet Petty advised that an analysis of the difference between these two sets of readings be carried out as standard practice.[23] By 1787, the level of magnetic variation in Dublin was noted to be 14°13' west,[24] in 1752 the variation was 19° west[25] and by 1817 the figure was 28°30' west.[26] In a stand-alone survey,

19 Joseph Moland, 'Map of Lusk' (1716), reproduced in Refaussé and Clark, *A catalogue of the maps*, p. 59, pl. 8. **20** John Brownrigg, 'Little Mary Street' (1804) (NLI Longfield papers, MS 21F86(30)). **21** John Longfield, 'Constitution Hill' (1816) (NLI Longfield papers, MS 21F86(40)). **22** John Roe, 'Map of the Palace, Tallaght' (1811), reproduced in Refaussé and Clark, *A catalogue of the maps*, p. 85, pl. 37. **23** Marquis of Lansdowne, *Petty Papers*, i, p. 83, quoted in Andrews, *Plantation acres*, p. 305. **24** *Freeman's Journal*, 30 Aug. 1787. **25** Roger Kendrick, 'Map of Glanas Moin in the parish of Tallaght' (1752), reproduced in Refaussé and Clark, *A catalogue of the maps*, p. 73, pl. 18. **26** John Longfield, 'Map of lands in Louth' (1817) (NLI Christ Church papers, MSS 2789–90(45)).

such variations would not merit comment, but if the surveyor was using data from a map produced years or decades previously, evidence that the surveyor took such variation into account or at least acknowledged its presence without necessarily giving figurative evidence would be advantageous. John Longfield produced a map of lands belonging to Christ Church Cathedral in 1816,[27] based on an original 1762 map by Byron. Longfield included a north/magnetic north arrow that indicated the use of a circumferentor during the survey. As a significant period of time had elapsed, during which magnetic north would have moved, this feature showed his acknowledgment that such variations had to be taken into account when comparing the two surveys. Longfield clearly understood the importance of the issue.

Another survey by Longfield of lands in Tipperary[28] included a value of magnetic variation in degrees and minutes. This, coupled with a small note indicating that parts of this survey were duplicated from a Down Survey map, adds evidence not only that Longfield was using a circumferentor during his surveys, but that he also understood that magnetic variation changes over time and the impact this had on surveys. In 1807, Longfield produced a series of eight maps of Glasnevin,[29] in which magnetic variation was displayed on the north arrow, but a figure of this variation, while measurable from the north arrow using a protractor, was not given. John Roe produced a map along similar lines, this time of a section of land belong to the Hatch Estate in Kilmainham in 1812.[30] While not referencing which map or original survey he had consulted, Roe did include the deviation between true and magnetic north. Longfield and Roe's awareness of this issue, and their inclusion of it in their maps, gives clear indication that the two men wished to reduce the chance of legal disputes based on their mapping:

> From what has been already laid down, we may see the absolute necessity of allowing for the variation of the magnet, in comparing old surveys with new ones; for want of which, great disputes may arise between neighbouring proprietors of land: and it were to be wished that our honourable and learned judges would take this matter into consideration whenever any business of this kind comes before them.[31]

AREA CALCULATION

Determination of magnetic variation was not the only technique used by surveyors for which evidence can occasionally be found on maps. Area measurement lines, of immense importance to practical surveying, can occasionally be seen on surviving

---

27 Ibid. **28** John Longfield, 'Lands in Killenaule in Tipperary' (1817) (NLI Christ Church papers, MSS 2789–90(59)). **29** John Longfield, 'Lands in Glasnevin' (1807) (NLI Christ Church papers, MS 2789(106–14)). **30** John Roe, 'A map of a piece of ground at Kilmainham in the county of Dublin' (1812) (NLI Cloncurry papers, MS 16G50(1)). **31** Noble, *Geodæsia Hibernica*, pp vi–vii.

drafts. These simple lines were of fundamental importance not only to the landowner, but to the wider Irish economy. Area was the vital component in order to calculate the value of land, establish rents for tenants and estimate crop yields – all of which were core issues of Ireland's agricultural based economy at the time.

Bernard Scalé highlighted the important role that surveyors played in the lucrative business of landownership and rental in his *Tables for the easy valuing of estates* (Dublin 1771):

> The increasing value of lands in this kingdom demands the particular attention of every person, anywise concerned therein; from the nobleman of the most extensive estate, down to the holder of a few acres … The author's extensive business in land surveying and valuation, gave him many opportunities of seeing how essentially necessary such a work is as the following would be to every proprietor to land, to clergymen, barristers, agents, attorneys, public notaries, stewards and also to the farmer, who has frequent occasion to let out small parcels of land, to those in a subordinate state. It is likewise an invariable guide to those concerned in dividing common fields, where the value of one part and the other, so materially differ; it will guard against unavoidable errors proceeding from hasty and inaccurate calculations. In fine, it is a standard to correct errors, and detect impositions; particular care has been taken in the accuracy of all the calculations, and in arranging the whole in such a familiar manner, that gentlemen will surely be pleased in being saved the trouble of calculations.[32]

There were several techniques for producing area values from surveys during this period, and physical evidence of such calculations can be observed in manuscript estate maps of Peter Callan,[33] Alex Stewart,[34] John Brownrigg[35] and John Longfield.[36] Among the most highly regarded techniques was that of Thomas Burgh, who, as surveyor general in the 1720s, published a method of area calculation determined by angle of measurement, length of measurement and a localized coordinate system. Like Scalé earlier, Burgh was also acutely aware of the importance of accurate area calculations from surveys:

> There is reason to wonder that an essay towards a geometric and universal method to determine the areas of rectilinear figures hath been so far neglected that it does not appear to have been thought of at a time when the methods of obtaining the quadrature of curvilinear spaces have been carried

---

32 Scalé, *Tables for the easy valuing of estates*, p. i.   **33** Peter Callan, 'Map of lands in Kilbany' (1750) (NLI Hatch papers, MS 21F112(5)).   **34** Alex Stewart, 'Map of Ballymun' (1724) (NLI Domville papers, MS 11,937(71)).   **35** John Brownrigg, 'Old Church Street' (1812) (NLI Christ Church papers, MS 21F86(22)); John Brownrigg, 'Beresford Street' (1790) (NLI Longfield papers, MS 21F86(8)); John Brownrigg, 'Holding on Charlemont Street' (1795) (NLI Longfield papers, MS 21F87(104)).   **36** John Longfield, 'Ellis Quay' (1813) (NLI Longfield papers, MS 21F86(34)).

to so great a degree of perfection. And the want of such a general rule must be well known to those who are acquainted with the inaccuracies of common surveys.[37]

Several surveyors[38] wrote on the problem of area calculation and offered solutions, usually from a limited selection of theorems not necessarily developed by themselves. Of note is Gibson's *Treatise in practical surveying* (Dublin, 1763), which Gibson himself directed towards 'persons who have property in land, to lawyers in controverted surveys and to practical surveyors'.[39] Gibson demonstrated five distinct methods to calculate area, of which several were highly practical and accurate, while some were highly unusual and verged on the ludicrous, due to the difficulty with which they were implemented and the potentially dubious results that would be obtained. Gibson's series of calculations gives a broad cross-section of the various methods of area calculation being employed in Ireland during the eighteenth century and, as such, are worth analyzing.

   Gibson's most practical solution is his first theorem – the division of the survey area into regular figures such as squares and triangles, whose areas can be calculated separately and the area of the whole obtained by combining the separate regular-shaped areas. William Petty referred to this method as 'laborious prostapheresis of triangles'.[40] Yet this method is not too far removed from the modern surveying equivalent of converting surveys into a series of triangles knows as a Triangulated Irregular Networks (TIN) to determine contour lines. Given the large number of calculations involved in this method, Gibson advised:

> The lines of the maps should be drawn small, and neat, as well as the bases; the compasses really pointed, and scale accurately divided; without which you may err greatly. The multiplication should be run over twice at least, as also the addition of the column content.[41]

Samuel Wyld was also a supporter of this method, encouraging readers of his surveying treatise to actually survey irregular-shaped features in a way that would allow them to be drawn as regular shapes.[42]

   This method was not the only technique of area determination using triangles that Gibson suggested. A second method involved converting a piece of land into one large triangle, regardless of its original shape, and from there using a standard

---

37 Thomas Burgh, *A method to determine areas of right-lined figure universally* (London, 1724), p. 1. **38** Jacob Neville, *New tables* (Dublin, 1762); Thomas Power, 'The universal land surveyor' (proposed) (Cork, 1767); William Hawney, *The complete measurer*; Thomas Harding, 'The practical surveyor's best companion' (proposed) (Dublin, 1784); Thomas Power, 'The universal land surveyor' (proposed) (Cork, 1786); Nicholas Walsh, *A treatise on surveying* (Dublin, 1787). **39** Gibson, *Treatise of practical surveying*, p. 196. **40** *Report from select committee on survey and valuation of Ireland*, p. xvi [445], H.C. 1824, viii.79. **41** Gibson, *Treatise of practical surveying*, p. 196. **42** Wyld, *The practical surveyor*, appendix A, p. 4, fig. 22.

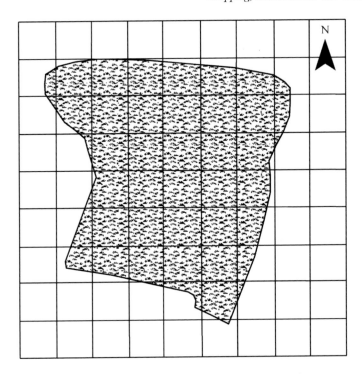

12.6 Example of Gibson's second method of area determination using a square grid.

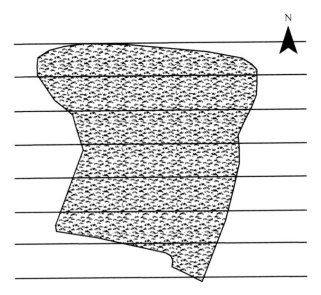

12.7 Area determination through the use of parallel lines.

triangular area calculation to determine the new object's shape. The area of the actual land in question was then worked out from this overall figure. In comparison to Gibson's other suggested triangular method, however, this second method is overly complex, with a significantly higher chance of errors being introduced. Gibson's own brief comments were that:

> This method will be found very useful and ready in small enclosures, as well as very exact, it may also be used in large ones, but great care must be taken of the points on the extended line, which will be crowded, as well as of not missing a station.[43]

Gibson's third method involved a grid of squares being laid over a plot of the survey area 'to determine in the area of a piece of ground from the map therefore, by the *square horn*'.[44] The square horn was a transparent or semi-transparent grid divided into inch squares so that scale transformations between the map and the real-world area could be easily determined:

Horn = 100 perches, map scale = 10 perches to an inch

By calculating the number of whole squares (fig. 12.6) and then using the method of triangular division for the remaining areas on the edge of the survey whose irregular shape does not suit this second method, the total area can be determined. This method appears to have been slightly outdated by Gibson's time, but he defended its inclusion in his treatise:

> I am confident I shall be judged to be too prolix on this head but as this method has stood the test of many ages, and is still used by many, I have for the benefit of those of the slowest capacity, explained it as fully as I was able.[45]

At least one eighteenth-century surveyor, Alexander Stewart, operated this method for calculating areas.[46]

Another method for which there is evidence of usage in eighteenth-century surveying in Ireland, places horizontal lines to divide the area in question into regular rectangular shapes and calculates the remainder using the triangular method (fig. 12.7). While there exists little, if any, evidence of the use of other methods mentioned by Gibson in eighteenth-century manuscript maps, there are many examples of parallel lines being drawn on drafts or rough final maps of at least two major period surveyors: John Longfield[47] and Thomas Reading.[48] A series of horizontal parallel

43 Gibson, *Treatise of practical surveying*, p. 211.   **44** Ibid., p. 201.   **45** Ibid., p. 207.
46 Alexander Stewart, 'Map of Ballymun' (1724) (NLI Domville Estate, MS 11,937(71)).
47 John Longfield, 'Lands in Crumlin' (1813) (NLI Christ Church papers, MSS 2789–90(27)); John Longfield, 'Ellis Quay' (1813) (NLI Longfield papers, MS 21F86(34)); John Longfield, 'Holding on Charlemont Street' (1795) (NLI Longfield papers, MS 21F87(104)).
48 Thomas Reading, 'A map of part of Rathmines' (1742) (NLI Hatch papers, MS

lines appears on several maps produced by these surveyors, with no indication that they were used for anything other than area calculation. Unfortunately, the actual area calculation figures were not included on any of these drafts. Peter Callan was another surveyor who appears to have supported a more widespread use of this method, as he advised that:

> one surveyor should be appointed to furnish all the surveyors of the kingdom with paralleled paper, drawn with one general correct instrument, as afore described; which paper should be stamped, and sold at such a reasonable rate as should be approved by the Dublin Society.[49]

It could be argued that, due to the lack of evidence of other area calculation methods on maps, this parallel method was the most popular. The lack of written evidence, however, does not mean that such methods as the highly practical triangular method were not widely practised. Quite simply, proof of its use could be on discarded draft copies, or the calculations may have been transcribed off the actual map sheet. The parallel method was merely one of several methods in use throughout this period for simple area calculations.

Despite Gibson's listing and description of several practical area calculation methods, he did include one that is almost as bizarre as it is unrealistic. Gibson's final method determined the area of a piece of ground by using one variable that is rarely associated with mapping – weight. The map is divided into a regular grid of squares with every square that is not contained within the area of land in question removed. The map is then weighted. By comparing the initial weight of the map to its final weight the area can be calculated:

> Weight of the paper = 74.6 grains; weight of the map = 59.2 grains; then 74.6 = 223 square, 59.2 = 179.96 square in the map, and each square being 100 perches, makes 17969 perches or 110A 2 R 16P, differing from only 16 perches from the true content.[50]

This method bears a striking similarity to Archimedes' volume calculation using water displacement, however its practical use in surveying is highly dubious. Gibson was aware that this method would meet with disapproval and commented:

> Tho' this method of weighing may seem whimsical and ridiculous, yet if experiments be made with wine scales and weights, upon maps laid down by large scales, and drawn upon good even writing Demy paper, the contents produced will be found to be much nearer the truth than imagined.[51]

21F112(3)). **49** Callan, *A dissertation*, p. 45. **50** Gibson, *Treatise in practical surveying*, p. 217.
51 Ibid., p. 218.

There is no evidence of this method being employed in the Dublin land surveying community during the eighteenth century.

Aside from evidence of a surveyor's artistic capabilities or calculation techniques, evidence of methods of practical land surveying is regularly found on the manuscript maps. Observation lines connecting widely separated tracts of land within the same survey can occasionally be found on draft maps. These lines were measured in the field using either a theodolite or, more often, a circumferentor to establish the relative angular position of dispersed areas of land and a chain to determine the distances separating them. This method of survey control can be found on draft maps of Reading,[52] Byron[53] and Brownrigg.[54] Given the often dispersed nature of landownership in eighteenth-century Dublin and its surrounding areas, connecting areas of land under the same ownership in one survey is a practical and efficient method and it is surprising that evidence of its existence is not more regularly observed on draft maps.

52 Thomas Reading, 'Several parcels of land in Dalkey' (1769) (NLI Christ Church papers, MS 2789(3)).   **53** Samuel Byron, 'Ballymore Eustace' (1791) (NLI Christ Church papers, MS 2789(17)).   **54** John Brownrigg, 'Several holdings on north side of Channel Row' (1804) (NLI Christ Church papers, MS 2789(57)).

Part IV
The city

13 Charles Brooking: Dublin in 1728

Much of what is known about how eighteenth-century Dublin looked comes from historic town plans of the entire city. These works were more than cartographic ventures; they were complex and intricate logistical exercises requiring astute business management, elegant and beautiful works of art and commercial products designed to entice and enthral the reader. They were often beyond the range, skill and ability of most period surveyors. Original city plans were as unique as they were rare. They were complicated to survey and expensive to print, with such difficulties often explaining how there are so few maps covering all of Dublin prior to 1800. Yet, despite these problems, such maps reflect the skill and professional prowess of the surveyor who created them and ensure that their name is forever connected with the city. Such plans tell the story of the city. They reflect what the citizens of Dublin wished to show and what they wanted to hide.

For the modern reader, these town maps represent cartographic waypoints in the city's life with the map coming to symbolize and embody a particular era. For Dublin, the years 1728 and 1756 have become stamped with the names of surveyors Charles Brooking and John Rocque respectively. Their maps form a backdrop to any story of the city and provide intricate and absorbing information about Dublin in a manner that is unique and unlike any other source. Each came at an important time in the city's urban development. Brooking's map showed the city at the beginning of its eighteenth-century expansion, while Rocque's displayed Dublin as it was at the dawn of the work of the Wide Streets Commission and before their radical redevelopment of its thoroughfares. Aside from their cultural and historical significance, it is the fact that these maps were surveyed, rather than compiled, that singles them out for specific focus as part of any analysis of the cartographic history of eighteenth-century Dublin. Both Brooking's and Rocque's maps of Dublin were produced in radically different styles, yet each to the highest standards available and far beyond the realms that had existed for everyday map production in Ireland.

There were, of course, maps of Dublin before 1728. The city had a rather late cartographic debut compared to other major European capitals, with the first comprehensive survey only being completed by John Speed in 1610 for his *Theatre of the empire of Great Britain* (London, 1611). Other seventeenth-century surveyors and engineers followed in Speed's wake. William Petty used eight surveyors, not including their assistants, for the Down Survey maps of Dublin in 1655.[1] These focused primarily on the rural parts of the county, however, with the city only being represented as a simple town marker. Bernard de Gomme's *The city and suburbs of Dublin*

---

1 Robert Girdler, Jonas Archey, William Stock, Thomas West, Edward Wilson, Thomas Clarke, Patrick Allen, William Wright, Down Survey of Ireland, 1655 (NLI, MS 714).

(London, 1673) was probably the most cartographically important map of the city between Speed (1610) and Brooking (1728), as it presented the evolution of the city from a walled Elizabethan town to the more suburban sprawl of the eighteenth century. Thomas Philips' 'An exact survey of the city of Dublin and part of the harbour' (1685) displayed Dublin in an unusual east/west orientation, with much of the map's focus being placed on the harbour and bay. A far less grand map in terms of both size and cartographic detail is Herman Moll's map of Dublin in his 1714 atlas of the principal ports of Britain and Ireland.[2]

CHARLES BROOKING

Charles Brooking's *A map of the city and suburbs of Dublin and also the archbishop and earl of Meath's liberties with the bounds of each parish* (London, 1728) was the first major map of Dublin city in the eighteenth century, and the first of the city since Speed (fig. 13.1). While de Gomme and Philips had also produced maps of the city in the meantime (as noted already), neither was as detailed or focused on the city. Brooking, from the outset, was keen to present evidence of his authority in no uncertain terms by stating in the title: 'Drawn from an Actual SURVEY'.[3] Brooking's work was an all-encompassing map of Dublin's civic, architectural, parochial and business worlds, giving it a far greater cultural depth than the work of those who had preceded him, or of many of those, including Rocque, who followed. His map contained two separate forms of boundaries – the city liberties and parishes, all of which were named. Along the edges of the map were profile views of Dublin's principal buildings, each referred to in the actual body of the map. Dublin's rich business world was represented by coats of arms of twenty-four separate guilds and the striking prospect of the city across the top served to complement the basic, but thorough, cartographic representation of the city within the main portion of the map. The dedication was as ambitious as the map's content:

> To his excellency John Lord Carteret, baron of Hawnes, one of the lords of His Majesties most honourable privy council & lord lieutenant general and general governor of His Majesties kingdom of Ireland. This map is humbly dedicated by Charles Brooking, 1728.

The most unusual feature of Brooking's map is its orientation – south/north rather than north/south. There is no rule of cartography stating that a map must be orientated with north at the top of the page, considering that once a directional north arrow is included, the physical orientation of the map is arbitrary. One possible reason for this break from tradition may be that the prospect of the city that covers

---

2 Herman Moll, [untitled] (London, 1714), Marsh's Library, Y.6.20.   3 Brooking, *A map of the city and suburbs of Dublin*.

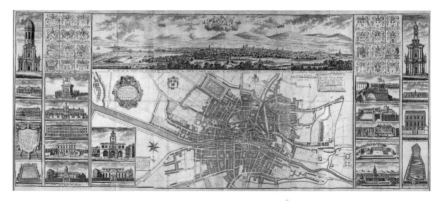

13.1 Charles Brooking, *A map of the city and suburbs of Dublin* (London, 1728)
(courtesy of the Royal Irish Academy © RIA).

the top portion of the map is directed towards the Wicklow Mountains, which lie to
the south of the city, giving a good view of the improvements being made at the time
to Dublin's quay and harbour, as well as the progression of the northern suburbs and
providing a vista of the city's taller buildings. Brooking presumably chose to orientate
both map and prospect to face in the same direction, thus reducing confusion for his
readers.

SURVEYING METHOD, 1728

As Brooking stated that he actually surveyed Dublin, it is useful to examine what
techniques he may have used. There is no direct evidence in his 1728 map of the
instrumentation he used or methods he applied, however a contemporary author
provides a detailed examination of urban surveying, which may have been similar to
the system used by Brooking. Samuel Wyld's *The practical surveyor* gives a clear explanation of the preferred instruments and methods of urban surveying at this time.
Urban surveying was considered to be a far more complex form of surveying than
work in the countryside, as

> the performance of this work is very laborious, and you must be careful to
> keep the field-book in a plain and regular manner, otherwise the multitude
> of observations and offsets will be apt to breed confusion.[4]

The theodolite was the preferred instrument to record angular measurements, with
the establishment of a station network using city streets and lanes as lines of sight (fig.
13.2). Due to the increased presence of metal in an urban environment, a circumferentor would have encountered significantly more interference from local magnetic
sources than it would in a rural one.[5] It would be useful, however, as lines of sight

4 Wyld, *The practical surveyor*, p. 150.   5 Ibid.

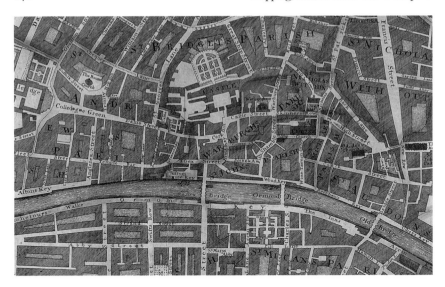

13.2 Detail of Dublin's city centre (from Charles Brooking, *A map of the city and suburbs of Dublin* (London, 1728), courtesy of the Royal Irish Academy © RIA).

were more limited at street level and magnetic bearings could aid the surveyor immensely. To measure offsets from a line of sight between two stations, Wyld suggested the Gunter chain, as

> the ground-plott of the houses, pavements &c. are generally laid out by foot measure; therefore let every link thereof be a foot long, and fifty of these links will make the chain of a sufficient length.[6]

Prior to a survey of the size and scale of Brooking's map of Dublin, a detailed reconnoitre of the main streets and lanes of the city would have been necessary. The establishment of a survey control grid of stations was also vital to the success of a large urban survey. The creation of a loop of survey stations whose positions could be checked by means of a traverse would also enhance the accuracy of the entire survey. Wyld strongly advised that

> Before you begin your work, it will be necessary to walk about the town, and choose 4 or 5 principal streets that lead out of one into another, enclosing between them several by-lanes, alleys &c. and contrive your first station in such a manner, that when you come round these 4 or 5 streets, the last station-point; and observe, that the fewer angles you make in going round these streets before you close, the better.[7]

Once a network of survey stations had been set up, the next phase was to record the positions of street corners or 'remarkable houses &c.'[8] that lay on these main streets.

6 Ibid., p. 151.   **7** Ibid., p. 153.   **8** Ibid., p. 152.

The number of observations that a surveyor recorded was entirely dependent on the detail of the final map. Rocque, for example, recorded the position of every individual building in Dublin during his 1756 survey of the city,[9] whereas Brooking seems to have followed Wyld's method of only measuring buildings of note and street corners, resulting in the block layout of his map. It was considered advisable to draw a rough draft of the survey in the field to prevent confusion when completing the map.[10]

Town and market squares required a different surveying methodology than street surveying. Wyld was aware of this issue and advised that

> When the station-line leads you into a square, you may plant the theodolite in the middle thereof, and from that one station direct the telescope to the corners (very often there are but four, and the sides all strait) and measure the distance from the station to the corners ... But if you would take notice of particular houses therein, or if the sides are very irregular, then go round it: but lanes and alleys are laid down by offsets only, from the station line through the middle.[11]

With the majority of problems encountered within an urban environment accounted for, the surveyor was advised to draw what had been measured at the end of each day's surveying, paying particular attention to the ground-plots of churches.[12]

Brooking completed his survey of Dublin in 1727 and, given the prestige of his work, sought funding from the city for its publication:

> Certain of the commons, setting forth that Thomas Brooking hath completely finished the map of the city and suburbs, and therefore prayed that some of the said maps be taken from said Brooking, or such that gratuity as should be thought proper: whereupon do pay to alderman Humphrey French, for the use of the within named Thomas Brooking, £10 sterling, towards defraying the expense he was at making a map of this city, the same to be allowed the treasurer on his accounts.[13]

It seems almost insulting that Brooking was referred to as Thomas rather than Charles in reference to his cartographic masterpiece. Given the minimal level of biographical detail known about Brooking, however, it cannot be stated with certainty that his first or middle names were not Charles Thomas or Thomas Charles or that the city officials did indeed make a complete mistake. For example, Scalé is regularly referred to as Bernard, whereas in fact his first names were Peter Bernard[14] and the same may be the case for Brooking.

9 Rocque, *An exact survey.* **10** Wyld, *The practical surveyor*, p. 152. **11** Ibid., p. 153. **12** Ibid., p. 154. **13** Gilbert (ed.), *Ancient records*, vii, p. 443 (1727). **14** Bendall (ed.), *Dictionary of land surveyors*, ii, p. 460.

CARTOGRAPHIC STYLE

Of the main seventeenth- and eighteenth-century maps of Dublin, Brooking's is the only one to show administrative boundaries and to list them in his legend, or 'explanation' as Brooking preferred. A total of eleven separately named and distinct parishes are presented in Brooking's map. The 'bounds of ye parishes' are represented by a narrow dotted line and are at first glance difficult to view, but they do not interfere with or distract from the geographic data through which they run. Each parish name was orientated with respect to the parish's shape, resulting in a series of randomly aligned texts throughout the map. The Dublin city liberty, for which the municipal council of the city was responsible, is more clearly marked with a heavy chain running primarily around the perimeter or outer suburbs of the city. A section of the archbishop of Dublin's liberty was also highlighted by Brooking. He included the archbishop's coat of arms inside this boundary and the crest of Dublin city within the city liberty border. While Brooking refrained from any form of detailed explanation of the city's civic workings, his basic division of the city into its various administrative areas provides a greater indication of the city's internal workings than was supplied by Speed, de Gomme and even Rocque.

As mentioned, Brooking's version of the city's physical urban landscape was made up of blocks rather than individual buildings. This creates an interesting visual effect in which emphasis is placed on street layout rather than the city's buildings. Several buildings did merit particular consideration, however, and these are shown in profile along the map's edges. Churches were awarded special attention by Brooking, but the old Four Courts in the grounds of Christ Church Cathedral and the Playhouse in Smock Alley, neither of which appear in Brooking's detailed building profile drawings, are identifiable by being assigned letters that are referred to in the map's legend.

Infrastructural developments were also clearly highlighted by Brooking, with his inclusion of the new section of the north bank of the Liffey running along what is known today as the North Wall and Dublin Port. Brooking's insertion of the phrase 'this part is walled in but as yet overflowed by ye tide' in the modern Sherriff Street area, then simply a mud-flat, indicates that land reclamation was in progress but, as of 1728, had not been completed. Brooking's map was also the first major Dublin cartographic project not to include any portion or mention of the city's medieval wall or any form of proposed fortification. His map was a radical step away from the earlier militaristic maps of de Gomme and Philips, who both suggested positions for defensive structures in the city. This, coupled with the expansion of the city's suburbs presented Dublin in a far more civil and residential/mercantile light. Brooking's only mention of military presence in the city is his inclusion of the Royal Barracks, now Collins Barracks, in Oxmantown.

PROFILED BUILDINGS

The inclusion of profile images of some of the most important buildings in the city at the time is a unique feature of Brooking's map. There appears to be no hierarchy or special focus to any of the twenty building profiles included, however their insertion gives a better understanding of the city's social structure than would have been available from Brooking's survey detail alone. Brooking included two churches: St Ann's on Dawson Street and St Werburgh's on Werburgh Street. Unusually, neither of Dublin's two cathedrals was shown. One possible explanation for the selection of these two churches out of the many in Dublin is their modernity at the time – St Ann's having been constructed in 1719 by Isaac Wills and St Werburgh's also in 1719 by the surveyor general, Thomas Burgh.[15] St Werburgh's was still unfinished when Brooking was conducting his survey, most likely in 1727, so his view of the church does not match that of the finished building. Figure 13.3 displays Brooking's version of St Werburgh's with a cupola, perhaps due to the assistance of Alessandro Galilei, a Florentine architect[16] connected to the project. In 1729, the year after Brooking's map appeared on the market, it was decided to erect a stone tower instead of the planned steeple.[17] Joseph Tudor's 1750 view of Dublin Castle presents this alternative design of St Werburgh's tower, indicating that the original design copied by Brooking was not followed.

Aside from Brooking's Werburgh mistake, his series of profiles gives an insight into buildings and structures that have either been radically changed in appearance by the twenty-first century or no longer exist (fig. 13.4). Brooking's representation of Trinity College is a unique view of the college's western façade constructed in stages between 1670 and 1699 by Thomas Lucas and Sir William Robinson, before its remodelling in the late 1750s.[18] Dublin Castle is also shown as a dilapidated building, with a large section of its exterior wall missing and with a medieval gate still present. The statute of King George I on its own pedestal off Essex Bridge no longer exists and despite the bridge being the subject of a large treatise by George Semple in 1780,[19] Brooking's image gives us one of the most detailed profile views of the statue.

Brooking's profile view of St Stephen's Green shows that several plots had yet to be built on, adding weight to the argument that the map was surveyed by Brooking himself. Among the other buildings included are the Blue Coat Hospital, Dr Steeven's Hospital, the Mansion House, the Corn Market, the Custom House and the Royal Hospital in Kilmainham (the profile of which is the same as in Brooking's prospect of the city).

Building profiles were not the only ancillary items to be included by Brooking along the edges of his Dublin map. Two adverts for maps of Dublin and Ireland were

15 Christine Casey, *The buildings of Ireland: Dublin* (London, 2005), pp 342, 469.   **16** Letters of Robert Molesworth to his wife, 16 Oct. 1716 (NLI P3752).   **17** Kenneth Severns, 'A new perspective on Georgian building practice: the rebuilding of St Werburgh's Church, Dublin (1754–1759)', *IGSB*, 35 (Dublin, 1992), 3–16 at 4.   **18** O'Dwyer, 'Building empires', 108.   **19** Semple, *Treatise of building in water*.

13.3 St Werburgh's Church (from Charles Brooking, *A map of the city and suburbs of Dublin* (London, 1728), courtesy of the Royal Irish Academy © RIA).

13.4 Images of important and notable Dublin buildings (from Charles Brooking, *A map of the city and suburbs of Dublin* (London, 1728), courtesy of the Royal Irish Academy © RIA).

included – the map of Ireland being produced by Brooking's own publisher Bowles, which consisted of:

A geographical description of the kingdom of Ireland newly corrected and improved by actual observation. Containing 1 general map of ye whole kingdom, 4 provincial and 32 county maps, divided into baronies, wherein are carefully laid down all the cities, towns, boroughs, barracks, rivers, harbours, headlands, the noted ferries &c. together with the principle roads and the distances in common reputed miles &c. with a description of each county collected from the best accounts extant.

This 'geographical description' was probably the 1728 edition of an original 1689 map credited to Francis Lamb.[20] The second map mentioned by Brooking is 'a new and exact map of the harbour & bay of Dublin', which included depth soundings and was also sold by John Bowles.

Another aspect of Dublin's social framework included by Brooking are the crests of Dublin's guilds either side of the Dublin map. Twenty-four were depicted and, as with Brooking's profile views, there appears to be no obvious order or grouping. The insertion of these coats of arms added greatly to the map-readers' knowledge of the manufacturing and service industries within Brooking's Dublin

PROSPECT OF DUBLIN, 1728

A distinctive feature of Brooking's Dublin was his inclusion of the words 'a prospect of the city of Dublin from the north' across the top of his map (fig. 13.5). Prospects of cities were not unique, but his is the only major map from either the seventeenth or eighteenth century to show one of Dublin. John Green (an Irish-born cartographer also known as Braddock Meade), writing in 1717, highlighted the advantages of including such prospects in cartographic works:

> The plan and prospects of cities which are sometimes set about maps are very useful, as well as ornamental. A certain another speaking of the usefulness of maps, very well observes, that the eye will learn more in one hour by observation than the ear will benefit in a day by discourse. Is it possible for all the words in the world to give such an idea of St Pauls as the draught of it?

Green continued, rather profoundly:

> One may describe a place from a prospect, but it is impossible to draw a prospect from the description. In short, a draught shows at once what many words cannot express, and the best one can have is but a confus'd idea without it.[21]

Brooking capitalized on Green's theory with the prospect of Dublin. By placing the city within the geographical reference of both the Dublin/Wicklow Mountains and the Irish Sea, he removed the need to create a reference map of the entire Dublin region. The prospect was either created from more than one location or created away

---

20 J.H. Andrews, *Sir William Petty's* Hibernia Delineatio (Shannon, 1969), Introduction.
21 Green, *The construction of maps and globes in two parts*, p. 154.

13.5 Brooking's panorama of Dublin (from Charles Brooking, *A map of the city and suburbs of Dublin* (London, 1728), courtesy of the Royal Irish Academy © RIA).

from the field, as it is not possible to view the city from Ringsend to Kilmainham from the relatively flat north side of the Liffey. The road running through the centre of the prospect towards the viewer is most likely the Drumcondra Road, given its position in relation to the coast and the city. The structure of Dublin's buildings is visible from Brooking's prospect, with several distinct types of houses, churches and centres of industry (such as windmills) visible. The original 1728 edition of the map lacked a reference table for the easy identification of prominent buildings such as Dublin Castle or the city's cathedrals. In a counterfeit version, however, nineteen buildings were numbered and listed in a reference table crudely etched on top of the original engraving.

Brooking's 1728 map of Dublin perhaps lacks the cartographic and artistic sophistication of Rocque's later maps of the city, but the real value of his work is that it captured the city before the rapid expansion of the northern suburbs in the first half of the eighteenth century, in addition to representing the architectural and commercial make-up of Dublin on a far deeper social scale than Rocque was able to do.

14 John Rocque: Dublin in 1756

While the maps of his predecessors, such as Speed and Brooking, may have been era defining, John Rocque's work was century defining. No other city plan of eighteenth-century Dublin has been referenced or reproduced as often as Rocque's 1756 masterpiece – *The exact survey of Dublin*. Rocque was a skilled surveyor, a shrewd businessman, a marketing expert and a rather large cartographic fish in the small Irish surveying pond. The *Exact survey of Dublin* can be considered the apex of the city's eighteenth-century mapping. A section of this map even graced the reverse of the late twentieth century pre-Euro Irish £10 note. Rocque's professional and proficient ability to organize substantial survey operations and overcome their inherent logistical problems separates him from contemporary Irish surveyors and elevates him to the zenith of eighteenth-century surveying in Dublin. Even the direct competition of Dubliner Roger Kendrick (see above, pp 37–41) paled in comparison to Rocque's grasp of the project. He applied both Continental flair and English pragmatism to his work in Dublin. His royal references and previous Hanoverian patronage could not be matched by any Irish practitioner. He introduced a revolutionary change in cartographic style, method and relationship with geographic data to Ireland and promoted the greatest transformation in Irish mapping since the arrival of William Petty almost a century before. Rocque, a Londoner of French origin, left a lasting legacy in the form of his independent French School[1] of surveying, which carried on his styles and practices well into the following century (fig. 14.1).

JOHN ROCQUE (C.1709–62)

Unlike many other surveyors who operated in Ireland at the time, there is a ready source of information on Rocque's family and his origins. Rocque was a French Huguenot and was either born in London or moved there as an infant from the Continent around 1709. He is known to have had at least two siblings: brothers Bartholomew and Claude. Bartholomew Rocque (d. 1767) was a designer of decorative gardens,[2] who published at least one book[3] while living at Walham Green in London. It was perhaps through Bartholomew that John became involved in surveying practise – with many surveying techniques being applied to garden design at the time. The Rocque family maintained some link with their homeland, as Bartholomew is known to have visited Provence in 1738.[4]

---

1 Andrews, 'The French School of Dublin land surveyors', 33–41. 2 Mauro Ambrosoli, *The wild and the sown: botany and agriculture in western Europe, 1350–1850* (Cambridge, 1992), p. 358. 3 Bartholomew Rocque, *A practical treatise of cultivating Lucern grass* (London, 1765).

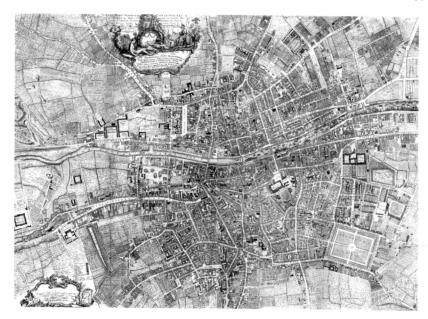

14.1 John Rocque, *Exact survey of the city and suburbs of Dublin* (Dublin, 1756) (courtesy of the Royal Irish Academy © RIA).

John Rocque's personal connections with France remain unclear. He was the godfather to the son of the French landscape engraver François Vivares;[5] he included the French measurement system of *toise* on his map of Dublin; his first known professional description of himself was as a '*dessinateur de jardins*';[6] and his last will and testament was witnessed by three men, two of whom, Jas Dorrett and Pierre Andre, were either French or of French descent and most probably fellow Huguenots. He was also known to have written in 1753 to his nephew Bartholomew, son of his brother Claude, in Switzerland, using adequate written French, which, as Varley points out, may simply indicate that he had not written in French on a regular basis but may have had a better grasp of the language in its spoken form.[7]

John Rocque is known to have been married at least twice. His first marriage to Ann Bew was childless[8] and it is not known if there were any children from his second marriage, to Mary Ann Scalé. Mary Ann carried on Rocque's business in

4 '… when I was at Monosque, a city in Provence, which was about twenty-seven years ago': Rocque, *A practical treatise of cultivating Lucer*, quoted in Varley, 'John Rocque: engraver, surveyor, cartographer and map-seller', p. 83. **5** Michael Bryan, *Dictionary of painters and engravers* (London, 1904). **6** John Rocque, *Plan of the house, gardens and hermitage of their majesties at Richmond* (London, 1734). Colm Lennon and John Montague, *John Rocque's Dublin: a guide to the Georgian city* (Dublin, 2010). **7** Varley, 'John Rocque: engraver, surveyor, cartographer and map-seller', pp 83–91. **8** Letter from John Rocque to Bartholomew Rocque dated 11 May 1753, quoted in Varley, 'John Rocque: engraver, surveyor, cartographer and map-seller', p. 85.

London after his death, publishing reproductions of many of his maps,[9] while also expanding the engraving business. John Montresor had many of his maps engraved by Mary Ann in 1766 and was more than happy to assist

> them in the execution of several draughts I have given them to engrave for me viz. one of Nova Scotia, one of the province of New York, one of Canada from the first island to Montreal and on the city of New York and environs with the Boston harbour and channel from the Hook.[10]

Rocque began his career as a surveyor, engraver and seller of maps and prints in London during the first half of the 1730s. The majority of his work at that time was co-produced with Thomas Badeslade and focused on country homes and decorative gardens. Badeslade is known to have produced work for George I,[11] and may have been his gateway to Hanoverian patronage. Rocque's and Badeslade's maps produced during this period were compiled and published in *Vitruvius Britannicus* (London, 1739), 'a collection of plans, elevations and perspective view of the royal palaces of Great Britain'. It is unclear if Rocque and Badeslade surveyed every map contained in this collection, however several of the maps[12] do contain strong Rocque-like traits, such as detailed terrain shading, uniformly planimetric buildings and ornate and highly decorative baroque cartouches. During this period, his employees are known to have numbered at least ten, all foreign, 'as many draughtsmen as engravers',[13] many probably of the same French Huguenot origin as Rocque himself.

Possibly his greatest cartographic achievement was his *New and accurate map of London* (1746) produced in both 16- and 24-sheet formats. This map was engraved on a massive scale, with every city block in London surveyed, and streets, laneways, alleys and docks individually named. His London map may have caught the attention of Robert Viscount Jocelyn and the earl of Kildare, as they were most likely involved behind the scenes in inviting Rocque to Dublin. This would explain his dedication to them in the Dublin cartouche.

9 M.A. Rocque, *Berkshire: reduction of actual survey published* (London, 1762); M.A. Rocque, *The small British atlas: a set of maps of the counties of England and Wales* (London, 1764); M.A. Rocque, *Cadiz: plan of the city and environs with harbor, bay etc.* (London, 1762); M.A. Rocque, *Post-roads of Great Britain and Ireland* (London, 1763). **10** Quoted in Towner et al., *Mapping the American revolutionary war*, p. 85. **11** Thomas Badeslade, *Chorographia Britanni* (London, 1742), title page. **12** T. Badeslade and J. Rocque, *A plan of the gardens and view of the buildings ... at Echa, Surrey* (London, 1737); T. Badeslade and J. Rocque, *Plan of the palace and gardens of Hampton Court* (London, 1736); T. Badeslade and J. Rocque, *Plan du jardin et vue des maisons de Chiswick* (London, 1736). **13** John Rocque to Bartholomew Rocque, dated 11 May 1753, quoted in Varley, 'John Rocque: engraver, surveyor, cartographer and map-seller', p. 85.

SURVEYING DUBLIN, 1756

The *Exact survey of Dublin* is a superbly detailed and striking map of Dublin as it was in the mid-eighteenth century. Originally published on four separate sheets, each representing a quarter of the city and suburbs, it was laid out at a scale of one inch to ten Irish perches and covered the entire city and sections of surrounding country-side. Rocque's highly developed artistic flair can be found throughout this piece, not only in the intricate map detail but also in the unobtrusive map decoration. His cartouche was wonderfully executed and visually enthralling yet lacked the same refinement and finesse found in his London masterpiece surveyed several years before. For the *Exact survey*, Rocque described himself with the eloquent title of 'chorographer to their royal highnesses the late & present prince of Wales', referring to the late prince of Wales, Frederick (1707–51)[14] (eldest son of George II) and the future George III (1738–1820),[15] who became prince of Wales upon his uncle's early death. The first official use of this title occurred in 1751,[16] when he was listed as a member of the household of George III, then prince of Wales.[17] Despite such high official references, there was no evidence that Rocque received royal support or funding during his mapping of Dublin.

The *Exact survey* was dedicated 'to their excellencies Robert Viscount Jocelyn, Lord High Chancellor James, earl of Kildare, and Brabazon, earl of Bessborough, lords justices general and general governors of Ireland. This plan is most humbly inscribed by their excellencies most dutiful and most obedient humble, John Rocque'. The rationale behind the creation of this map can be found throughout the physical detail contained within its borders. The word *border* is relevant to the nature of the *Exact survey*, as Rocque did not include any civic or ecclesiastical boundaries anywhere within his map. This stands in stark contrast to Brooking's 1728 map of Dublin, in which organizational boundaries are dominant, giving a more practical administrative usefulness to Brooking's map. Rocque's map was a commercial product rather than one commissioned by the city or government. It was multipurpose to its core. The inclusion of four sets of units of measurement – British feet, Irish and English perches (which were common in eighteenth-century Irish mapping), and the more unusual French *echelle de toise* – indicates that he intended this map to be circulated not only in Ireland and Britain, but also in Continental Europe (fig. 14.2). The lack of hydro-graphical data in Rocque's version of the River Liffey adds weight to the argument that the *Exact survey* was a commercial product designed to appeal to as wide an audi-ence as possible, rather than to be reserved for mariners, engineers or civic authorities. Rocque funded the map through subscription,[18] which was raised to twenty-five shillings in January 1755,[19] owing to a mistake in Rocque's determina-

14 Jeremy Black, *The Hanoverians* (London, 2004), p. 83.   **15** Ibid., p. 115.   **16** Varley, 'John Rocque: engraver, surveyor, cartographer and map-seller', p. 87.   **17** Chamberlyne, *Magnae Brittanniae nottia or the present state of Great Britain* (London, 1755), p. 116.   **18** *Dublin Journal*, 2 Nov. 1754; Colm Lennon and John Montague, *John Rocque and the exact survey of Dublin* (Dublin, 2010), p. x.   **19** *Dublin Journal*, 2 Nov. 1754.

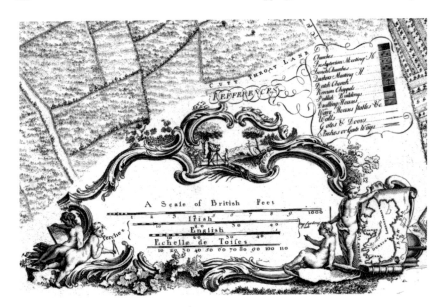

14.2 Scale bars in Rocque's *Exact survey of the city and suburbs of Dublin*
(Dublin, 1756) (courtesy of the Royal Irish Academy © RIA).

tion of the number of pages required for the map. Over three hundred and fifty
people subscribed to his work, including surveyors such as Jonathan Barker, George
Semple and Bernard Scalé, who was Rocque's brother-in-law and apprentice.[20] In
1757, when Rocque reduced the *Exact survey* onto one sheet for publication, he
approached Dublin city council to assist him financially with his endeavour. They
agreed to his request:

> John Rocque, topographer to his royal highness the prince of Wales, praying
> to be considered for taking and publishing an exact survey of this city and its
> environs (agreeable to his great plan of the city of London) in four sheets,
> which with great pains, labour and expense, he reduced into one sheet, and
> that the subscriptions for this work have not in any sort answered his expec-
> tation. Ordered, that the city treasurer do, on the Lord Mayor's warrant, pay
> the petitioner twenty guineas, the same to be allowed on his accounts.[21]

There is no direct evidence showing that he used existing estate maps of various
sections of the city to compile his *Exact survey*. These maps may have been more of
a hindrance than an advantage to Rocque (if he did have access to them), as they
were of widely dispersed sections of the city and may have spoilt the homogeneity
found in his work.[22]

20 J.H. Andrews, *Two maps of eighteenth-century Dublin and its surroundings by John Rocque*
(Dublin, 1977), p. 5. **21** 11 Jan. 1757: Gilbert (ed.), *Ancient records*, x, p. 252. **22** 'Manuscript

Evidence of Rocque's method of surveying the city is clearly visible – in fact, unlike other similar surveys, it is rather blatant. Inside a compartment within the scale bar was placed a vignette of two small human figures – presumably Rocque with an assistant – operating what appears to be a theodolite. Rocque was known to have worked with theodolites in other surveys in Ireland,[23] and his history with the instrument dates back to his map of London in 1746 when he established a trigonometrical skeleton of the city using this instrument to conduct his survey.[24] Rocque was known to have used chains in his survey of Dublin,[25] and there is a strong indication that a circumferentor may also have been among his equipment, as the *Exact survey*'s north arrow contains allowances for magnetic variation. The near drowning of Rocque's survey assistants during the measuring of a baseline is another indication that a trigonometrical method using theodolites was employed for his Dublin survey – a baseline being a vital component in this process. It is possible that Rocque operated both theodolites and circumferentors during the course of his survey of Dublin, however there is no evidence to indicate which was the preferred instrument or if the theodolite was used in the city while circumferentors were used in the more open areas of the surrounding countryside.

CARTOGRAPHIC STYLE

The most striking difference between Rocque's Dublin and his London surveys was the level of detail that he included in his Dublin work (fig. 14.3). No effort was made in his London map to distinguish between different buildings except for stately homes or buildings of importance. Ordinary shops and houses were omitted, and city blocks dominated the map's surface. Rocque's Dublin map, in contrast, included virtually every building within the city, 11,645 in total,[26] with separate hatching markers included to distinguish between residences and businesses. Indeed, unlike the majority of his Irish contemporaries and predecessors, Rocque simply seems not to have liked to leave blank areas on his maps. In Rocque's own words, the map was designed to show 'public buildings, dwelling houses, warehouses, stables, court yards', which his *Exact survey* did in abundance. Andrews speculated that the detail at the rear of the majority of the buildings, coach houses and stables included in the *Exact survey* was partially measured by eye rather than being surveyed.[27] Even with the

maps of the Domville Estate in Dublin city, Dublin county and Meath' (1655–1816) (NLI, MS 11,937); 'Manuscript maps of the Hatch estate' (1727–1871) (NLI, MS 21F112); 'A book of maps of the several estates of the Rt Hon. and Rt Rev. dean and chapter of Christ Church, Dublin' (1800) (NLI MS 2789). **23** John Rocque, 'A survey of Tullagorey' (Kildare, 1756): a surveyor operating a theodolite is included in the map's cartouche. **24** Andrews, *Two maps of eighteenth-century Dublin*, p. 2; John Rocque, *London and ten miles around* (London, 1746). **25** *Dublin Journal*, 14 Sept. 1754. **26** Ferguson, 'Rocque's map and the history of nonconformity in Dublin: a search for meeting houses', pp 129–65. **27** Andrews, *Two maps of eighteenth-century Dublin*, p. 3.

14.3 The Abbey Street area of Dublin (from John Rocque, *Exact survey of the city and suburbs of Dublin* (Dublin, 1756), courtesy of the Royal Irish Academy © RIA).

various contents of the fields surrounding the city remaining dubious and unable to be proven, the *Exact survey* still offered an unprecedented view of the city.

Gardens can be found in many portions of the map, particularly around Trinity College and the Lying-in Hospital, showing that the city was not simply a solid urban mass but also contained open and green spaces (fig. 14.4). Rocque's attention to the detail of these features may reflect his early career designing decorative grounds in England. Gardens at the rear of residential houses appear to be a similar generic size and design, which supports the theory that only the fronts of buildings were surveyed, not the rears. The city's graveyards were shown with gravestones in profile. Apart from trees and tenters for drying cloth, the gravestones appear to be the only profile items in the *Exact survey*. Many of the graveyards were left unnamed. The fields surrounding the city were shown to represent a mixture of pasture and orchards with the highest concentration of arable farming to the south-west of the city. Rocque may have also employed an engraver's stamp for some repetitive city features, as he appeared to use standardized symbolism when representing construction sites. The majority of these sites were located in and around the quays, particularly to the east of the city, and, at first glance, they appear to be shipyards, symbolized by crossed timbers similar to features found in ship construction. The same symbol can be found away from the river, for example on Meath Street and St Stephen's Green, meaning that this symbol was meant to represent any form of construction other than shipbuilding.

Despite Rocque's unsurpassed attention to detail in the *Exact survey*, there are several mistakes. Precise details such as the presence of bollards on Henrietta Street

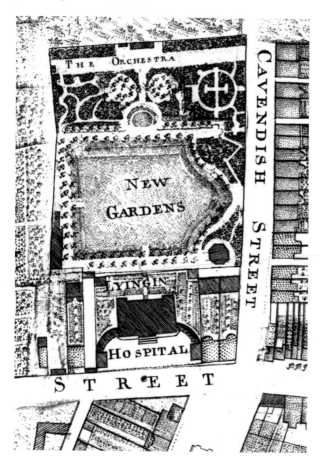

14.4 Rocque's inclusion of decorative gardens behind the Lying-in Hospital (modern day Rotunda hospital) (courtesy of the Royal Irish Academy © RIA).

and in front of Trinity College must be weighed against his omission of the Long Stone off College Green and the absence of surviving sections of the city wall. A section of St Patrick's Lane crossed the map's border, which is a poor cartographical trait. Bow Lane was spelt *Beaux Lane* – a forgivable inclusion considering Rocque's French background and a common mistake, as even one of France's greatest eighteenth-century cartographers noted that 'it is so easy to err when one is in a region whose language and pronunciations are not familiar'.[28]

Rocque took the decision to include the equestrian statue of George II in St Stephen's Green, which was not erected until after the *Exact survey* appeared on the market.[29] With the statue's inclusion, Rocque took the same gamble that Brooking had taken with his inclusion of the then-uncompleted St Werburgh's Church in 1728.

---

28 'Il est si facile de pécher quand on est dans un pays dont la langue et la pronunciation ne sont pas familières': C.R. Cassini to the Procureurs du Pays de Provence (2 Aug. 1785), quoted in Sponberg-Pedley, *Commerce of cartography*, p. 186. 29 Maxwell, *Dublin under the Georges*, p. 211.

Unlike Brooking, Rocque won his gamble. There was also the unfortunate yet unavoidable repetition of 'Stable Lane', as so many minor streets and alleys at the rear of town houses had not yet been assigned their own nomenclature and were in fact lanes that granted access to stables.

Rocque's map of Dublin highlighted its importance as a trading hub. Commercially, eighteenth-century Dublin was very successful, as indicated by a visitor in 1732:

> The merchants, citizens and manufacturers in Dublin are very numerous, and many of them rich and in great credit, perfectly well understanding every branch of trade of which their linen, woollen, silken and hair-manufactured goods are specimens.[30]

Rocque's cartographic interpretation of this wealth of trade can be found in the many brigs and sloops present along the city's quays and docks. In the section of the Liffey below the old Custom House beside Essex Bridge, a total of ninety-five ships and boats of various descriptions can be found in the Liffey. Below Essex Bridge, under which sailing ships could not pass due to its height, smaller row boats are shown transporting goods and people (fig. 14.5). Rocque did not survey these docked ships; it is against surveying logic to record vehicles for inclusion in a map and if he had done so the streets of the *Exact survey* would be thronged with stationary carriages and coaches. Instead, Rocque's purposeful inclusion of these vessels demonstrated cartographically both the success of Dublin as a port and the fact that the Liffey was navigable up to Essex Bridge.

Important public and civic buildings were paid special attention to in the *Exact survey* and were highlighted by particularly dense hatching. The Four Courts, Dublin Castle, Kildare House, the Blue Coat Hospital, the King's Inns, the Custom House, the Lying-in Hospital and Dr Steeven's Hospital were among the many non-ecclesiastical structures highlighted and named. The Parliament Building on College Green was given particular attention, as it was the only building on the map to contain an internal layout, which Rocque probably obtained from another source rather than his own hand. He also noted religious diversity, including a wide variety of places of Christian worship (fig. 14.6).

Aside from public and religious structures, Dublin's various industrial and guild buildings were included. Alms houses, carpenters' halls, glass houses, music halls, printing houses, bowling greens, watch houses, shoemakers' halls, tailors' hall and particularly meeting houses of various religious groups were among the many features of Dublin's commercial and social fabric noted by Rocque. This is more representative of the physical structure of the city than the guild coats of arms included by Brooking.

One of Rocque's most recognizable trademarks was the inclusion of terrain

30 Edward Lloyd, *A description of the city of Dublin* (London, 1732).

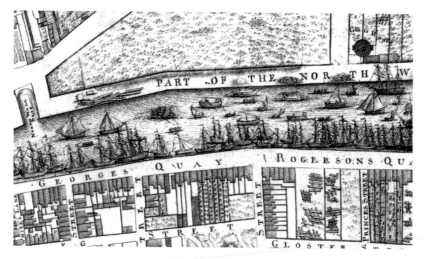

14.5 Ships in the River Liffey showing Dublin's strength of commerce
(from John Rocque, *Exact survey of the city and suburbs of Dublin* (Dublin, 1756),
courtesy of the Royal Irish Academy © RIA).

14.6 Legend to
Rocque's map of
Dublin showing
religious sites (from
John Rocque, *Exact
survey of the city and
suburbs of Dublin*
(Dublin, 1756),
courtesy of the Royal
Irish Academy ©
RIA).

shading,[31] yet the *Exact survey* contains sparse terrain information. Rocque failed to
show the obvious slope that leads from Christ Church Cathedral to the Liffey which

---

31 John Rocque, *A map of County Armagh* (Dublin, 1760); John Rocque, 'A plan of the
gardens and view of the buildings at Esher, Surrey' (1737); John Rocque, 'A survey of
Moortown, Kildare' (1757).

may have been excluded as he may not have wanted terrain shading to interfere with
map detail such as buildings, yet he specifically included the central hill on which
Armagh town and cathedral sit in his map of Co. Armagh in 1760. The only terrain
features displayed within dense urban areas were dung hills, earth works, brick yards
and quarries, one of which was located on Sackville Street. Areas outside the city,
such as the Phoenix Park or the Dodder River valley, contained terrain shading
which was aided by the orientation of text with terrain and other local features.

The *Exact survey* was engraved by Andrew Dury, who had a similar style to
Rocque, especially concerning terrain shading,[32] if not so refined. Rocque originally
planned to produce his Dublin map on two sheets, however, finding that the scale at
which it was to be engraved would suit four sheets better, he advertised his mistake
but assured his subscribers that those who had already paid would not be affected by
a change in price.[33]

ROCQUE'S *CITY AND ENVIRONS*, 1757

The *Exact survey* was not Rocque's only map of Dublin. In 1757, *A plan of the city of
Dublin and environs* was published, giving a wider view of the area surrounding
Dublin as well as the city itself. The *Dublin and environs* map again demonstrated
Rocque's uniqueness in the Irish surveying market, as it was published with a wider,
possibly international, audience in mind – this is demonstrated by the presence of
English and Irish mile scale bars in addition to yard and *echelle de toise*, a reference in
the title to the map being produced in the same scale as Rocque's maps of London,
Paris and Rome, and the bilingual, if simple, title in English and French. The map
covered a wide area, far beyond the then limits of the city – from Harold's Cross in
the south to Glasnevin in the north and from the Phoenix Park in the west to Dublin
Bay.

Rocque's presentation of terrain made his contributions to the cartographic
heritage of Dublin unique. Areas such as the Tolka, Liffey and Dodder river valleys,
in addition to the undulating hills and steep banks in the Phoenix Park, gave an
element of dimension and realism. The crest of the hill on which Christ Church
Cathedral sits was included by Rocque in his *Dublin and environs* map, although it had
not been shown in his *Exact survey*. The mud-flats and rocky shoals of Dublin Bay
and the channel of the River Liffey were shown in detail, but depth readings were
missing, thus reducing the map's usefulness to navigation and highlighting a more
multipurpose and commercial function. *Dublin and environs* differed from the *Exact
survey* primarily in its representation of buildings, which were no longer shown as
individual properties but as city blocks reminiscent of Rocque's 1746 map of
London. Many individual buildings were represented in the city's hinterland, mostly

---

32 A. Dury and W. Herbert, *A topographical map of the county of Kent* (London, 1769). **33**
Dublin Journal, 2 Nov. 1754.

manor houses and important civic and religious buildings. Within the bounds of the city, such sites were distinguished from the dot hatching of the surrounding residential and commercial city blocks by being shaded in solid black. Rocque noted only one historical site – 'Baggot & Rath Castle' – outside of the city and, like de Gomme, he included a proposed fortification located within the Phoenix Park. Unlike de Gomme, Rocque is not known to have performed any military services, nor to have produced any real engineer works, so the inclusion of fortifications is something of a mystery.

Rocque brought more than an eloquent artistic style and Continental cartographic fashion to Dublin. His ability to organize a large and highly detailed survey project, involving many individuals, within a defined and concise timeframe, demonstrated his strong managerial traits. His flair for marketing can be found in the upbeat and highly positive articles he published during the course of his survey – this in spite of the several problems he encountered. The professional manner in which he dealt with Kendrick and the unfortunate lack of tolerance from certain sections of the Irish surveying community helped to reinforce his expertise in the business and practise of surveying.

Few surveyors operating in eighteenth-century Ireland had the impact of John Rocque, or left a legacy like his. His apprentice, Bernard Scalé, trained others in Rocque's style, and the many reprints of his *Exact survey of Dublin* in the centuries since its creation are testimony to his greatness. J.H. Andrews perhaps best summed up Rocque's work when he wrote:

> Despite his Continental origins, he had absorbed enough of the spirit of English empiricism not to make a parade of general principles or to insist on pressing them to their logical conclusions. The principles were made manifest in his maps, however, and much of their substance can be conveyed in three words: intelligibility, visibility and plainiformity.[34]

---

34 Andrews, *Two maps of eighteenth-century Dublin*, p. 3.

15 Eighteenth-century Dublin city estates: urban metamorphosis through mapping

Maps of the urban estates of eighteenth-century Dublin often resemble a patchwork quilt rather than a cartographic exercise. Scattered, isolated and random clusters of properties cover large portions of the city, offset by more concentrated and larger estates primarily in the suburbs. Most of the land within the city was in the hands of a few individual estate owners, including Dublin Corporation, thus making rent and leases the norm for residents. The estates of Dublin city and county, of which those of the Gardiners, Fitzwilliams/Pembrokes, and the archbishops of Dublin are three well-documented examples, were regular sources of employment for Dublin's eighteenth-century surveyors. The land owned by these estates generated massive incomes, and the maps and measurements made of these assets by Dublin surveyors were key to their successful management.

URBAN ESTATES

As noted already, Dublin was divided into many privately owned urban estates during the eighteenth century. Some of these, such as the Hatch Estate, consisted of dispersed plots of land, whereas others, such as the Gardiner Estate, were more concentrated. With Dublin's population almost quadrupling to nearly 200,000 residents during the course of the eighteenth century,[1] the city expanded from its medieval core into the surrounding countryside.[2] With modernization being difficult within the oldest part of the city due to narrow streets and dense population, owners of the new suburbs had an opportunity to lay out lands following their own personal tastes in the latest town planning and architectural designs. An English visitor in 1797 described the differences between the then two sections of the city, old and new:

> The general appearance of the city of Dublin ... is extremely beautiful, from the number of public building[s] and the principal streets are well paved and lighted, and the flagged way at either side, with some exceptions, broad and tolerably clean, which is a difficult matter to preserve ... but the inferior streets are equally filthy and diabolical.[3]

---

1 Sheridan, 'Designing the capital city', p. 68. **2** Clarke, *Dublin part 1, to 1610* (Irish Historic Towns Atlas, no. 11), p. 3. **3** Anon., *Dublin and its vicinity in 1797* (London, 1797).

Independently owned estates led to a disjointed level of urban advancement, with sections of undeveloped and older areas between modernized estates.

GARDINER ESTATE

The Gardiner Estate, located in the north-eastern portion of the city – including the areas now covered by Mountjoy Square, Dorset Street, O'Connell Street and Gardiner Street – was one of the largest Dublin estates. The progenitor of the Gardiner estate was Luke Gardiner; a shrewd banker who married a wealthy heiress and bought the Drogheda estate[4] in 1714. He was MP for the boroughs of Tralee and Thomastown between 1725 and 1755 and at one time held the office of vice-treasurer of Ireland and surveyor general of customs.[5] One of his lasting legacies is Henrietta Street, off Bolton Street – a superb example of early Georgian architecture, where Luke was a resident. His son Charles (1720–69) followed in his father's foot-steps, expanding the family's properties, not only in Dublin but also in Ulster and elsewhere in Leinster. But it was Charles' son Luke (1745–98) who developed the Gardiner Estate to its greatest extent.[6] Luke was MP for Co. Dublin as well as sitting on the board of the WSC. As a commissioner, he used his influence to benefit his own holdings within the city.[7]

From the 1780s onwards, Thomas Sherrard, along with his various partners and assistants, became the primary surveying force for the Gardiner family. Sherrard not only worked on the estate, he also he lived on it – being based on Blessington Street, which fell within the Gardiner's sphere of influence from 1800 onwards. He was also connected with the Gardiners directly through his work with the Wide Streets Commission, of which Luke Gardiner was a member.[8] It may be suggested that either Sherrard's surveying role with the WSC or his work on the Gardiner Estate helped him land the other position. It is clear that he was extensively involved with developments that helped shape the north inner city, producing multiple maps of Bolton Street,[9] Capel Street,[10] Dorset Street[11] and Gardiner Street.[12] His sons and

---

4 This area covered the modern day O'Connell Street/Henry Street/Moore Street region. See Sheridan, 'Designing the capital city', p. 91. 5 *Dictionary of National Biography*, vols 2, 5, 7. 6 Mary Clark and Alastair Smeaton (eds), *The Georgian squares of Dublin* (Dublin, 2006), p. 35. 7 WSC/Mins/6, p. 182. 8 Both Sherrard's and Luke Gardiner's signatures are found on at least one WSC manuscript map, Thomas Sherrard, Great Britain Street and Cavendish Row, 1787 (DCA WCS/Maps/206). 9 Thomas Sherrard, 'Lease of premises … to Alexander Lynar' (1791) (NLI Gardiner papers, MS 36,516/7); Thomas Sherrard, 'Lease for lives renewable forever … to Richard Trench' (1794) (NLI Gardiner papers, MS 36,516/12). 10 Thomas Sherrard, 'Lease … to Thomas Pilkington' (1790) (NLI Gardiner papers, MS 36,520/2); Thomas Sherrard, 'Lease for three lives … to Michael Heron' (1804) (NLI Gardiner papers, MS 36,520/5). 11 Thomas Sherrard, 'Lease for three lives … to Rev. Christopher Wall' (1805) (NLI Gardiner papers, MS 36,524/17). 12 Thomas Sherrard, 'Lease for three lives … to William Duke Moore' (1788) (NLI Gardiner papers, MS 36,532/1); Thomas Sherrard, 'Lease for three lives to John Cash' (1791) (NLI Gardiner

business partners slowly took over these responsibilities by 1810.[13] Sherrard also bears
the unusual distinction of being the only surveyor to have a street named in his
honour. Sherrard Street just off Dorset Street, still comprising mostly Georgian era
buildings and which once lay within the Gardiner Estate, is named after him.[14] The
Gardiner Estate slowly fell into decline after the death of Luke Gardiner at the Battle
of New Ross in 1798.[15]

FITZWILLIAM/PEMBROKE ESTATE

The Fitzwilliam/Pembroke Estate, in the south-eastern portion of the city, had a
longer and more diverse relationship with surveyors than the Gardiners'. Like other
contemporary estate owners,[16] the Pembroke family tended to retain the services of
a surveyor for a number of years and thus a lineage of their estate surveyors can be
traced. Such retention of service had benefits for both client and surveyor – the client
could depend on a surveyor who knew their tastes and requirements and who would
gain first-hand knowledge of the estate's properties over their years of service.
During the eighteenth century, the Fitzwilliam/Pembroke Estate developed both
Merrion and Fitzwilliam squares in the city, but also maintained a large rural tenant
population on their lands, which included most of Donnybrook, Merrion and
Dundrum.

Some of the earliest recorded surveying on this estate is by James Cullen, who
conducted extensive work around Ringsend and Irishtown from the 1690s until
approximately 1710.[17] A solid practitioner and competition estate surveyor, Cullen
was succeeded by his son Edward, who was recorded as working for the estate in
1731.[18] Surveyor Thomas Cave worked for both the estate of Christ Church
Cathedral and the Pembroke family until his unexpected death, referred to as a
'sudden disorder', in 1749, which was marked by the estate agent's hasty rush to find
a new surveyor.[19] During the 1760s, Jonathan Barker produced a series of superbly
detailed maps of the entire Fitzwilliam/Pembroke Estate from the Liffey to
Dundrum (pl. 9). Barker's maps were excellently produced and represent a form of
cartographic stock-taking for the estate owners. They betray the sole concern of the
proprietor for his own lands. Barker's maps are almost entirely focused upon the
Pembroke properties, with only minimum detail being supplied for the neigh-

papers, MS 36,532/5).   **13** Sherrards, Brassington and Greene, 'Mabbot Street' (1810) (NLI
Gardiner papers, MS 36,545).   **14** The naming of this street may also be connected with
property owned by Sherrard.   **15** Charles Mosley (ed.), *Burke's peerage, baronetage and
knightage* (107th ed., 3 vols, Wilmington, 2003), ii, p. 2748.   **16** The liberty of Christ
Church, Domville Estate etc.   **17** James Cullen, 'Map of Baggot Rath' (NAI Pembroke
papers, 1692 (2011/2/1/1)), James Cullen, 'A map and survey of Ringsend and Irishtown'
(1706) (NAI Pembroke papers, 2011/2/1/6).   **18** Edward Cullen, 'River Dodder from Balls
Bridge to Ringsend Bridge' (1731) (NAI Pembroke papers, 2011/2/1/8).   **19** Letter of
Richard Mathews, 1 May 1749 (NAI Pembroke papers, 97/46/1/2/5/64).

bouring areas of the city and county.[20] They include local amenities useful to estate development, such as extensive brickfields in Sandymount,[21] in addition to standard surveying features such as field areas, buildings and land classification.[22] This leads us to the realization that, like the Gardiner family, the Pembroke family was primarily concerned with the developments and rents within its own sphere of influence rather that a citywide development plan.

The Down Survey was occasionally referenced by the surveyors employed by the Pembroke/Fitzwilliam Estate as a reference for older leases and field layouts. Official copied Down Survey maps, signed by deputy surveyor generals Jerome Smith[23] and Andrew Chaignean,[24] can be found in the estate's mapping records, while the process of simply viewing the Down Survey maps may have occurred on a regular basis.

Father-and-son surveyors Pat and John Roe became the surveyors of choice for the estate during the 1790s, continuing well into the following century. One major development with which they were involved was the laying out of the Georgian urban masterpiece of Fitzwilliam Square in 1791:

> A new square is planned at the rere of Baggot Street, in which lots are rapidly taken and the buildings are to be immediately commenced. The design is not without elegance and the execution, it is believed, will be correspondent.[25]

The Roes' involvement with the Fitzwilliam/Pembroke Estate continued until the 1820s. Following Pat's death, John Roe continued by himself, with the assistance of his father's catalogue of maps.[26] Arthur Neville, city surveyor, also took advantage of the existing Roe maps,[27] as well as producing many maps of the estate during the 1820s and 1830s. Neville regularly used his official title after his name while surveying in a private capacity,[28] with his duties being taken over in the early 1830s by the surveying firm of Sherrard, Brassington and Gale,[29] who proceeded to resurvey the

20 Jonathan Barker, 'A plan of Merrion Square' (1764) (NAI Pembroke papers, 2011/2/2/10); Jonathan Barker, 'Plan of Merrion Square and adjacent neighbourhood' (1762) (NAI Pembroke papers, 2011/2/2/8); Jonathan Barker, 'A map of Dundrum' (1762) (NAI Pembroke papers, 2011/2/2/4). **21** Jonathan Barker, 'A map of Baggotrath' (1762) (NAI Pembroke papers, 2011/2/2/6). **22** Jacinta Prunty, *Maps and map making in local history* (Dublin, 2004), p. 102. **23** Jerome Smith, 'Survey taken in Parish of Tanee' (1753) (NAI Pembroke papers, 2011/2/4). **24** Andrew Chaignean, 'Survey taken for the parish of Donnybrook' (1770) (NAI Pembroke papers, 2011/2/4). **25** *Dublin Evening Post*, 18 June 1791. **26** John Roe, 'Map ... in the barony of Rathdown, Co. Dublin, copied from Pat Roe's map drawn in 1780 with additions and alterations' (1815) (NAI Pembroke papers, 97/46/4/15); John Roe, 'Map of Ringsend' (1821) (NAI Pembroke papers, 97/46/4/16). **27** Arthur Neville, 'Part of the estate of the Rt Hon. the earl of Pembroke, surveyed by John Roe, revised by Arthur Neville' (1826) (NAI Pembroke papers, 97/46/4/17). **28** Arthur Neville (city surveyor), 'Map of ... Grand Canal, Sideny Crescent, Warrington Place' (1830) (NAI Pembroke papers, 97/46/4/18); Arthur Neville (city surveyor), 'Plan for the improvement of that part of the estate of the hon. Sidney Herbert' (1830) (NAI Pembroke papers, 97/46/4/19). **29** Sherrard, Brassington and Gale, 'Survey of Bray Co. Wicklow'

entire estate. This is reminiscent of the project conducted by Jonathan Barker sixty years previously and indicates that, as with the organizations such as the Ordnance Survey, map revision cycles were conducted by large estates. Thomas Sherrard would have been elderly during this time,[30] but Brassington continued to be associated with the Fitzwilliam/Pembroke Estate until the 1860s.[31]

ESTATE OF THE ARCHBISHOP OF DUBLIN

One of the largest estates in the county belonged to the archbishop of Dublin. Predominately rural, the archbishop's estate covered large swathes of Swords, Lusk, Finglas, Tallaght, Clondalkin and Rathcoole, and was a productive employer of surveyors from the 1650s onwards.[32] The estate had not remained static from the Reformation to the eighteenth century, with property being sold and bought. The lengths of leases on this estate were set by the Irish parliament in 1634,[33] using a time-frame of twenty-one years for agricultural land and forty years for urban plots.[34] Such leases were not always enforced strictly, however, or returned to the archbishop and instead were inherited by the tenant's relatives or offspring, resulting in a lease passing through several hands over many decades. Archbishop William King (1650–1729) complained in 1723 that he was only receiving a rent of £7 10s. per annum on land worth over £300, due to the lease still operating on terms set 160 years previously.[35]

The archbishop of Dublin did not derive his entire income from rents. He was also entitled to a tithe, accounting for approximately one tenth of the produce of each parish.[36] This was not popular with tenants who were not members of the established church. A Mr Brown of Trinity College addressed the Irish parliament in 1788 in relation to the difficulties that were encountered in trying to collect tithes. He mentioned the resentment felt by tenants towards this ecclesiastical charge and those who encouraged such resentment for their own benefit:

> The real cause of oppression was the land-jobber or middle-man, he having racked the tenant to the utmost, knew not how to increase this rent but by robbing the parson. He teaches the foolish peasant to curse the parson for the weight of his spade and the scantiness of his meat, though he has only to lift up his eyes to his tithe-free neighbour, and see him labouring under equal

---

(1830) (NAI Pembroke papers, 97/46/4/23).   **30** The 'Sherrard' in this case may also have been Thomas' sons William and/or David Henry.   **31** Richard Brassington, 'Map of part of the lands of Old Merrion' (1861) (NAI Pembroke papers, 97/46/4/30).   **32** Robert Newcomen, 'The lordship of Tahhagh latlie belonginge to the bishope of Dublin' (*c.*1654), reproduced in Refaussé and Clark, *A catalogue of the maps*, p. 43, pl. 22.   **33** 10 and 11 Chas I, c.3. [Ire.] (1634).   **34** Raymond Gillespie, *The first chapter act book of Christ Church Cathedral, Dublin, 1574–1634* (Dublin, 1997), p. 146.   **35** TCD MS 2537/32, quoted in Refaussé and Clark, *A catalogue of the maps*, p. 24.   **36** G. O'Brien, *The economic history of Ireland from the Union to the famine* (London, 1921), p. 494.

want of comfort, and heavier load of rent. The rent of land tithe-free is always much higher than of other land; it follows plainly that not a holder in Ireland would be advantaged by the abolition of tithe tomorrow.[37]

The establishment of land acreage, type and presence of buildings in addition to traditional terriers,[38] fell to the land surveyors in the employment of the archbishop. There is a strong connection between the surveyors who worked on the archbishop's lands and those who were employed by Dublin Corporation and other major surveying enterprises, such as the Down and Trustees surveys during the seventeenth and eighteenth centuries. Such a connection is not surprising considering the high social status of the archbishop of Dublin, not only as a senior member of the Church of Ireland, but also as one of the major landowners in Co. Dublin. Archbishop King felt strongly about the necessity of hiring surveyors, urging the bishop of Cloyne in 1717 to hire them 'as to maps it will be very necessary to have them'.[39]

Surveyor Robert Newcomen produced several maps for the archbishop's estate in the 1650s[40] and was also employed by both the Down Survey and Dublin Corporation.[41] Joseph Moland[42] and John Greene,[43] both city surveyors in the course of their careers, produced maps for the archbishop from c.1710 to 1716, in addition to their previous work for the Trustees' Survey in the first years of the eighteenth century.[44] Other city surveyors employed during the course of the eighteenth and nineteenth centuries included Roger Kendrick,[45] also verger of St Patrick's Cathedral, in the 1750s and A.R. Neville[46] in the early 1800s.

In addition to the connection to the office of city surveyor, there appears to be a distinct trend towards the employment of surveying lineages over time. Moland's apprentice, Gabriel Stokes, was employed by the archbishop during the 1730s, while Moland himself was originally John Greene's assistant during the 1690s.[47] Father-and-son surveying duos can be seen in the maps of Thomas Logan,[48] A.R. Neville,[49]

---

37 *Freeman's Journal*, 19 Feb. 1788. **38** A land terrier is a record system for an individual's land and property holdings. **39** TCD, MS 2534/148, quoted in Refaussé and Clark, *A catalogue of the maps*, p. 24. **40** Newcomen, 'The lordship of Tahhagh', reproduced in Refaussé and Clark, *A catalogue of the maps*, p. 43 & pl. 22. **41** 10 Dec. 1668: Gilbert (ed.), *Ancient Records*, iv, p. 456. **42** Joseph Moland, 'A survey of part of the lands of Drumeen' (1713), reproduced in Refaussé and Clark, *A catalogue of the maps*. **43** John Greene, 'A survey of the towne and lands of Kilpatrick' (1715), reproduced in Refaussé and Clark, *A catalogue of the maps*, p. 56, pl. 3. **44** The Trustees' Survey (1700–3) was named after the trustees of estates forfeited in the aftermath of the Williamite Wars (1689–91). It was in many ways similar in scope to Petty's Down Survey of the 1650s. **45** Roger Kendrick, 'A map of part of the land of Glanasmoin, Tallaght' (1752), reproduced Refaussé and Clark, *A catalogue of the maps*, p. 73, pl. 41. **46** A.R. Neville CS and Son, *A map of the mansion house and ground of the earl of Clonmel* (Dublin, 1807). **47** 24 Apr. 1698: Gilbert (ed.), *Ancient records*, vi, p. 196. **48** Thomas Logan and Son, 'Map of lands in Templeogue' (1813), reproduced in Refaussé and Clark, *A catalogue of the maps*, pl. 33. **49** A.R. Neville CS and Son, 'A map of the mansion house and ground of the earl of Clonmel, Dublin' (1807).

Pat Roe[50] and Thomas Sherrard.[51] Sherrard's apprentices, Richard Brassington and
Clarges Greene, as well as his former partner John Brownrigg,[52] were also employed
by the various archbishops of Dublin. Adhering to such lineages was not a universal
theme, however, and many unconnected surveyors[53] were also employed by the
archiepiscopal estates during the seventeenth and eighteenth centuries.

---

50 Pat Roe, 'A map of part of the lands of Tallaght belonging to his grace the archbishop
of Dublin' (1774); John Roe, 'A survey of the demesne of Tallaght' (1811), reproduced in
Refaussé and Clark, *A catalogue of the maps*, p. 85, pl. 37. **51** Sherrard, Brassington and
Greene, 'Survey of Burgagemolye' (1810), reproduced in Refaussé and Clark, *A catalogue of
the maps*, p. 83, pl. 35. **52** John Brownrigg, 'A map of part of the farm of St Sepulcher's'
(1793), reproduced in Refaussé and Clark, *A catalogue of the maps*, p. 80. **53** Elyard Arnoldi,
'Ballymore' (1668); Peter Duff, 'Map of Clondalkin' (1703); Thomas Cave, 'Map of
Belinstown and Loughmarting' (1728); Francis Mathews, 'Map of lands in Templeogue'
(1783), reproduced in Refaussé and Clark, *A catalogue of the maps*, maps 9, 15, 33 and 46
respectively.

16 Dublin city surveyors, 1679–1828

The highest civic position an eighteenth-century surveyor could attain in Dublin was city surveyor. This office existed for a period of 178[1] years, starting in 1679 with John Greene Jr, and was held by at least eleven individuals,[2] each of whom left his own distinct mark on surveying in Dublin. The role of city surveyor was not as broad as that of surveyor to the Wide Streets Commission, yet what makes it important is that it was the highest civic office held by a practitioner of surveying within the bounds of Dublin city. His main task was to provide Dublin Corporation with its mapping requirements, primarily involving the plotting of leases. As the corporation was also responsible for the provision of services, such as piped water, the city surveyor could be called upon to provide technical expertise with such engineering works.

Table 16.1 List of Dublin city surveyors (1679–1857). Dates from J.T. Gilbert (ed.), *Ancient records* and Mary Clark, *The book of maps of the Dublin city surveyors, 1695–1827* (Dublin, 1983).

Dublin city surveyor	Years in office
John Greene Jr	1679–98
Barnaby Hackett	1689–90
Joseph Moland	1698–1718
James Ramsey	1718–35
Roger Kendrick	1735–64
Thomas Mathews	1764–82
Samuel Byron	1782–95
D.B. Worthington	1795–1801
A.R. Neville	1801–28
Arthur Neville	1828–57

The first occupant of the position of Dublin city surveyor was John Greene Jr., who petitioned Dublin Corporation to create the position in late 1679 (fig. 16.1).[3] As part of the office of city surveyor, the occupant had to swear to:

> execute their trust according to the best of their skill and knowledge, that his authority might be viewed and knowne for the better satisfaction of those persons who shall employ him, and for that the petitioner is desirous to survey and make an exact map of all the cittee tenures, and for this satisfaction to

1 1679–1857. **2** Possibly more: Joseph Moland was appointed 'one of the city surveyors': see Mary Clark, *The book of maps of the Dublin city surveyors, 1695–1827* (Dublin, 1983), preface. **3** 25 Dec. 1679: Gilbert (ed.), *Ancient records*, v, p. 183.

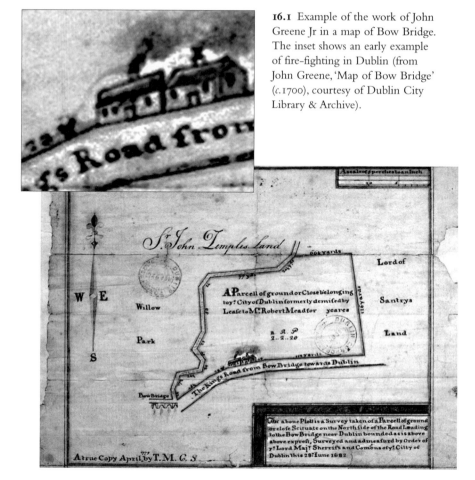

16.1 Example of the work of John Greene Jr in a map of Bow Bridge. The inset shows an early example of fire-fighting in Dublin (from John Greene, 'Map of Bow Bridge' (*c*.1700), courtesy of Dublin City Library & Archive).

submit himselfe to the pleasure of the assembly's commission to be sealed the next post assembly.[4]

Greene's employment was entirely at the pleasure of the lord mayor, city sheriffs and members of Dublin Corporation. Dublin's municipal corporation at the time was divided into two chambers or houses, the higher consisting of the lord mayor and twenty-four aldermen, while the lower[5] consisted of forty-eight sheriff's peers and ninety-six members of Dublin's various guilds. The corporation met four times per year[6] in the tholsel near Christ Church Cathedral, with many 'post-assembly' meetings taking place sporadically during the remainder of the year.[7]

Greene's first decade in this new role was relatively unremarkable, however events

---

4 Ibid.   **5** Also known as 'the sheriffs and commons'.   **6** Christmas, Easter, Midsummer and Michaelmas.   **7** Sheridan, 'Designing the capital city', p. 73.

occurring far from Dublin were to have a major impact on his immediate future. In 1685, James II, a Catholic, ascended to the throne of England. This event radically altered the sectarian divide that existed in the civic make-up of cities across Britain and Ireland. In Dublin, the oath of supremacy was removed after insistence from the king, allowing Catholics to be given the freedom of the city.[8] The new Catholic regime, which had in the past been curtailed and discriminated against, now had the ability to control civic bodies and appoint its own people, Catholics, to positions of power. All appointments to Dublin Corporation were to have vice-regal approval and any existing appointments, including the position of city surveyor, could be removed at will. As Sir Ellis Leighton commented, 'corporations are the creatures of the monarchy, and therefore, they have a particular obligation beyond other subjects at large to depend upon the monarchy and to uphold it.'[9]

In December 1687, Greene was removed from his official role, and Barnaby Hackett, a Catholic, was appointed in his place. There is a strong possibility that Hackett was a relation of Thomas Hackett, a banker and money lender who was appointed lord mayor of Dublin in October 1687 by a charter of James II.[10] There is no record of Barnaby Hackett's work in surveying during this period, possibly because there was little need for surveys, with no leases being sealed between November 1687 and May 1691.[11] He may have simply been someone with the right family connections and of a suitable religion tasked with occupying the position, with no intention of performing the city surveyor's duties.

This incident is one of the very few in which religion affected a professional surveyor's work. Overall, little is ever mentioned about surveyors' religious backgrounds, and it tended not to play an issue during the course of their duties. For Dublin-based surveyors, the assumption that most were Protestant is not without support. Known Protestant surveyors operating during this period included Jonathan Wight, an English Quaker working in Cork in the eighteenth century, and John Rocque, who was a French Huguenot.[12]

Hackett's role as city surveyor came to a sudden end with the ascension to the throne of Protestant William III in (1689) and James II's final defeat at the Battle of the Boyne the following year. Hackett's position became untenable, with the corporation calling for 'the forfeitures of those Papists who illegally succeeded in the ... corporation.'[13] When Hackett disappeared from the records in 1691, Greene resumed his old role as city surveyor.

Greene was a businessman, and his role as city surveyor did not prevent him from working in a private capacity in land surveying. At times, however, this negatively affected his ability to fulfil his official duties. Thomas Sherrard, surveyor to the Wide Streets Commission from the 1780s onwards, also combined official and private surveying work.[14] The situation grew so bad that by 1698 there was a need to hire a

8 Ibid., p. 74.   **9** 4 Apr. 1672: Gilbert (ed.), *Ancient records*, iv, p. 599.   **10** Oct. 1687: Gilbert (ed.), *Ancient records*, i, p. 73.   **11** Clark, *The book of maps of the Dublin city surveyors, 1695–1827*, p. x.   **12** Wight's diary is in the Religious Society of Friends Library, Ballyboden, Dublin.   **13** 20 Oct. 1690: Gilbert (ed.), *Ancient records*, v.

full-time assistant for Greene, as he was 'often out of town when he is wanted'.[15] This assistant, Joseph Moland, was admitted to the post of 'one of the city surveyors',[16] without an official salary and being paid only a commission based on the number of surveys he completed. Greene and Moland are known to have produced at least one survey in 1704,[17] but by 1706 Moland was referred to as city surveyor, indicating that Greene had either retired from the role, reduced his level of involvement or been dismissed due to his focus on his private practice.[18] Greene is known to have continued to work as a surveyor for both the archbishop of Dublin until 1715[19] and Trinity College until 1724.

Moland's payment on a piece-work basis suited him for small cadastral surveys within the city; however, it was less appropriate for larger projects that the city surveyor had to perform occasionally. One such example is a map of Dublin Bay and harbour that Moland had been working on:

> [at] great expense and labour in making an actual survey (by chain and instrument) … with the adjacent coasts and country, all rivers and exact situation of all gentlemen's houses, and other places of note within the extent of the said map.[20]

Moland was paid the sum of fifty pounds sterling for his efforts. The following year, however, having recently completed his map of Dublin Bay, he was again requesting additional payments from the corporation, with the sum of thirty pounds sterling being approved.[21] He was not the only surveyor working on Dublin Bay and harbour at the time. Thomas Holt was appointed surveyor and gauger for the recently formed Ballast Office, and may have conducted his work alongside Moland, or in addition to the work that Moland had just completed.[22] Other surveys conducted by Moland as city surveyor include work in Temple Bar,[23] Lazy Hill (modern Pearse Street)[24] and Donnycarney.[25]

For the majority of those who occupied the role of city surveyor, the position was for life. Moland died in office in late 1717 or early 1718 and his apprentice, James Ramsey, was appointed in his place. Records of Ramsey's work as city surveyor indicate that he had wider scope than his predecessors, as he was busy enough to have to

---

14 13 Mar. 1789 (DCA WSC/Mins/8).   **15** 24 Apr. 1698: Gilbert (ed.), *Ancient records*, vi, p. 196.   **16** Ibid.   **17** John Greene and Joseph Moland, 'A survey of lands of Donnycarney in the county of Dublin' (1704) (DCA C1/S1/130).   **18** 24 Mar. 1706: Gilbert (ed.), *Ancient records*, vi, p. 349.   **19** John Greene, *Details of houses at Tutestown* (Dublin, 1715).   **20** 24 Mar. 1706: Gilbert (ed.), *Ancient records*, vi, p. 349.   **21** 16 Jan. 1698: Gilbert (ed.), *Ancient records*, vi, p. 378.   **22** 16 Jan. 1707: Gilbert (ed.), *Ancient records*, vi, p. 378.   **23** Joseph Moland, 'Survey of several parcels of ground situate on north and south side of Temple Bar' (1707) (DCA C1/S1/30).   **24** Joseph Moland, 'Survey of a piece of ground on south side of River Liffey near Lazy Hill' (1709) (DCA C1/S1/52).   **25** John Greene and Joseph Moland, 'A survey of lands of Donnycarney in the county of Dublin' (1704) (DCA C1/S1/130).

hire more than one assistant.[26] Perhaps Ramsey's greatest contribution to surveying was his technical support in establishing standard yard measurements for the corporation (see above, p. 52). Ramsey occupied the post of city surveyor for seventeen years until his death in 1735.

Roger Kendrick, verger of St Patrick's Cathedral and Rocque's competitor, was appointed Dublin city surveyor on Ramsey's death in 1735.[27] During the late 1730s, Kendrick's work appears to have been focused on long levelling runs, possibly in relation to piped water, which is dependent on height values. In 1738, Kendrick was paid twenty-five pounds sterling for conducting a levelling run between Straffan, Co. Kildare, and Dolphin's Barn in Dublin city.[28] The following year, Kendrick was again surveying in Kildare, this time being paid thirty pounds for his 'extraordinary trouble'.[29] The extra effort that he went to during the course of his surveys, for which he charged the corporation, was not always welcomed by the city, and Kendrick was officially reprimanded by the corporation in relation to charging for several unauthorized surveys for the city paver.[30]

Aside from his attempts to obtain extra payment on the side, Kendrick's best documented work was his effort to produce a city plan of Dublin in direct competition with John Rocque in 1754. While Kendrick's map never materialized, there is strong evidence to suggest that he had amassed a large amount of data from his role as city surveyor on which to base his proposed Dublin map. Kendrick had been paid £12 15s. 6d. to create a map of the city in nine parts four years previously, 'thereby describing the precincts of the several districts, as they are now cleansed by the several persons who have undertaken that work.'[31] Kendrick's map of Dublin, for waste collection and other municipal purposes, was completed long before Rocque arrived in Dublin, and so his inability to produce a finalized map of the city for mass production remains a mystery.

Kendrick's professional defeat by Rocque in no way affected his position with the corporation, but, by 1757, the subject of city leases and in turn the city surveyor's role was placed under review. The matter behind this review was the 'preservation of the city estate'[32] by reconsidering the terms of leases and the actual boundaries of corporation-owned lots, in response to the rapid development and expansion of the city. Under the new structure, leases were to be reviewed after three lives or seventy years, whichever came first, while the role and products of the city surveyor were also taken into consideration:

> 1) The annexing of maps to the original leases is in no sort a provision in the latter case, and not without something further, an effectual one in the former.

---

26 17 Jan. 1717: Gilbert (ed.), *Ancient records*, vii, p. 54.   **27** 18 Jul. 1735: Gilbert (ed.), *Ancient records*, viii, p. 173.   **28** 14 Apr. 1738: Gilbert (ed.), *Ancient records*, viii, p. 286. **29** 19 Oct. 1739: Gilbert (ed.), *Ancient records*, viii, p. 350.   **30** 5 Dec. 1743: Gilbert (ed.), *Ancient records*, ix, pp 131–2.   **31** 4 May 1764: Gilbert (ed.), *Ancient records*, ix, p. 357.   **32** 21 Jan. 1757: Gilbert (ed.), *Ancient records*, x, p. 263.

2) That upon the fall of every life within the 7 years, and before any renewal is granted, the city surveyor shall be directed to survey the premises and to report particularly all such changes he finds thereon.[33]

These were the most significant changes made to the role of city surveyor since the time of John Greene.

Kendrick was suggested as a possible judge in the detracted public battle between Peter Callan and John Bell, which was fought in the press during the 1750s. Bell, in reference to the two men's conflicting field notes, suggested that 'the same exact field-notes be sent to be cast up by the surveyor general, or by the city surveyor of Dublin, which, I think, will determine that affair'.[34] Peter Callan was not supportive of Bell's suggestion; however, under the forged name of his employer Bartholomew O'Brien, Callan wrote that he was in no doubt as to how he felt about Kendrick's role:

> By what motive can we be induced to believe that there is a surveyor general and a city surveyor of Dublin, lawfully empowered to determine the contents of field-notes? And if there be such superior officers, how can we know who they are, and by what law are they so established?[35]

Despite Callan's aggressiveness, he did make a valid point – there was nothing in the job description of Dublin city surveyor that meant he could interfere between two surveyors in dispute, and if he did so, any judgment would not have enforceable legal support. Kendrick may have also been asked to become involved due to his official position rather than his personal qualities as a surveyor. It is important to note that Bell considered the role of Dublin city surveyor second only to the surveyor general, which is understandable, given the relative lack of official civic surveyors.

Kendrick had been city surveyor for almost thirty years by 1764. Unlike his predecessors and the majority of his successors, he opted to retire rather than continue indefinitely. The midsummer assembly accepted Kendrick's option to retire and awarded him an annual pension:

> Roger Kendrick is grown old and unable to procure for himself an independent subsistence for the remainder of his life, do recommend that he be allowed an annuity of £20, during his natural life. We observe that he has given up such maps and papers as he had relative to the city estates.[36]

Kendrick's city surveyor career may have overlapped with that of his successor, Thomas Mathews. Mathews was already operating in a surveying capacity before Kendrick's retirement, producing a survey of the Grafton Street area in 1752.[37] He

---

33 Ibid.   **34** *Universal Advertiser*, 7 Nov. 1758.   **35** Ibid., 21 Nov. 1758.   **36** 20 Jul. 1764: Gilbert (ed.), *Ancient records*, xi, p. 226.   **37** Dublin city surveyor maps (DCA C1/S1/69).

may have been an assistant of Kendrick's before his retirement and replacement in 1764.[38] From the perspective of cartographic conservation, possibly Mathews' most valuable act for students of eighteenth-century surveying was his compilation of a book,

> wherein shall be entered by him all the maps, surveys and levels which he has hitherto made, or shall hereafter make, upon such occasions, the same to be left in the tholsel office, to be produced at any time hereafter.[39]

Mathews was paid a fee of £100 for compiling this book of maps, of which the corporation 'much approve'.[40] Possibly due to this act of preservation, many of Mathews' maps survive to this day.[41] Mathews would only receive his fee for maps he produced if they were handed in to the town clerk, who in turn would give Mathews a certificate stating that the maps had been registered at the tholsel.[42]

Aside from his acts of preserving the city's cartographic heritage, Mathews was often occupied with setting out lots and dividing sections of land. In 1771, he was directed to lay out lots for building on Oxmantown Green. On Mathews' surveys, the land was noted to have 'been waste and unserviceable', but through planned building projects it would become 'an ornament to that part of your honours' estate and greatly increase the rental thereof'.[43] Mathews was also active in setting out lots on South Great George's Street.[44]

His activities as city surveyor required him to use his skills for tasks not always associated with traditional land surveying. In 1772, stables belonging to a Mr Mahon of Islandbridge were damaged, possibly by a waste water outlet built by the piped water committee of Dublin Corporation. Mathews and Joseph Parker, possibly an assistant or a surveyor hired by Mr Mahon 'were directed to make out an estimate of such damages, which said estimate, so returned ... amounts to the sum of £94 1s. 61/2d'.[45] An additional report determined that waste water had 'sapped the foundation' of the stable and Mr Mahon was paid the sum determined by Mathews.

Mathews' connection to Parker is unclear, and the two are only mentioned together in this one incident. Mathews was known to have had at least two assistants during his career as city surveyor. Isaac Gladwell, in an advertisement in *Finn's Leinster Journal*, was keen to show off his 'apprenticeship to Mr Thomas Mathews, late surveyor to the corporation of the city of Dublin, where he has been employed in his profession for many years past'.[46] Another assistant, R. Lewis, signed at least one map for Mathews in 1781,[47] only one year before Mathews' death. This may have

---

38 4 May 1764: Gilbert (ed.), *Ancient records*, xi, p. 208. **39** 11 Apr. 1766: Gilbert (ed.), *Ancient records*, xi, pp 326–7. **40** 20 Jul. 1781: Gilbert (ed.), *Ancient records*, xiii, p. 197. **41** Dublin city surveyor maps (DCA C1/S1/4–5, 12, 38, 41, 46, 47, 54–6, 79, 80, 90, 91, 96, 99, 106, 114, 116, 120, 131, 133). **42** 20 Oct. 1769: Gilbert (ed.), *Ancient records*, xii, p. 39. **43** 17 Oct 1771: Gilbert (ed.), *Ancient records*, xii, p. 156. **44** Gilbert (ed.), *Ancient records*, xi, pp 115, 166–7, 203. **45** 16 Oct. 1772: Gilbert (ed.), *Ancient records*, xii, p. 224. **46** *Finn's Leinster Journal*, 18 Sept. 1784. **47** Dublin city surveyor maps (DCA C1/S1/69).

been connected with Mathews' age, infirmity or indeed absence on business, as there is no record stating that Mathews' death was sudden or expected.

Mathews died in 1782, but Lewis never became city surveyor. The role instead passed to Samuel Byron. A former student of the Dublin Society's school of landscape and ornament,[48] which apart from teaching fine art, also provided courses in geographical studies, Byron served an apprenticeship under Scalé in England during the 1770s.[49] While Sherrard and Brownrigg may have inherited Scalé's penchant for business, it was Byron who continued the sophisticated cartographic style of Rocque and Scalé. His detailed and striking work can be said to represent the pinnacle of cartographic output of city surveyor. Unlike previous occupants of the position, Byron was originally hired on a one-year contract that was reviewed on an annual basis.[50] He was granted entry into the guild of cutlers, painter-stainers and stationers,[51] which, according to Andrews, was 'an honour not known to have been shared by any other surveyor'.[52]

Much of Byron's work was in and around the St Stephen's Green area. One of his early products was a detailed survey of the green, which was well received by the contemporary media:

> The survey of Stephen's Green, which was presented by Mr Byron to the lord mayor ... is the most singular as well as beautiful production of the kind that can be imagined. Surveys and plans give in general little more than sites, boundaries and contents; while this artist has extended his art infinitely beyond their mere rule and compass. In the above view, mathematical accuracy, it seems, is not only critically preserved, but by a pencil unknown before in this line, we are delighted with an actual portrait of the celebrated square, in its most beautiful dress.[53]

Unfortunately, no copy of Byron's map of Stephen's Green is known to have survived.

Apart from creating beautiful maps, Byron also helped uphold the corporation's legal rights against holders of leases. Two months after completing his Stephen's Green survey, Byron was asked to examine a lot leased by a Mr Myers on Grafton Street. Myers was accused of not complying with the terms of his agreement with the corporation, in that he blocked access to neighbouring lots. He was found guilty and Byron was paid £20 19s. 9d. for his services.[54] Never media shy, Byron also announced his marriage to a Miss Church in 1787 and continued with his work on the newly emerging sections of the city.

His extensive workload took him to the reclaimed sections of land in modern East Wall in 1788, where

---

48 *Dublin Journal*, 7 Mar. 1780.   **49** *Dublin Journal*, 28 Apr. 1781.   **50** 17 Oct. 1782: Gilbert (ed.), *Ancient records*, xiii, p. 261.   **51** 18 Oct. 1780: Gilbert (ed.), *Ancient records*, xiii, p. 261. **52** Andrews, *Plantation acres*, p. 276.   **53** *Dublin Journal*, 21 Aug. 1783.   **54** 17 Oct. 1783: Gilbert (ed.), *Ancient records*, xiii, p. 337.

A gentleman yesterday riding by Summer Hill and the Strand, observed Mr Byron, the city surveyor, with his attendants, striking out lines for new streets, to be laid out in lots for building. The beautiful situation of the place made him pay attention, when he found that Mr Byron had staked out a street of eighty feet wide ... This will certainly be as elegant a street as any in London, and it is understood the proprietors intend calling it Buckingham Street, in compliment to our illustrious viceroy ... Gloucester Street is intended to extend to the Circular road, and between it and Summer Hill there are intervening streets intended, which are to be called Nugent Street and Grenville Street.[55]

Another of Byron's works to be featured in the media during the 1780s was his design of the ornamental grounds in Merrion Square, which were 'universally approved and adopted by the gentlemen of the square, and ... put into immediate execution'.[56]

During the last years of his life, he began to work with Arthur Richard Neville. Neville would eventually occupy the post of city surveyor in the early nineteenth century, but the first record of his work with Byron dates to 1791, when the two surveyors were tasked to 'ascertain the mears and bounds' of lands leased to John Coghill in Clonturk.[57] In January 1795, Byron's contract with the corporation was renewed for the last time[58] He died, at a relatively young age, in September of that year.[59]

Little is known about Byron's successor, David Worthington. He was appointed to the post on Byron's death and his position was also renewed annually.[60] Worthington was known to use the initials CS after his name, denoting this official title,[61] a trend begun by Mathews.[62] Aside from Barnaby Hackett, Worthington held his official role for the shortest period, only six years, before his death in 1801.[63]

Byron's old colleague Neville was appointed city surveyor on Worthington's death (pl. 10). Neville's association with Dublin Corporation can be traced to 1704, when his grandfather, John Neville, was admitted as a freeman.[64] This honour would also be bestowed on Arthur in January 1795,[65] and followed the same recognition given to him by the people of Monaghan following a survey he conducted of the county in 1791.[66]

Neville's practices as a surveyor can occasionally seem somewhat questionable, as

55 *Dublin Chronicle*, 31 Jul. 1788. **56** Ibid., 4 Oct. 1788. **57** 22 Jul. 1791: Gilbert (ed.), *Ancient records*, xiv, p. 209. This is now in the Drumcondra area. **58** 16 Jan. 1795: Gilbert (ed.), *Ancient records*, xiv, p. 416. **59** *Dublin Evening Post*, 8 Sept. 1795. **60** 16 Oct. 1795: Gilbert (ed.), *Ancient records*, xiv, p. 429. **61** D.B. Worthington, 'Map of piece of ground part of Sutor's Lane' (1801) (DCA C1/S1/103). **62** Thomas Mathews, 'Map of a piece of ground on the north side of Thomas Street' (1778) (DCA C1/S1/90). **63** 1801: Gilbert (ed.), *Ancient records*, xv, p. 216. **64** Clark, *The book of maps of the Dublin city surveyors, 1695–1827*, p. xv. **65** 16 Jan. 1795: Gilbert (ed.), *Ancient records*, xiv, p. 398. **66** *Dublin Evening Post*, 25 Aug. 1791.

his high costs and a habit of mixing private surveying business with his official work emerge throughout his career. As Clark mentions, Neville's combined payments over his twenty-eight-year occupation of the position of city surveyor exceed £2,000, with the largest being £817 18s. 6d. in 1819.[67] The corporation, alarmed at such high costs, sought to 'prevent the bringing forward of any bills from the city surveyor in future',[68] but this attempt met with little or no success. Neville also had a habit of drawing maps for his private practice on the rear of maps of the city estate,[69] which is something that even John Greene never attempted, despite his attention to his private career. Neville died in 1828, and the role of city surveyor passed to his son Arthur Neville Jr. Arthur Jr was the last Dublin city surveyor, and the post was discontinued in 1852.[70]

Dublin's city surveyors span the entire length of what is sometimes called the 'long' eighteenth century, and overall they represent a broad cross-section of professional surveyors operating in the city during that time. From the political and religious turmoil of the 1690s to the expansion of the city in the 1770s and the Victorian metropolis of the 1850s, the city surveyor held the city's highest official surveying position and represents one of the longest traceable lineages in Dublin surveying.

67 Clark, *The book of maps of the Dublin city surveyors, 1695–1827*, p. xv.   68 28 Apr. 1752: Gilbert (ed.), *Ancient records*, xvi, p. 87.   69 Clark, *The book of maps of the Dublin city surveyors, 1695–1827*, p. xvii.   70 *Thom's Irish almanac and official directory* (Dublin, 1852).

Part V
The future

17 'To remedy some of those inconveniences': surveying and the Wide Streets Commission, 1758–1810

It is near impossible to travel through modern Dublin city centre without being affected by the works of the *Commissioners for making wide and convenient streets and passages*, or, as they came to be known, the Wide Streets Commission. This body was responsible for massive changes to Dublin's cramped and dense urban core during the eighteenth and nineteenth centuries. Indeed, they shaped much of Dublin to what it is today, giving it many of its most important streets and thoroughfares (fig. 17.1). Originally established to create a single street leading from the newly reconstructed Essex Bridge to Dublin Castle in 1758, the WSC eventually transformed large portions of Dublin to their own style and taste by widening narrow streets,[1] creating new ones[2] and simultaneously enhancing their own properties,[3] to both the convenience and the condemnation of Dublin's citizens. Their task of implementing rigid Georgian designs in a city that had grown organically and at times chaotically over nearly a millennium was fraught with difficulties, but in the end they, with extensive assistance from several surveyors, provided the city with a lasting legacy.

But why did Dublin need redevelopment? Was it really so different from its modern layout? Prior to 1758, parts of Dublin were simply not suited to a large, growing, cosmopolitan city. Streets were too narrow for coaches, dangerous for pedestrians, dirty, dark and acted as a beacon for some of the city's more disreputable trades and citizens. Even by the end of the century, visitors to the city found sections of it not to their liking: '[The] narrowness and populousness of the principle thoroughfares, as well as ... the dirt and wretchedness of the canaille ... was a most uneasy and disgusting exercise'.[4] An anonymous visitor to the city in 1797 described Powerscourt house:

> Being situated in one of the narrowest streets, together with one of the most crowded meat markets in that city, being within a few feet of the hall door, renders it almost wholly unpleasant, and unworthy of notice.[5]

There were many traffic black spots in the narrow and crooked streets:

1 Dame Street, South Great George's Street.　2 Frederick Street North, Parliament Street. 3 Developments in the Gardiner estate were funded by the WSC; of note is the continuation of Sackville Street to the Liffey and the construction of Carlisle Bridge, now O'Connell Bridge.　4 Arthur Young, *A tour of Ireland* (2 vols, London, 1780), i, p. 6.　5 Anon., *Dublin and its vicinity* (London, 1797).

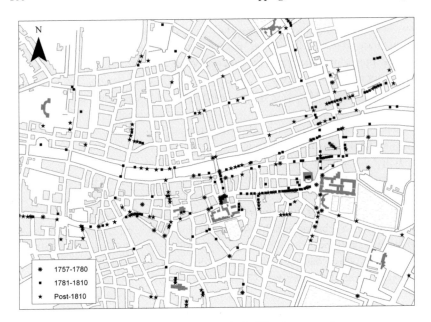

17.1 Location of all WSC maps in Dublin city centre from
1757 to the mid-nineteenth century.

> Much pestered with hucksters sitting under bulks and stalls in the streete,
> whereby the streetes are made soe narrow that coaches or carts cannot well
> passe or turne, which is a great annoyance to the inhabitants of this citty.[6]

The southern junction of Essex Bridge had been highlighted as causing particular
problems for people and vehicles wishing to cross from the major thoroughfare of
Capel Street to Dublin Castle via one of the few bridges to span the Liffey in Dublin.
Crossing Essex Bridge, traffic met a T-junction at Essex Street and was funnelled
through the narrow Blind Quay to Cork Hill, where it merged with traffic from
Dublin's then main east–west passage, Dame Street, which at the time was significantly narrower than it is today. Such problems did not go unnoticed, and in 1757
the Irish parliament created the WSC to deal with the Essex Bridge bottleneck.[7]

PARLIAMENT STREET, 1758

Surveyors and surveying had an unusually heavy influence on the initial work of
commissioners. A portion of Essex Bridge had collapsed in 1751 and the bridge
became unusable for both pedestrians and coaches. George Semple, an engineer who

6 1670: Gilbert (ed.), *Ancient records*, iv, p. 489.   7 Given royal approval in 1757; *Statutes at
large*, 31 Geo. II, c.19. [Ire.] (1757).

was also an accomplished architect, builder and surveyor, was invited by Dublin Corporation to rebuild the bridge.[8] After encountering problems with the surviving piers of the bridge, Semple went to London to examine documentation on the construction of Westminster Bridge which had been recently completed. His time in London also allowed him to consult a wide range of international literature on the subject of bridge-building that was not readily available in Dublin, including a manual by Italian Leon Battista Alberti, who stated that 'a bridge must be made as broad as the street which leads to it'.[9]

It appears that the reconstruction of the bridge had the additional advantage of causing an examination of the state of the streets at its southern junction. Semple's proposed design for the new street, later named Parliament Street (pl. 11), followed Alberti's advice. Being the same width as the new Essex Bridge, Parliament Street would remove a substantial traffic problem by providing a direct passage between the bridge and Dame Street.

The new street was to be the same width as his new bridge (51ft or 15.5m), and its construction was supported with logical arguments:

> 1st that the royal palace or castle is of a very difficult access and almost totally concealed by means of the old Cork House on Cork Hill;
>
> 2nd that the passage from the castle to Essex Bridge (a very great thorofair) is extremely crooked and narrow, not being more than eighteen feet broad at the end of Copper Alley on the Blind Quay;
>
> 3rd that at the north end of Ormond Bridge, the passage for the publick is not more than twenty one feet in breath, but at the head of the King's Inn Quay, and about the south end on the old bridge, is very dangerous and great thorofair, it is only about fifteen or eighteen feet broad, and that out of all said widths, the projection of palisades, posts &c. are to be deducted.[10]

His new street was designed to 'contribute to the ease and safety of passengers, the adorning [*sic*] those parts of the city, and will be of use and benefit to the publick'.[11] In May 1758, advertisements appeared in the *Dublin Journal*, the *Dublin Gazette* and the *Universal Advertiser* requesting landowners and residents who were to be affected by the creation of the new street to voice their concerns directly to the clerk of the newly formed WSC, Mr Howard, who had been appointed the same month.[12] The creation of Parliament Street was the beginning of the most ambitious redevelopment plans in eighteenth-century Dublin, and surveyors would have a major role to play in the success of the WSC.

The commissioners had significant legal clout behind them. The legislation that created the body gave it the right to initiate compulsory purchase orders to buy land

---

8 Semple, *A treatise of building in water*, p. 2.   **9** Ibid., p. 8.   **10** Anon., *Scheme for opening an approach to Dublin Castle* (Dublin, 1757).   **11** *Statutes at large*, 31 Geo. II, c.19 clause I. [Ire.] (1758).   **12** 6 May 1758 (DCA WSC/MINS/1, p. 2).

and plots that were required for their developments. Detailed accounts were made of the revenues of such plots, including their rent and value, beginning with the residents in the Essex Bridge area in June 1758.[13] Where residents refused to move, or when ownership could not be determined, a jury of twelve, appointed by the city sheriffs, would examine the resident's case and determine a value for the land, which the WSC would pay.[14]

Considering his wide-ranging work on the subject of passages to Essex Bridge, and his familiarity with the practicalities of executing the plan, it was unsurprising for George Semple to be appointed the first surveyor to the WSC. He wasted no time and by December 1758 he was in the process of preparing official maps for the project to be presented to an assembled jury.[15] Not all was going to plan, however. Despite his extensive work on the project, which, by the end of 1758, had both legislative and financial support, a serious and unexplained disagreement erupted between Semple and the WSC. Having twice refused to hand over maps to both the WSC clerk Mr Howard, and the commissioners themselves, Semple was informed on 22 January 1759 that the commissioners were 'resolved that he shall be no further employed by them'.[16] The nature of the disagreement is unknown, and in his extensive *Treatise of building in water* (London, 1780), in which Semple detailed many aspects of his career, he failed to mention either his time with the WSC or his work on Parliament Street.

Semple's dismissal from the WSC was not a unique occurrence among the surveying community of eighteenth-century Dublin, but it was rare. Another notable case was that of Thomas Owen, surveyor to the Paving Board. His case sheds light on the level of disagreement between Semple and the WSC and how serious and pressing the situation must have been to lead to Semple's dismissal.

Owen, a relative unknown, was selected ahead of fellow surveyors Thomas Mathews and William Cox for the position of Paving Board surveyor in 1774,[17] and went on to have a complicated and turbulent career. Trouble was not long in finding Owen. The first official complaint against him came in 1776 when a Mr James Kelly of Church Street protested that Owen had given him incorrect advice as to the finished level of the paving of Church Street. Owen's defence to the board was that 'in the variety of the questions asked him when in the [middle] of business [he] could not be accountable for every answer, especially before his level was completed'.[18] Having visited the site, the board found in Owen's favour and withdrew the charges against him. A second complaint came the following year when Major John Butler criticized Owen's 'misbehaviour' – whether professional or personal is not noted – and Owen was required to make a full apology to the members of the board and Major Butler, which was accepted by all parties.[19] In 1780, Owen was once again in

13 30 June 1758 (DCA WSC/Mins/1, p. 6).   **14** 24 July 1761 (DCA WSC/Mins/1, p. 88).
15 9 Dec. 1758 (DCA WSC/Mins/1, p. 7).   **16** 22 Jan. 1759 (DCA WSC/Mins/1, p. 18).
17 8 June 1774 (DCA PB/Mins/1, p. 10).   **18** 9 Aug. 1776 (DCA PB/Mins/2, p. 186).
19 13 June 1777 (DCA PB/Mins/3, p. 157).

trouble with the board, on this occasion relating to negligence of duty. It was reported that 'a number of people who they employ have been long kept out of their money, on account of Mr Owen not having measured their work'.[20] Owen's work was checked and the charges against him were again dropped.

Despite having avoided reprimand on two occasions, Owen's financial issues and continual troublemaking would eventually wear out the Paving Board's patience. Having been warned of possible dismissal in 1784 if he continued to look for payment outside of normal channels, which was seriously frowned upon,[21] the board resolved in 1787 to close the position of Paving Board surveyor.[22] Owen's impassioned response was surprisingly one of shock and astonishment. In a letter to the board, he highlighted his thirteen years service, the improvements he had made to the city, his lack of money to provide for his family, his poor health and the future career of his son, who he had been training as his replacement. The board was unmoved by Owen's plight, but awarded him £30, or four months' wages, as a redundancy payment.[23] Owen again complained that his dismissal had ruined his reputation, however the board contested this fact and issued Owen with a certificate stating the details of his dismissal.[24] Given Owen's dubious record, with many complaints and evidence of financial irregularities, Semple's removal from office from the WSC in so short a space of time must be seen in a different light. The possibility of tensions, arguments, conflicting agendas and personality clashes or a combination of these, may have led to Semple's discharge. These are not recorded, however, and any further discussion would be speculative

Semple's replacement, measurer William Purfield, carried on work on the Parliament Street project and was retained by the WSC into the 1760s.[25] Purfield was a respected measurer, rather than a surveyor,[26] and he may have been hired by the commissioners following his exemplary work on the new western façade of Trinity College in 1752.[27] Nonetheless, his position as the WSC surveyor did not go unquestioned or unexamined. While finishing work on Parliament Street, a map of Essex Street and Cork Hill produced by Purfield was scrutinized by the commissioners. There is a clear indication that his work on this map did not meet with their confidence, as the then city surveyor, Roger Kendrick, and the deputy surveyor general, George Gibson, were asked jointly to produce their own survey of the same area, which was to be compared to Purfield's original.[28] Purfield's work appears to have passed the test, as he was retained by the WSC and produced further work on the Essex Street/Parliament Street area with prominent surveyor, Jonathan Barker.[29]

20 8 Apr. 1780 (DCA PB/Mins/7, p. 50).   **21** 27 Jun. 1784 (DCA PB/Mins/11, p. 6).
22 14 Feb. 1786 (DCA PB/Mins/19, p. 258).   **23** 21 Feb. 1787 (DCA PB/Mins/19, p. 272).
24 12 Apr. 1787 (DCA PB/Mins/1, p. 391).   **25** 28 July 1761 (DCA WSC/Mins/1, p. 109).
26 The equivalent of a quantity surveyor.   **27** O'Dwyer, 'Building empires', 123.   **28** 8
Oct. 1762 (DCA WSC/Mins/1, p. 180).   **29** 8 Nov. 1762 (DCA WSC/Mins/1, p. 182).

THE WIDE STREETS COMMISSION AND ITS POWERS

The commissioners themselves were a group of wealthy landowners who were often members of parliament and among the upper echelons of Dublin society (fig. 17.2). The initial panel of commissioners included Arthur Hill, commissioner of revenue and later chancellor of the exchequer; Thomas Adderley of the Barrack Board; Philip Tisdall, later attorney general; and John Ponsonby, speaker of the House of Commons.[30] Later members included Frederick Trench, David La Touche, John Beresford, who was instrumental in the construction of the new Custom House, and landowner Luke Gardiner, who oversaw WSC work on his estate in the northern section of Dublin city. Some commissioners were more active than others, with La Touche and Trench being particularly active during the 1790s. Others appeared to have only a passing interest in the work of the organization.

The commissioners met at irregular intervals until the 1780s, when meetings between some of them occurred several times a week. The location of these meetings alternated between the tholsel, the chambers in Dame Street[31] and the royal exchange.[32] Maps produced by the WSC were often hung in the coffee room of the royal exchange for public viewing, thus exposing a surveyor's work to a wide, audience.[33] The involvement of such high-powered individuals emphasizes the importance of the redevelopment of the city's infrastructure through the WSC, and the political power, and resources, upon which the body could depend.

As the members of the commissioners changed through the decades, so did the legislative power given to them. The initial act enabling the WSC to create Parliament Street was expanded in 1759 to allow the commissioners to examine the possibility of developing more than one street.[34] Their finances were boosted with another act[35] in 1781, enabling them to receive a sum of one shilling per ton of coal imported into the city, which would eventually cause significant political fallout. The WSC's financial position was further enhanced in 1790, with an act allowing it to borrow the large sum of £100,000.[36] Such acts indicated that there was a definite need and desire to redevelop many sections of Dublin city, as

> there are many narrow streets, lanes and passages in the city of Dublin, and the liberties thereof, where there are waste and unbuilt grounds, or where houses and buildings have been heretofore made, and such houses or buildings have fallen or are going into decay, and the opening and widening of such narrow streets, lanes and passages would be of great benefit to all and every inhabitant of such narrow lanes, streets and passages, and also to the owners

30 Edward McParland, 'The Wide Streets Commissioners: their importance for Dublin architecture in the late 18th-early 19th century', *IGSB*, 15 (1972), 1–31 at 2. **31** 15 Mar. 1762 (DCA WSC/Mins/1, p. 146). **32** 14 Jan. 1785 (DCA WSC/Mins/6, p. 104). **33** 21 Feb. 1804 (DCA WSC/Mins/19, p. 167). **34** *Statutes at large*, 33 Geo. II, c.15, clause v [Ire.] (1759). **35** *Statutes at large*, 21, 22 Geo. III, c.17. [Ire.] (1781). **36** *Statutes at large*, 30 Geo. III, c.19. [Ire.] (1790).

17.2 Signatures of the wide streets commissioners, Thomas Sherrard, 'Great Britain Street and Cavendish Row' (Dublin, 1787) (WCS/Maps/206, Dublin City Library & Archive).

and proprietors thereof, and of such waste or unbuilt grounds or houses and would be a great improvement to the said city.[37]

After the commissioners' initial flurry of action in the late 1750s and early 1760s, there was a period of sluggishness and inactivity during the 1770s. This can be most readily observed in the minute books of the WSC as, during the 1780s, 1790s and early nineteenth century, the commissioners used one minute book per year, whereas only four books were completed for the period 1758–81 – an average of 5.75 years per minute book. Despite the relative quietness regarding the work of the WSC, the effects of the construction of Parliament Street appear to have encouraged discussion on how best other sections of the city could be developed.

In early 1769, a series of surprisingly forward-thinking and disturbingly accurate articles on proposed developments for Dublin's main streets appeared in the *Freeman's Journal*. What makes these articles unique is that many of the suggestions were implemented decades later by the WSC. This suggests that the anonymous author may have been a member, or possibly a future member, of this body. The author was evidently aware that changes to the city could not be completed overnight:

> Amongst a refined and civilized people, in great and opulent cities, all improvements and alterations should be carried on, with a view towards something more extensive on a *future day*. The expense of pulling down houses and purchasing ground renders it impossible to complete a scheme of magnificence at once, but everything may be accomplished by time and perseverance, by gradual and repeated effort. If this principle had been early enough attended to, what prodigious advantages might have been gained in the situation of Parliament House![38]

The insightful author proposed that if Sackville Street had been continued to the river (now Lower O'Connell Street) and if a street had been built on the opposite, southern, side of the river, it would have given a splendid view of Trinity College (figs 17.3, 17.4). This proposed street on the south bank of the Liffey would indeed be built and named Westmoreland Street, however, such work would not be finished

---

37 *Statutes at large*, 30 Geo. III, c.19, clause, xxvii, [Ire.] (1790), quoted in Sheridan, 'Designing the capital city', p. 120. **38** *Freeman's Journal*, 21 Jan. 1769.

17.3 *Sackville Street and Gardiner's Mall* (now rebuilt as O'Connell Street),
Dublin, by Joseph Tudor (*c.*1750). Line-engraving with watercolour (24.4 x 39.6cm)
(NGI 11633; photograph © National Gallery of Ireland).

until the early nineteenth century, nearly a half century after the article was
published.

The author made several other creative suggestions that also became realities in
the coming decades. Regarding the position of the Custom House, which at the
time was located on what is now called Wellington Quay, the author wrote:

> From the strong tendency that the city discovers to enlarge itself eastwards,
> and to push down to the sea, I foresee, with much concern, that the bridge
> [modern O'Connell Bridge] so frequently mentioned, will at length from
> necessary force itself. If it must be, no avenues more convenient or more
> beautiful than those two streets could possibly be laid out [Sackville/
> O'Connell Street and Westmoreland Street]. A bridge being erected, the
> Custom House must be removed, the consequence of which is, that the
> merchants will follow.[39]

Other future works of the WSC were foretold including the widening of Dame
Street and improvements to College Green.

Aside from correctly predicting the future growth of Dublin, the author also
discussed theories of city expansion and the need for such developments in Dublin.

39 Ibid.

17.4 The Sackville Street/Trinity College axis in 1756 (from John Rocque, *Exact survey of the city and suburbs of Dublin* (Dublin, 1756), courtesy of the Royal Irish Academy © RIA).

These discussions provide insight into the reasons for the WSC's existence in the eighteenth and nineteenth centuries, and the fact that discussions of the development of the city were not always conducted behind closed doors but in the press for the general public to see. Philadelphia, Pennsylvania, 'a remarkable instance of the beauty a metropolis may receive', was suggested by the author in the *Freeman's Journal* as a role model for Dublin, due to its large, uniform streets and the strategic positioning of its public buildings. Dublin had

> hitherto felt severely the great inconveniences, of the want of such a scheme; and experience has of late convinced us of the advantages of such a measure, by the few alterations we have been obliged to make to remedy some of those inconveniences.[40]

40 Ibid., 11 Feb. 1769.

Using Parliament Street as an example of the positive effects of the WSC's work, the author continued:

> the city is more airy, and consequently more healthy, as well as more conven-
> ient and pleasant, since one street has been opened [Parliament Street] and
> part of another widened [Dame Street] – no individual has suffered, many
> have gained.[41]

Despite the improvements so far highlighted, the city was still in need of extensive work. The author listed public buildings such as the tholsel, the mansion house and the Four Courts (at the time located in the grounds of Christ Church Cathedral) as being in poor state of repair – with even the city marshal being unable to provide decent accommodation for his family. Although some work had already been under-taken on Dame Street, significant developments were still necessary. The author also wrote:

> let us turn our eye down the hill; and enjoy the prospect along Dame Street,
> properly widened and regularly levelled in a direct line ... has any city in
> Europe anything that can surpass (or perhaps equal) such a vista?[42]

The author obviously had a vested interest in the city's development and seemed well versed in civic development and architecture, not only in Ireland but also further afield. It appears that he had also taken the 'Grand Tour' of Europe, as visits to Florence, Genoa and Venice were also mentioned. His membership or future membership of the WSC is not an unreasonable assumption. Despite the logical arguments and obvious knowledge, the author concluded that he 'shall no longer give a loose to my ravished imagination'. Modern Dubliners owe a lot to that 'ravished imagination'.

THE WORK OF THOMAS SHERRARD (1750–1838)

Survey work for the WSC was undertaken by several men during the first three decades of its existence. George Semple, William Purfield, Roger Kendrick, George Gibson and Jonathan Barker were early providers of maps to the commissioners. One man was to dominate the position of surveyor to the WSC for nearly half a century – Thomas Sherrard. He was a product of John Rocque's 'French School' of surveying and was the apprentice of Bernard Scalé during the 1770s. His joint position of surveyor and clerk to the WSC during the later eighteenth and early nineteenth centuries makes him one of the most prominent surveyors to help shape Dublin into its current layout.

41 Ibid.   42 Ibid.

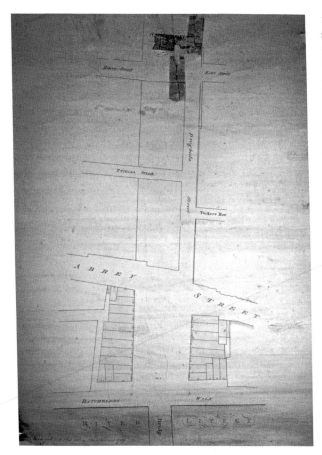

17.5 Map by Sherrard showing the continuation of Sackville Street to the River Liffey (from Thomas Sherrard, 'Sackville Street' (1789); WSC/Maps/39, Dublin City Library & Archive).

Sherrard's work for the commissioners was well respected, with one member commenting 'he is a man very much confided in by the board for his knowledge in valuing ground'.[43] From map records, it appears that Sherrard first began to work with the WSC around 1780, when he was in his early thirties, producing maps of Dame Street[44] and Rutland Square (modern Parnell Square),[45] and drawing up plans for the completion of Sackville Street (modern O'Connell Street) by continuing it to the Liffey (fig. 17.5).[46]

Sherrard's Sackville Street continuation plan represents an excellent example of the role of surveyor to the WSC, not only in laying out new streets, but also establishing property boundaries and ownership before development work began. Sherrard's map of the proposed improvements to Sackville Street shows the street's

43 Evidence of Andrew Caldwell: Anon., *Remarks on the agreement between the commissioners for making wide streets and Mr Ottiwell* (Dublin, 1794), p. 8.   **44** DCA WSC/Maps/115, 1784. **45** DCA WSC/Maps/41, 1789.   **46** DCA WSC/Maps/78, 1786.

layout in 1786. At that time, Sackville Street stopped at Henry Street, with Drogheda Street, which was half the width of Sackville Street, continuing to the Liffey. Sherrard's map identified a total of twenty-three proposed lots to be laid out after the widening of Drogheda Street to the same width as Sackville Street. The proposed work would remove two 'blocks' of Drogheda Street between Henry Street and Princes Lane, between Princes Lane and Abbey Street. The precision with which the WSC worked is revealed in the request that the buildings on the eastern side of Drogheda Street would have to be moved back one or two feet from their current positions to maintain the new street's symmetry. Such exactness was not restricted to the Sackville Street continuation, but can be found throughout the records of the WSC during the eighteenth century. Architect Samuel Sproule once reported that the windows of a house built on Dame Street had to be altered as they were 'a few inches too low, & ... the windows of Mr Colles' house adjoining ... are too high by four & an half'.[47]

While Sherrard's work on Sackville Street may represent one of the most prominent instances of the WSC's use of surveyors, it accounted for only a small portion of his tasks. In one of his earliest jobs for the WSC in 1782, Sherrard was requested to conduct a 'survey of the houses and grounds' between Cavendish Row and Dorset Street, so that Mr Adams, the WSC valuation surveyor, could establish the costs of purchasing the properties.[48] This project eventually led to the construction of North Frederick Street (fig. 17.6). Apart from Mr Adams and the commissioners themselves, Sherrard worked closely with many other WSC employees, such as Samuel Sproule, who produced architectural plans for the commissioners. The work of Sherrard and Sproule was important to the widening of Dame Street. Sproule produced the architectural plans, while Sherrard conducted levelling runs between Cork Hill and Trinity College.[49] Their combined work passed the high standards of the commissioners.[50]

Sherrard appears to have also been involved with the improvement of Dublin's streets outside of his role in the WSC. In January 1782, he wrote to Dublin's Paving Board, to discuss his new residence on Capel Street. He informed them that

> he has taken the house within Michael Swift Esq. formerly dwelt in Capel Street & is willing to give up the pallisadoes (so justly deemed a nuisance), if the board will be at the expense of removing them, turning the arches over the areas & flagging & paving the footway; which must be the normal size & done under his approbation & he will give the rails towards the expense.[51]

Sherrard worked with the Paving Board as part of his role with the WSC, however it is interesting to note his interaction with them as a private citizen also. As clerk

---

47 26 Sept. 1783, quoted in McParland, 'The Wide Streets Commissioners', 11. **48** 3 May 1782 (DCA WSC/Mins/4, p. 59). **49** 17 May 1782 (DCA WSC/Mins/4, p. 52). **50** 24 May 1782 (DCA WSC/Mins/4, p. 67). **51** 11 Jan. 1782 (DCA PB/Mins/9, p. 191).

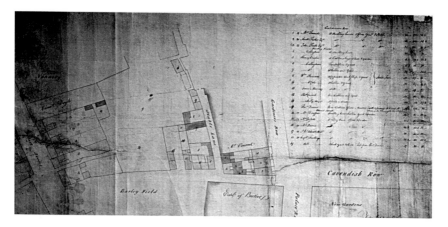

17.6 Sherrard's map of the Barley Field, now the site of North Frederick Street (from Thomas Sherrard, 'Survey of the Barley Field' (1782); WSC/Maps/18, Dublin City Library & Archive).

and surveyor to the commissioners, he often found himself involved in roles that departed greatly from traditional land surveying. In 1786, Sherrard informed the commissioners that he had supervised the demolition of no. 36 Bachelors Walk and that the neighbouring house, no. 37, was now unfortunately in danger of collapsing. The commissioners immediately ordered that:

> Mr Sherrard do take the most speedy & effectual measures to prevent any injury to the public from said house & do pull down, if necessary, so much of said house as may prevent any danger and dispose of the materials to the best advantage.[52]

Sherrard does not appear to have been formally reprimanded for this mistake, but the incident reappeared before the commissioners in the following month. A Revd Carey, who lived in no. 37, seriously protested to the damage caused to his home by the demolition of the neighbouring house. Carey was unexpectedly willing to move from his home, however he insisted on being paid extensive compensation by the WSC. Something was not right. Further investigations by the commissioners' valuation surveyor determined that Revd Carey was in fact a tenant in no. 37 only, and that he had no genuine claim to compensation.[53] Sherrard paid £10 for the materials taken from no. 36, including doors and locks, indicating that he may have had connections in the building trade or possibly owned houses himself. Aside from occasionally demolishing buildings, Sherrard was regularly required to hire watchmen to protect houses that were bought by the WSC and lay vacant for long periods.[54]

52 10 Jan. 1786 (DCA WSC/Mins/6, p. 254).   **53** 17 Feb. 1786 (DCA WSC/Mins/6, p. 261).   **54** 11 July 1791 (DCA WSC/Mins/10, p. 166).

Sherrard's role as clerk to the WSC was a profitable addition to the revenue generated by his successful private surveying business. Being a multi-faceted position, dealing with some of the most powerful individuals in eighteenth-century Ireland, it often involved a high degree of personal responsibility, as noted when Sherrard's role was renewed in 1789:

> Business of the clerks department: to fill up and serve summons upon the several commissioners each time of their meeting, to attend said meetings, take down minutes of the proceedings, enter them in the minute book and copy them into a fair book if necessary. To copy, make out and sign the several resolutions and orders of the board for the several parties and to prepare drafts on the sectary or treasurer for the several sums ordered to be paid by him . . . To write and forward all the letters ordered by the board and to keep copies thereof . . . The clerk is not required to give attendance upon the valuation by jurys, issue summons for that business or have any interference whatsoever therein more than to enter verdicts when returned by the law agent and confirmed.[55]

Sherrard was a key man in the WSC's operations. He was entitled to £50 per annum for the role of clerk, in addition to being paid for every survey he conducted for the WSC, which was proving to be a lucrative and steady income. Maps produced for the WSC were stored by Sherrard 'in his office',[56] but it is unclear whether he had a specific office for his role as clerk or if this referred to his own surveying offices in Capel Street and later on Blessington Street.

SHERRARD'S 'GREAT MAP'

Dublin was rapidly changing and the work conducted by the WSC could sometimes surpass the available maps of Dublin. By 1791, they were in need of 'an accurate and general map of the city'. This proposed map was to cover the area enclosed to the north by the Royal Canal and the south by the Grand Canal, showing

> the extent or front of each house and distinguishing the dwelling houses from the stables or warehouses and also waste ground not built upon: the whole to be laid down upon a scale of eighty feet to an inch; would be a very desirable object to obtain.[57]

This map, having apparently being proposed by Sherrard himself, was awarded £1,000 to be paid at three hundred guineas per annum until the map was completed.

55 13 Mar. 1789 (DCA WSC/Mins/8, p. 224). **56** DCA WSC/Mins/10, p. 200. **57** 1 July 1791 (DCA WSC/Mins/1, p. 161).

The most recent large mapping project to have taken place in the city was Rocque's *Exact survey* in the 1750s, and despite Scalé's production of an updated version of this map in 1773, it was obvious that a new, complete survey of the city was required. Sherrard surveyed the city according to its six divisions, which equally divided the city north and south of the Liffey. These were local government administrative areas and, by January 1795, Sherrard had completed the north-eastern division of his 'great map' at a cost of £200 sterling.[58] The entire project lasted until 1797, when

> Mr Sherrard laid before the Board the north section of the great map of Dublin and its environs, being the sixth and last section of said work done pursuant to resolution of the 13th April 1792, finished in the same style as the sections already done.[59]

Little is known about the 'great map' produced by Sherrard and no complete copy of it has survived. The only known portion of it is the nineteenth-century duplicate of a small section around Christ Church Cathedral included in Andrews' *Plantation acres*.[60] The map appears to have been more detailed than Rocque's survey of the city, as the rear buildings and walls of houses and businesses were also obviously measured, unlike Rocque's practice of estimating their positions. At a scale of eighty feet to one inch, Sherrard's map would have been much larger than Rocque's and, as such, more buildings could be labelled while individual buildings could be numbered and refer-enced on a separate index. Shortly after the Great Map was presented to the commissioners, they sent a request to parliament requesting that funding be made available for the publication of the map and that the map be copyrighted to the WSC.[61] Nothing else is mentioned in the minutes of the WSC about the 'Great Map', and, in view of how little information about it survives, it may not have been published. Considering the attention and praise that Brooking's and Rocque's maps of the city receive, it seems a pity that the most detailed map of eighteenth-century Dublin has been virtually forgotten.

THE OTTIWELL INCIDENT

The work undertaken by surveyors in determining the extent, and therefore the value, of land could have serious legal and financial repercussions. In the early 1790s, Sherrard became an unwitting central character in a complex price-fixing scandal involving the Wide Street Commission and a property developer named Henry Ottiwell, which was referred to by one contemporary author as 'the grossest act of improvidence that ever public men were guilty of'.[62] This incident would eventually

---

58 30 Jan. 1795 (DCA WSC/Mins/13, p. 36). **59** 16 Jun. 1797 (DCA WSC/Mins/14, p. 160). **60** Andrews, *Plantation acres*, p. 281. **61** 4 May 1798 (DCA WSC/Mins/14, p. 330). **62** Anon., 'An impartial view of the conduct of the commissioners of wide-streets, in their bargain with Mr Henry Ottiwell' (Dublin, 1796), p. 9.

see Sherrard summoned and intensively questioned before no fewer than three parliamentary investigative committees between 1791 and 1795. It began with a survey by Sherrard of several lots belonging to the WSC on Beresford Place. Sherrard valued the ground for sale at 30s. per square foot and the ground was brought forward to auction in February 1791.[63] The prospective buyers felt that the valuation was too high, and the lots were unsold. Such failed auctions were not unheard of during the course of the WSC's work. During a similar auction several years previously, for lots along what is now North Frederick Street, the commissioners held two auctions, both of which were unsuccessful.[64] The sale of the Beresford Place lots had added importance, however, as the WSC were experiencing financial troubles. Throughout the winter of 1790/1, Sherrard had regularly met with wide streets commissioner Marquess Henry Beresford to discuss the body's financial difficulties and their future improvements to Abbey Street.[65] It appears, however, that Beresford had a plan in place to obtain immediate funding for the WSC through back channels, by selling the Beresford Place lots at a lower price to Henry Ottiwell, who was known as 'a person of very considerable property'.[66] This would provide the WSC with Ottiwell's immediate and secure funding and avoid potential problems as the WSC had encountered with investors in the past: 'they had been harassed and disappointed by the paltry proposals of insolvent adventurers, and men of straw, without property or security'.[67]

As part of the deal, Ottiwell, who might have been representing several other developers, had also bargained for a preferential price on property in any future dealings with the WSC.[68] The legal issue with this was that the commissioners were in effect agreeing to sell land to Ottiwell that they did not yet own. The problem of whether such questionable secret dealings between a public body and a private developer were in the citizens of Dublin's best interests brought the attention of the Irish parliament.

Sherrard had never been consulted by the commissioners on the price of the land offered to Ottiwell, however it was he who was brought before several committees as a central witness to an investigation surrounding the deal.[69] Sherrard testified that his initial valuation of the Beresford lots might have been high, but that the price paid by Ottiwell may have been reasonable for the ground.[70] Despite Sherrard's frequent meetings with Henry Beresford in the months previous to the deal, the commissioner had never consulted Sherrard on any details relating to Ottiwell, and Sherrard's valuation of the land had also only ever been given to Beresford himself and never to the rest of the WSC board.[71] Commentators at the time agreed that Sherrard's

---

63 Ibid., p. 12.   **64** Anon., 'A refutation of the "Remarks on the agreement between the Commissioners for Making Wide Streets and Mr Ottiwell"' (Dublin, 1795), p. 7.   **65** Anon., 'Remarks on the agreement between the commissioners for making wide streets and Mr Ottiwell' (Dublin, 1794), p. 8.   **66** Anon., 'An impartial view', p. 17.   **67** Anon., 'A refutation of the "Remarks"', p. 35.   **68** Anon., 'An impartial view', p. 6.   **69** Investigations were held in 1791, 1794 and 1795: Anon., 'An impartial view', p. 12.   **70** Anon., 'An impartial view', p. 12.   **71** Anon., 'Remarks on the agreement', p. 13.

testimonies were given with 'his usual perspicuity' and that 'Sherrard did not know of any such sale, which implies there might have been such sale without his knowledge.'[72]

Ottiwell's own appearance before the same committees was less dignified. In June 1795, he refused to answer questions put to him as he felt that they may damage his property holdings, and ignored other summons to the extent that he eventually barricaded himself inside his home to avoid arrest by the Irish parliament's sergeant-at-arms.[73]

Despite his innocence in the Ottiwell affair, Sherrard's testimonies resulted in a substantial amount of his time being spent away from surveying and, by 1796, 'his private business remained totally neglected, to his very great prejudice'.[74] The commissioners saw fit that he should be awarded an extra fifty guineas for the earnings lost by his appearances in parliament. The WSC noted Sherrard's professionalism during the investigations:

> During the sitting of said committee he underwent very long and painful examinations in the most solemn manner, touching the proceedings of the board for a series of years past, as appears by said committee's report. And by their orders did prepare and lay before them several schedules and other papers ... That about the same period he received several orders from the House of Lords, and in obedience thereto, did prepare and present at their lordships bar, the several papers called for.[75]

The Ottiwell incident was not the only occasion on the work of the WSC came under the scrutiny of the Irish parliament. Lord Carhampton, a member of the Irish House of Lords, voiced his learned opinion about the commissioners and their work in a fascinating 1798 session reviewing a bill allowing taxation to be raised on coal imports for the financing of the WSC. Carhampton's appraisal, despite its wit and good humour, demonstrated that the works of WSC could be self-serving for the commissioners rather than strictly in the best interest of the general public. Carhampton noted that,

> as individuals, he lived amongst them in the habits of closest intimacy, nor were there men in the world with whom he would rather pass the remainder of his life as men of honour and deserved respect, but bound up together, and labelled with the title of Wide Streets Commissioners, he considered them as forming one of the most mischievous volumes extant in any country. Habitually improvident of their own private expenses, it was not very surprising if men became lavish of the public money, when trusted to their expenditure. Thousands upon thousands of the public money had already

72 Anon., 'A refutation of the "Remarks"', p. 7. **73** The parliamentary register: or, History of the proceedings, vols 14–15, June 1795, p. 401. **74** 22 Apr. 1796 (DCA WSC/Mins/13, p. 301). **75** Ibid.

been squandered by this board, not for the purpose of opening narrow and inconvenient streets obnoxious to the city of Dublin, but with erections of new streets and squares for the accommodation of the rich.[76]

Drawing on the amusing image of the commissioners closely gathered around a map, 'cutting and carving' the city up and 'endeavouring to influence his brother commissioner', Carhampton stated that all the commissioners did was begin work on narrow streets such as Cow Lane or Carrion Row – 'such places were too vulgar for pronunciation, and scarcely to be articulated without the risk of breaking gentlemen's teeth' – rename them and then divert funds 'to embellish the street of one gentleman's residence'.

Deploring the proposed doubling of the coal tax as a 'tithe upon a necessary of life', Carhampton reminded the commissioners that in order to complete Westmoreland Street, all that remained was to purchase 'wretched tenements' in Fleet Street for a few thousand pounds. Once completed, the new street might 'stay their lordships stomachs for superb embellishments'. He suggested that a vote on the proposed tax increase be delayed for three months. The chancellor declared that 'he would rather walk up to his knees in mud for the remainder of his life, and through the ... gloomy allies that could be ... the city of Dublin, than listen to ... all that he had heard in the house for months past, about wide streets and Wide Street Commissioners'.[77] The chancellor defended the commissioners, however, by pointing out that they received no reward, fee or 'interest he knew upon earth' and were dedicated to their public service. Acknowledging levels of corruption or rather lack of interest among members of the commissioners, including one recently elected commissioner who 'had not yet attended, nor did he know that he ever should' attend a WSC meeting, the chancellor requested of the board that,

> while they impeached the commissioners of that board with profusion, improvidence and tediousness in their works, they should look a little to facts, and before they indulged in those charges, it would have been well to read the papers on their table, from which it would be seen that they [parliament] had funds more than adequate to answer their [the WSC] debts.[78]

To conclude, the chancellor felt it was unfair to impeach men as dishonest on a collective basis, while at the same time declaring that individually they were respected.

Manuscript maps produced by the organization from 1778 to 1800 were mainly focused on Abbey Street, Dame Street, George's Street, Castle Street and Sackville Street. Despite the commissioners' interest in the city centre, their work also covered the entire area within their jurisdiction during this period. Isolated concentrations of maps were produced of Ringsend, Islandbridge and St James' Street, demonstrating

---

76 *Leinster Journal*, 22 Sept. 1798.   **77** Ibid.   **78** Ibid.

that their work was not entirely focused on major projects such as the creation of Parliament Street and the continuation of Sackville Street. Given the number of dated maps confirmed to be from this era, however, it becomes obvious that Lord Carhampton's arguments were not without merit. Aside from the high number of maps produced for the city's main thoroughfares, which is understandable for a body concerned with improving urban communications, there was also a disproportionately high number of maps produced of the city's more affluent and modern neighbourhoods compared to the poorer congested neighbourhoods in the southwest of the city.

The period 1800 to 1810 witnessed a change in the commissioners' efforts, with a general retraction in the scope of their work. New mapping projects tended to be concentrated around modern Westmoreland and D'Olier Streets, as well as Beresford Place. There was also a noticeable movement eastwards of the WSC's work, from the Parliament/Capel Street axis during the 1750s and 1760s, to the increasingly prominent Sackville Street/Trinity College axis of the early nineteenth century. The widening of narrow streets and construction of Carlisle Bridge (now O'Connell Bridge) opened up access to the eastern section of the city centre, assisting this transition.

THE WIDE STREETS COMMISSION IN THE EARLY NINETEENTH CENTURY

Despite Lord Carhampton's concerns about the commissioners' work, the design and construction of Westmoreland Street and D'Olier Street eventually began in late 1799 (pl. 12). By December, Sherrard had been ordered to prepare two designs for improving the approach to Trinity College (pl. 13) and from Grafton Street to Carlisle Bridge,[79] which had been built in the 1780s.[80] Considering the influence of the fellows of Trinity College, the WSC decided to consult them on the work.[81] The fellows were unhappy with the proposals, worrying that 'very great inconvenience may ensue to the college from complying'.[82] Such opinions were the least of the commissioners' concerns by the turn of the century, however. Following the political turmoil of the 1798 rebellion, during which commissioner Luke Gardiner had been killed at the Battle of New Ross,[83] the WSC were regularly encountering severe financial problems. In 1800, the commissioners wrote to Marquis Cornwallis, lord lieutenant of Ireland, about the work that they were undertaking on the approaches to Carlisle Bridge. The letter suggested that the confusion caused by the 1798 rebellion had resulted in a request for funds for this work to be either ignored or lost.[84]

---

79 5 Dec. 1799 (DCA WSC/Mins/16, p. 12). **80** DCA WSC/Maps/160. **81** 19 Dec. 1799 (DCA WSC/Mins/16, p. 24). **82** 23 Jan. 1800 (DCA WSC/Mins/16, p. 40). **83** Irish House of Commons, 1692–1800: www.leighrayment.com/commons/ireland commons.htm, 5 Jan. 1798 (accessed 1 May 2012). **84** DCA WSC/Mins/16, p. 56.

Political events were also conspiring against the WSC. The Act of Union (1800) stripped Ireland of its own independent parliament. With the country now being governed from Westminster, Dublin was in essence reduced to the level of a provincial capital. From 1801 onwards, funding for the commissioners' work would have to be approved from London. The post-union WSC would be a radically different organization, with few major projects undertaken and a general decline in the level of standards.

Finances were the focus of a major report produced by the WSC in 1802, much of which was documented by Sherrard. The *Extracts from the minutes of the commissioners* (Dublin, 1802) provided a summary of the main projects undertaken from the 1750s onwards, detailing costs and additional sources of revenues generated by the commissioners themselves. After the early work on Parliament Street, the commissioners' main focus was on Dame Street and George's Street (£11,029 6s. 3d.) during the 1760s and 1770s, Abbey Street (£88,430 7s. 1d.), Rutland Square and Parkgate Street during the 1780s, with improvements to Sackville Street (£84,767), Baggot Street and Skinners Row and the creation of Westmoreland Street, D'Olier Street (£45,335 13s. 5d.) and Frederick Street (£11,596 1s. 6d.) in the 1790s.[85] Work on Parkgate Street was partially financed by a nine-year toll on the Mullingar Road.[86] Lots on Dame Street were sold by the commissioners to raise funds, but most funding came from parliamentary legislation and the coal tax:

> The revenues with which the commissioners have been enabled to proceed upon these several plans of improvement have arisen partly from king's letter and partly from parliamentary aid, and the produce of appropriated duties.[87]

The *Extracts* also reported that the quays to the west of Carlisle Bridge had yet to be opened, which the commissioners felt would 'be objects of great utility'.[88] The quays were in a general state of disrepair, with one visitor to the city describing them thus:

> As if nothing in this capital was to wear the face of propriety, or consistency, much less of perfection, this noble structure [the Four Courts] is erected within a few feet of the dirtiest and most filthy part of the River Liffey, upon a piece of the ruined quay, which is actually like a rotten ditch tumbling piecemeal into the water.[89]

The widening and straightening of Lower Abbey Street was estimated by the commissioners to cost an additional £10,000; almost the same price as creating North Fredrick Street.[90] A major plan to build several new streets around Dublin Castle, isolating the castle from the surrounding areas and protecting it from acci-

---

85 Ibid., pp 2–34. **86** Wide Streets Commissioners, *Extracts from the minutes of the commissioners* (Dublin, 1802), p. 32. **87** Ibid., p. 1. **88** Ibid., p. 34. **89** Anon., *Dublin and its vicinity* (London, 1797). **90** 21 Dec. 1804 (DCA WSC/Mins/19, p. 167).

dental fire due to a number of 'forge manufactories' nearby, was never undertaken, possibly due to cost.[91] The Westmoreland/D'Olier Street project also encountered financial problems. In a letter to the sectary of His Majesty's revenue, Sherrard wrote:

> As to the opening of the avenues from the parliament house to Carlisle Bridge, there is no fund whatsoever in the power of the commissioners applicable to those purposes; but as it is a matter so absolutely necessary for the accommodation of the public, the commissioners will direct the grounds necessary for the said purposes to be valued, relying upon the assistance of government in any application that may be made to parliament, to institute a fund to carry these measurers into effect.[92]

By 1806, the financial restrictions placed upon the WSC were becoming evident. Even simple tasks such as advertisement of works were being curtailed, being viewed by the board as 'the very heavy and unnecessary expense'.[93] From January 1806, the WSC would only advertise in two newspapers[94] three times a week, rather than three newspapers, which had been the practice since the 1750s.

Sherrard was growing well into middle age by the turn of the nineteenth century, and there is evidence in the commissioners' minute books that he was not as sprightly as he had once been. In July 1803, he was allowed a leave of absence to go to England, 'for the recovery of his health',[95] and in December of the same year a motion by Frederick Trench to the board of commissioners appointed Sherrard's sons, William and later David Henry,[96] as joint clerks and surveyors. Sherrard's long term with the WSC had distinct advantages for the commissioners and their work. With the final developments on Lower Abbey Street beginning in 1804, Sherrard was asked to retrieve maps of the area that he had produced in 1784 and also his plans for laying out lots, produced in 1790.[97]

Despite the change of parliament and increasing financial pressure, the WSC still looked to London for inspiration as to how Dublin could be improved. Sherrard was asked by the commissioners in 1803 to purchase a newly published map of London and have it mounted on rollers.[98] His purchase might not have been of sufficient quality, or simply became outdated very quickly due to developments, as in 1808 the commissioners asked Sherrard to buy another new map of London, 'with the docks and other improvements to the present time and that he do dispose of the old map of London.'[99]

The end of the first decade of the nineteenth century saw the work of Sherrard and the commissioners focus on their new streets leading from Carlisle Bridge. Unlike their previous work, this was not always centred on widening streets or

---

91 15 Oct. 1801 (DCA WSC/Mins/15, p. 134). **92** Wide Streets Commissioners, *Extracts from the minutes*, p. 42. **93** 29 Jan. 1808 (DCA WSC/Mins/20, p. 382). **94** *Saunders' News Letter* and the *Correspondent*. **95** 14 July 1803 (DCA WSC/Mins/18, p. 321). **96** 7 Nov. 1810 (DCA WSC/Mins/22, p. 290). **97** 21 Dec. 1804 (DCA WSC/Mins/19, p. 167). **98** 20 Jul. 1804 (DCA WSC/Mins/19, p. 103). **99** 4 Apr. 1808 (DCA WSC/Mins/21, p. 38).

purchasing properties, but rather on general improvements to the area. Sherrard was sent to correct building sites on D'Olier Street that were causing a nuisance as they projected into the line of the road in 1808,[100] while two years previously he was also asked to produce a map of the Carlisle Bridge area to present before the Board of Revenue regarding the removal of obelisks that adorned the bridge, as they 'only serve more distinctly to show the obliquity of said bridge in regard to its situation with the course of the river and the several avenues leading thereto.'[101] While his father was busy taking down such features, William Sherrard had become involved with the creation of one of the city's iconic nineteenth-century monuments, Nelson's Pillar. In 1808, he received a letter from the secretary of the committees for erecting a statue of Lord Nelson, requesting that 'they have considered the intersection point of Henry Street and Sackville Street as the best adapted to the purpose and to request you will take the trouble to request their idea to the commissioners of wide streets'.[102]

Following 1810, there are few records of surveying in the minutes of the WSC. Work did continue with surveying, widening and straightening streets until the 1840s, albeit to a greatly reduced degree compared to the height of the commissioners' activities during the 1780s and 1790s.

During the period between 1758 and 1810, the WSC had many positive impacts on the surveying community in Dublin, and it was a regular employer of surveyors. Aside from Thomas Sherrard, who spent the majority of his surveying career with the commissioners, the WSC is known to have been involved with a minimum of twelve other professional surveyors during this period. Roger Kendrick,[103] Thomas Mathews,[104] D.B. Worthington[105] and A.R. Neville[106] all produced maps for the WSC while holding the position of city surveyor, as did assistant city surveyor Robert Lewis,[107] and deputy surveyor general George Gibson.[108] Surveying partnerships were also involved in map production for the commissioners, with Sherrard employing his business partners Richard Brassington and Clarges Greene[109] at various times. Sherrard also produced maps with architects Samuel Sproule[110] and Henry A. Baker,[111] who were among the chief architects working for the commissioners. Surveying with the WSC was also a multi-generational affair, with sons of both Sherrard[112] and Neville[113] producing maps for the commissioners.

Aside from employing surveyors, the work of the WSC heavily referenced maps made before the commission's foundation. Maps dating back as far as the 1680s[114] were regularly consulted for determining property ownership and leases. Early

---

100 13 May 1808 (DCA WSC/Mins/21, p. 56).   **101** 14 Feb. 1806 (DCA WSC/Mins/20, p. 17).   **102** 29 Jan. 1808 (DCA WSC/Mins/20, p. 380).   **103** DCA WSC/Maps/573, 576. **104** DCA WSC/Maps/545, 583, 590, 595, 719.   **105** DCA WSC/Maps/97, 617, 701.   **106** DCA WSC/Maps/27, 125, 126, 128, 129, 130, 139, 166, 189, 573.   **107** DCA WSC/Maps/547.   **108** 8 Oct. 1762 (DCA WSC/Mins/1), p. 180.   **109** DCA WSC/Maps/552.   **110** DCA WSC/Maps/115.   **111** DCA WSC/Maps/160.   **112** DCA WSC/Maps/124.   **113** DCA WSC/Maps/496.   **114** John Greene, 'Survey of corner house, fronting to St Nicholas Street' (1682) (DCA WSC/Maps/568).

eighteenth-century maps produced by Joseph Moland[115] and a possible progenitor of the Gibson surveying lineage, John Gibson,[116] were also reviewed by the WSC, making the commissioners the preservers of maps that otherwise may have been lost or destroyed.

The work of the Wide Streets Commission has had a monumental and ongoing effect on the population of Dublin. To this day, tens of thousands of the city's residents and visitors use the thoroughfares, streets and avenues that this body designed and built. Their influence on the modern city is undeniable. It is through the work of their surveyors that it is possible to see how this familiar landscape came to be, what existed before and how the city may have been. The heritage value of the commissioners' maps is unquestionable in the history of eighteenth-century Dublin, and these precious maps forever link its resident surveyors to the city's fabric.

115 Joseph Moland, 'Survey of a piece of ground on the south side of the River Liffey, near Lazer's Hill' (1709) (DCA WSC/Maps/651). 116 John Gibson, 'Map of portion of the lands and premises, the property of the parish of St Michael the Archangel' (1709) (DCA WSC/Maps/745).

18 'Distances are of so great importance': surveying and transportation

> The marking out of the road is indispensably requisite in maps, without which a geographer can never make them of much use to either a traveller or student.[1]

John Green, in characteristically philosophical form, penned the above statement in 1717 to emphasize the general importance of roads, and later canals, in eighteenth-century mapping. These structures made transport of people, goods, ideas, medicines and technology possible; they allowed the map reader to answer the vital questions of 'where am I and where am I going?' Roads, as linear features, required separate surveying techniques from those practised for the surveying of land. Canals, as complex engineering works, required additional levels of survey accuracy that were unprecedented at the time. Surveyors played a key role in both, with those involved in such projects using specialized equipment and techniques, while simultaneously moving their profession onwards into the depths of the Industrial Revolution.

ROAD SURVEYING

Roads create a skeletal network in a country. In essence, map detail is focused on human activities and allows the reader to determine not only their place in the world, but also where the rest of the world is in relation to them:

> What can a man learn from a multitude of places, confusedly scatter'd? Like a traveller in a pathless wood, he is at a loss which way to guide himself. Wou'd it not look very odd to see a plan of London (if it can be so call'd) without the streets? And yet it wou'd be equally instructive, for it is as impossible to judge rightly of the situation of places in the map of a country without the roads, as it would of churches, palaces and all public buildings, in the plan of a city, without the streets.[2]

Roads are relevant to any study of eighteenth-century surveying in Ireland for many reasons. Road mapping was a distinct part of business for eighteenth-century surveyors and its place in period surveying treatises indicates that there was a high possibility that a professional surveyor would undertake road surveying during his

---

1 Green, *The construction of maps and globes in two parts*, p. 151.   2 Ibid., p. 137.

career.[3] The main principles of road surveys relate to orientation and distance. Given the linear nature of roads, surveys could be rapidly conducted between towns with only minimum detail of the surrounding countryside being included. Road maps were complex documents, with multiple layers of information, such as town and village locations, geographic features and road type, being included in addition to the main features of distance and direction. Stylistically simple, yet of relatively high surveying complexity if trigonometrical methods were used, road surveys were a part of many surveyors' workloads, as demonstrated by surviving maps and records.

Roads in eighteenth-century Ireland varied from broad thoroughfares suitable for large carriages and carts to dirt tracks. Arthur Young described the poor condition of many of Ireland's roads on his journeys around the country in the late 1770s:

> This road is abominably bad, continually over hills, rough, stony and cut up. It is a turnpike, which in Ireland is a synonymous term for a vile road … It is the effect of jobs and imposition which disgrace the kingdom; the present-ment roads shew what may be done, and render these villainous turnpikes the more disgusting.[4] … I would often hear of roads being made over such quaking bogs, that they move under a carriage, but could scarcely credit it; I was, however, convinced now; for, in several places, every step the horse set, moved a full yard of the ground in perfect heaves.[5]

George Semple commented that many of the new roads constructed during the latter half of the eighteenth century were 'tolerable', but that they were narrow and crooked compared to those found in other European countries. He saw the improvement of roads as a necessity to make the country 'capable of answering [its] natural purpose … promoting the extension and good trade'.[6] His solution to Ireland's road network crisis was the suggested creation of a new road in a direct line between Derry and Cork, to be one hundred feet wide with spur lines joining it with Dundalk, Drogheda, Dublin, Limerick, Galway, Castlebar and Armagh. Semple's plan, apart from being overly simplistic, proved unnecessary, as the country already had a complex road network, albeit in a poor state of repair in many parts of the county.

One of the most detailed road surveys of Ireland conducted during the eigh-teenth century was that of George Taylor and Andrew Skinner in 1776. Taylor and Skinner were military men, George being the brother of Alexander Taylor, who conducted a survey of Irish post-roads in 1805 and also worked with Charles Vallancey on his military survey of Ireland.[7] Prior to Taylor's and Skinner's arrival in Ireland, they had produced a map book, *A survey and maps of the roads of north Britain,*

---

3 Wyld, *The practical surveyor*, p. 138. 4 Young, *A tour of Ireland*, p. 128. 5 Ibid., p. 206.
6 George Semple, *Hibernia's free trade* (Dublin, 1780), p. 169. 7 Bendall (ed.), *Dictionary of land surveyors*, ii, p. 502. There was also a third Taylor brother who was initially trained as a land surveyor but left the profession in 1773 and by 1781 was joint manager of an opera house in London.

or Scotland (London, 1776), which laid out each road in a linear design leading from one town directly to another, thus emphasizing major roads individually. This was not a unique method of displaying road layouts, and it had been championed by Scottish surveyor John Ogilby during the seventeenth century, his work appearing as an example of aesthetic excellence in Hume's *Standard of taste* (London, 1757). Taylor and Skinner repeated this technique for their map of Ireland's roads.

Maps of Ireland's roads did exist prior to Taylor and Skinner's work in Ireland, with Scalé's *Hibernian atlas* (London, 1776) being one of the most extensive, if slightly too generalized to be classified as a specific road map. Work began on the project in early 1777, with the assistance of two other surveyors and sixteen assistants. J.H. Andrews speculated that Taylor and Skinner used a theodolite instead of a circumferentor during their work, which may be true given the absence of magnetic north measurements in their final map and the popularity of the instrument in Britain compared to Ireland.[8] In the 1720s, Samuel Wyld advised that a combination of theodolite and 'the wheel', or perambulator, be employed during road surveys.[9] Working from major town to major town, prominent features such as church steeples would be utilized to provide a trigonometrical control network using theodolite bearings. Such a linear network of control points would be relatively weak geometrically. Given the nature of the maps produced by Taylor and Skinner, however, where the necessity to show the relationship between different road networks would have been minimal, such problems with survey reference points would not have had a major impact on their work. The series of maps created by the two men reads like a physical journey, being orientated from the town of origin to the town of destination, rather than being based on a north point.

Distances were determined using the perambulator,[10] and Taylor and Skinner paid particular attention to this issue. Their indices of the roads of Ireland list the distance of every market town from Dublin, in both English and Irish miles[11] and furlongs. All distances were measured in relation to Dublin Castle. The importance of recording distances on maps was further highlighted by John Green, who, referring to historical cartographic pioneers, highlighted the unfortunate absence of distances in their maps:

> Roads with the distances are of so great importance in maps, that should the journals from whence they were drawn happen to be lost, something of them would by that means be preserv'd, and some use might be made of them in another age. If Ptolemy had observ'd this method, his maps would have been abundantly more useful, and we might have been able not only to rectify them, but to improve the modern thereby.[12]

---

8 Preface to reprint of Taylor and Skinner, *Road maps of Ireland* (London, 1777, repr. Dublin, 1968). **9** Wyld, *The practical surveyor*, p. 138. **10** Ibid., p. 139. **11** Eleven Irish miles were equal to fourteen English miles: Taylor and Skinner, *Road maps of Ireland*, p. iv. **12** Green, *The construction of maps and globes in two parts*, p. 151.

Taylor and Skinner's road maps were relatively basic, yet clear and informative. Avoiding unnecessary textual clutter, each map linked two towns or cities, showing distance markers, stately homes[13] and points of interest. Natural features, such as rivers and hills, appear to have been sketched in, yet they add an element of realism to the work.

After their work in Ireland, the two military men departed for the North American colonies in 1779, which were at the time embroiled in the American Revolutionary War (1775–83). Based at the British stronghold in New York,[14] Taylor and Skinner produced maps of New York Harbour, while serving as officers with the duke of Cumberland's Provincial Regiment of Foot,[15] at the expense of work they had originally planned to complete in Scotland:

> Some years ago, Messrs Taylor and Skinner published proposals, and got many subscribers, for taking a survey and making a large map of this county [Perth and Clackmannan], which has never been hitherto done. These surveyors neglected the scheme for a more lucrative employ of publishing the roads of Ireland: since that was finished, they have gained some office in the army in America, and have quitted that project.[16]

CANAL SURVEYING (1751–1806)

> Commerce … is the most solid foundation of civil society, and the surest means of uniting mankind, even the inhabitants of the most distant countries; by commerce, the whole world in a manner becomes one single family.[17]

In the age before railways and high-speed motorways, transportation of goods, building materials and people was limited to either foot, sail or horse and carriage. The canal therefore represented a major technological and industrial breakthrough, with engineering surveying playing a vital role. Surveying techniques, primarily levelling, were paramount to the success of any Irish canal scheme. Given the ease of transporting of goods by canal and increase in commercial potential, there was great enthusiasm within Ireland for their construction:

> Again, if we consider and enumerate the chief sources of employment for this intended navigation, such as the natural production of the counties that lie near the canal, the cultivated commodities and manufacture, the imported

13 Many of which were included because of their association with subscribers to the work. 14 New York had fallen to the British Army in the aftermath of the Battle of Long Island (1776) and was in British hands until the end of the war: David McCullough, *1776* (London, 2005), p. 201. 15 R.H. Fairclough, 'Sketches of the roads in Scotland, 1785: the manuscript road book of George Taylor', *Imago Mundi*, 27 (1975), 65–72. 16 Richard Gough, *British topography* (London, 1780), p. 710. 17 Charles Vallancey, *A treatise on inland navigation* (Dublin, 1763), p. i. 18 Ibid., p. 12.

material and general commerce, all which are hereafter set forth, it must work up the imagination of every friend of Ireland, until he is wholly employed in projecting schemes to realize it, in the whole extent.[18]

While the relative area affected by canal construction was confined to the immediate region surrounding the structure, it was vital that land through which the canal passed was correctly mapped and its owners identified. Some of the earliest ideas for canals in Dublin emanate from Andrew Yarranton, who produced a map of Dublin in 1674 showing a series of proposed canals crossing the city to the east of Dublin Castle (fig. 18.1). Yarranton's plans were not feasible due to the dense urban nature of the land in question, however they demonstrate an interest in Irish canals dating back to the seventeenth century at least. Legislation for inland navigation projects was first introduced in 1715,[19] while the first operational canal was constructed in the 1730s from Newry to Coalisland. In 1729, engineer Thomas Bowen produced a map[20] showing details of two potential lines for a Dublin–Shannon canal, and by 1751 serious interest was being shown in a proposed canal between Dublin and the Shannon, with the *Corporation for promoting and carrying on an inland navigation in Ireland* being formed.[21]

Initially, Semple was asked his opinion on the route any Dublin–Shannon canal should take. There were regular debates in parliament between concerned parties as to whether a northern or southern route would be best suited, yet Semple was indecisive on the matter:

> My private opinion was asked by those on both sides of the questions; but not having applied my thoughts to anything of that nature, and not choosing to give a rash opinion, I set off, and took a cursory view of all the rivers worth my notice, between Dublin and Cork; then to Limerick and traced the course of the Shannon on the west side ... And on my return, having compared the opinions of several gentlemen that were employed and had wrote on it ... I was not able to determine which of those lines ought to obtain the preference; nor do I to this day.[22]

Despite his lack of commitment to either proposed line, Semple understood the importance of artificial inland navigation and wrote about its potential impact on trade later in his life.[23]

By the mid-1750s, the southern route had become favourite, with engineer Thomas Omer being placed in charge of the 'grand' southern route.[24] There were serious doubts raised about Omer's plans for the Grand Canal, with at least one anonymous author suspecting at worst that fraudulent maps were produced by Omer or that Omer was incapable of producing adequate maps for such a scheme:

19 Act 2 Geo. I, c.12 [Ire.] (1715). 20 Thomas Bowen, *A plan of the Grand Canal from the city of Dublin to the River Shannon* (Dublin, 1729). 21 25 Geo II, c.10 [Ire.] (1751). 22 Semple, *Treatise of building in water*, p. 1. 23 Ibid., p. 162. 24 Ruth Delany, *The Grand Canal of Ireland* (Dublin, 1973), p. 4.

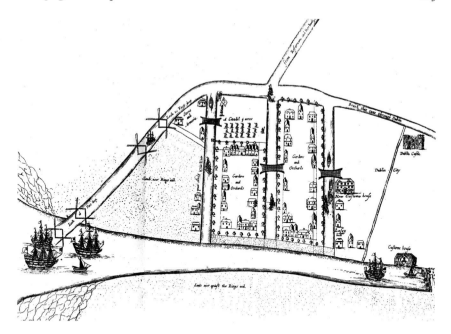

18.1 Proposed canal construction in Dublin city centre (from Andrew Yarranton, 'Dublin' (1674), courtesy of Dublin City Library & Archive).

> By considering what was Mr Omer's opinion, before he viewed and traced the southern line, without reflecting on his motives for such a rash declaration, we may account for some extraordinary appearances in the plan he now offers . . . this map, produced by Mr Omer, has no scale, it also has no latitudes, or bearing to any point of the compass, so, consequently, whether the rivers that intersect those lines are properly placed, it is impossible to know from his map.[25]

One of the best authorities on early canal surveying and engineering in Ireland was Charles Vallancey (1725–1812) (pl. 14). Vallancey was born in England of French descent. His father was a classical scholar who helped educate his son 'with the best Greek and Roman writers'.[26] These early lessons had unfortunate mixed results for Vallancey in his later academic work. During his formal education at Eton, Vallancey became close friends with the future lord lieutenant of Ireland, Marquis Townsend, and their friendship was said to have 'grown with their growth, and strengthened with their strength'.[27] In his early twenties, he joined the Royal Military Academy at Woolwich, where he received his training as a surveyor and engineering. By 1750, he was stationed in Gibraltar.[28]

25 Anon., *Observations on a pamphlet lately published entitled a description of the rival lines for inland navigation &c.* (Dublin, 1756), p. 7. **26** *Walker's Hibernian Magazine*, Nov. 1804. **27** Ibid. **28** William O'Reilly, 'Charles Vallancey and the military itinerary of Ireland',

It is possible that during his time in Gibraltar, with its proximity to north Africa, Vallancey developed his theories of the settlement of Ireland in antiquity that would later come to dominate his non-engineering career. Despite being an accomplished engineer and surveyor, Vallancey's keen interest in history brought him to theorize, after many years in Ireland, that the country had been settled by the Phoenicians, thus explaining the complexity of the Irish language.[29] Vallancey was a skilled scholar, being a founding member of both the Hibernian Society in 1779 and the Royal Irish Academy in 1785,[30] however his theories on an ancient Irish Phoenician link could find little enthusiasm, even among his supporters:

> This work, however, was not composed under the shades of academic bowes but amidst cares that would have discomposed the most philosophic mind. Yet it possesses great merit; although his zeal for the antiquity of his country blinds him to the truth.[31]

Historian William Jones referred to Vallancey's *A vindication of the early history of Ireland* (London, 1786) to a former student as follows:

> Have you met with a book lately published with the title of *A vindication of the ancient history of Ireland* [sic] ? It was written by a friend of mine, Colonel Vallancey; but a word in your ear – it is very stupid ... I ... am certain that his derivation from the Persian, Arabic and Sanscrit languages are erroneous. According to him, when silly people give me the surname of Persian, they in fact called me Irishman. Do you wish to laugh? Skim the book over. Do you wish to sleep? Read it regularly.[32]

Despite the inaccuracies and eccentricities of some of Vallancey's work, he was a prolific author during the late eighteenth century.[33] As such, he can be seen to have had a positive, if misguided, impact on eighteenth-century preservation of Irish culture and history.

Ancient Phoenicia aside, Vallancey's main skills lay in engineering and mapping.[34] In 1763, he published *A treatise on inland navigation* (Dublin, 1763), describing the main theories behind canal construction and included canal building projects from

---

PRIA, 106C (2006), 125–217 at 127. **29** *Walker's Hibernian Magazine*, Nov. 1804. **30** O'Reilly, 'Charles Vallancey and the military itinerary', 129. **31** *Walker's Hibernian Magazine*, Nov. 1804. **32** Cannon, 'Letters of Sir William Jones', ii, pp 768–9, quoted in O'Reilly, 'Charles Vallancey', 131. **33** Charles Vallancey, *A grammar of the Iberno-Celtic, or Irish language* (Dublin, 1781); Charles Vallancey, *Prospectus of a dictionary of the language of the Aire Coti; or, Ancient Irish* (Dublin, 1802). Charles Vallancey, *An essay towards illustrating the ancient history of the Britannic Isles* (London, 1786). **34** In the late 1770s, he conducted a military survey of Ireland, which he presented in person to King George III in 1782. He was promoted to colonel the following day: *Walker's Hibernian Magazine*, Nov. 1804.

antiquity to the eighteenth century. His understanding of the advantage that canals could bring to a country and the impact they could have on traditional means of transportation was stated from the very beginning of his work:

> Canals render carriages and beasts of burden less necessary ... it is by them that traffic can animate all parts of a state and produce plenty and happiness to the people, and thus extend a sovereign's power.[35]

Apart from canal building techniques and discussions on improvements in engineering, period canal publications made clear the role that surveying played in such projects. Primary importance fell to levelling. It is not economically viable to build canals in a straight line between two termini, as hills and valleys greatly increase cost. As such, the importance of surveying in the initial laying out of a canal was paramount: 'the country thro' which it is to pass, must be most exactly surveyed, and levels taken the whole extent, without [which] no judgment can be formed'.[36] A discussion of the importance of levelling in canal construction had previously been published in Ireland by Richard Castle in 1730, who gave a particularly detailed explanation of levelling techniques, noting the effect of the earth's curvature for long levelling runs.[37]

After the initial levelling run and survey of the surrounding areas, cross-sectional maps were required to analyze the amount of earth that need to be extracted, in addition to the volume of material needed for cut-and-fill section of the works. Vallancey's understanding of cross-sectional maps and their production gives a better insight into his skill as an engineering surveyor:

> Having determined the course of the canal according to the preceding consideration, a map should be added on a large scale; ... to this map should be added a section or profile of the ground from one end of the canal proposed to the other, passing through the middle of it, making the bottom of the canal, the soil, risings and gallows of the ground; from this may be determined the sinkings, position of locks, back drains, aqueducts, bridges etc.[38]

Cross-sectional maps are relatively rare in eighteenth-century Irish map collections outside of canal maps. Road surveying was another engineering field with a definite need for this type of map,[39] but such maps are seldom found in surviving map collections.

In 1771, Vallancey, by request of the Commissioners of Inland Navigation, authored a report on the proposed route of the Grand Canal (fig. 18.2). Following

---

35 Vallancey, *A treatise on inland navigation*, p. iv.   **36** Ibid., p. 123.   **37** Castle, *Essay on artificial navigation*, p. 9.   **38** Vallancey, *A treatise on inland navigation*, p. 134.   **39** Anon., 'Design of the Carlisle Bridge approaches, *c.*1800' (NLI Longfield papers, MS 21F87(101)).

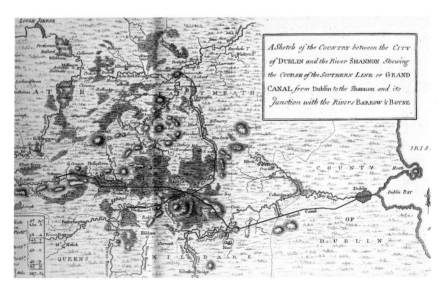

18.2 Proposed line of the Grand Canal (from Charles Vallancey, *A report on the Grand Canal* (Dublin, 1771), courtesy of the National Library of Ireland © NLI).

his own advice, he produced detailed surveys and levelling results on two separate routes, Dublin to the Shannon via Tullamore and Dublin to the Shannon via Mullingar. In addition to the main lines, he surveyed several 'collateral branches',[40] all of which were presented to the commissioners in map form as part of his report. Within Co. Dublin, the presence of several rivers was deemed to be problematic, but not overly complicated from an engineering perspective. The Liffey, which Vallancey described as 'difficult to be made navigable on account of . . . rapidity',[41] was crossed by the Grand Canal in Co. Kildare. The original crossing point was deemed to be too wide and deep, and Vallancey was able to find a narrower crossing point only two hundred yards upstream, with a water depth of only three feet.

Despite the benefit to commerce that would be enjoyed by the counties through which the canal would pass, there would inevitably be individuals who would lose land to the canal's construction. The purchasing of land was one of the highest expenses incurred with canal building, as it would 'nearly show the expense of the whole design'.[42] Castle, writing in 1730, also advised that the establishment of landownership should be a high priority in any canal mapping procedure: 'to the end that the damage done to every person may be obvious'.[43] Another writer also commented on the same problem over forty years later:

> The owners and occupiers of land through which the canal is to pass (I mean chiefly the small ones) have their minds perpetually employed how to make

---

40 Charles Vallancey, *A report on the Grand Canal* (Dublin, 1771), p. 3.   **41** Ibid., p. 4.
42 Ibid., p. 134.   **43** Castle, *Essay on artificial navigation*, p. 7 (NLI MS 2737).

the most of it, and are not only contriving every circumstance to exaggerate the purchase of the land.[44]

Vallancey's investigation into the course of the Grand Canal established that fifty-six landowners in Dublin would be affected by its construction, with fifty-five in Kildare and thirty-one in King's County (Offaly). His surveys allowed him to deduce the distance of the canal from Dublin to the Shannon,[45] the number of locks required,[46] and the difference in height between the Dublin city basin terminus and the Shannon.[47] Determination of statistical data such as this was vital in the overall planning of the Grand Canal; however Vallancey had one major adjustment that he felt the commissioners should make for the canal's design. The original plan was for the Grand Canal's terminus to be located at the city basin, near St James' Street in the south-west of the city. He felt that this was too distant from 'the usual abodes of the merchants and traders' of the city. The additional road transportation of goods would add significantly to the final price, thus reducing the economic viability of Ireland as a whole and 'thereby defeat the good intention of this navigation'.[48] He proposed continuing the canal parallel to existing roads to a new termination point at St Stephen's Green or Merrion Square,

> from when there will be so many direct avenues from its banks to various parts of town, as to lower the price of town carriage very considerably, as well as a favourable opportunity of letting the canal down to the river, between George's Quay and Ringsend, as may hereafter be found expedient.[49]

Vallancey's report was all-encompassing, covering in detail a wide range of subjects related to building a canal on the proposed route. A report published in the same year by Dublin Corporation engineer John Trail disagreed with Vallancey's choice of the location to cross the Liffey, however, preferring one selected by Omer that followed a straight line for the canal.[50] Trail suggested that an expert be brought in to settle the dispute, and Redmond Morres, a member of the fledgling Grand Canal Company, wrote to engineer John Smeaton, who at the time was involved with the Forth and Clyde Canal in Scotland. Smeaton was initially reluctant, with his responses often taking two or three months, however, the commissioners were determined to have his opinion due to 'the high character you have as to integrity, knowledge and experience in works of this kind'.[51]

By August 1771, Smeaton was still fully occupied but was willing to review the commissioners' reports, although he warned them that he was not familiar enough with the country for a complete review of the project. Despite the repeated requests to visit the project in Ireland, Smeaton's engagements meant that his actual visit to

---

44 Morres, *Letters on the Grand Canal*, p. 35. **45** 68 miles. **46** 46 Locks. **47** 59 feet.
48 Vallancey, *A report on the Grand Canal*, p. 66. **49** Ibid. **50** Delany, *The Grand Canal of Ireland*, p. 11. **51** Redmond Morres, *Letters on the Grand Canal* (Dublin, 1773), p. 5.

the site was looking less and less likely. As a result, he recommend that John Grundy, a Lincolnshire engineer, would be a suitable replacement for him in such a project.[52] Smeaton's letters to the commission throughout 1772/3 were much longer and more technically detailed than those that followed the initial enquiry into his availability, demonstrating his growing interest in the project. In a letter dated December 1772, he also suggested additional personnel that the project engineer would require around him, including a purveyor for material, a land valuer, a pay clerk and a store-keeper. Second on Smeaton's list of requested personnel was a land surveyor

> to measure the lands staked out, or proposed for purchase, temporary drainages &c., to measure the work of the artifices done by contract &c. and to take levels occasionally by direction of the engineer, together with plans and section of hill, hollows &c. through which the canal is to pass.[53]

An advertisement for a 'skilful engineer' published in 1787[54] by the Grand Canal Company emphasized many of Smeaton's recommendations for a surveyor, high-lighting the close ties between surveying and engineering in eighteenth-century Ireland. Smeaton eventually arrived to inspect the canal in September 1773 and suggested that Vallancey's Liffey crossing point was the most viable.[55]

John Brownrigg, former pupil of Bernard Scalé and onetime business partner of Thomas Sherrard, was an active surveyor for canal projects. Included in his work was the implementation of Vallancey's scheme for the extension of the Grand Canal further than the city basin,[56] and a recommendation to the Wide Streets Commission to construct a new street from Kevin Street to the canal dock at Portobello, with an accompanying bridge.[57]

The works of Skinner, Taylor, Brownrigg and Vallancey, coupled with the writings of Semple, clearly demonstrate the direct importance that surveying and mapping played in moving Dublin's transportation into the era of the Industrial Revolution. The promise of economic prosperity pushed road and canal construction onwards, but this was offset by the difficulties in purchasing land and the detailed and compli-cated surveying work that accompanied such large-scale engineering work. The absolute importance of maps to transportation schemes and the necessity of levelling meant that surveyors and their measurements were vital to such projects before the first sod of earth had been turned.

Transportation surveying highlights the gradual but inventible separation that the Industrial Revolution brought to surveying. The split between those who retained the traditional surveying techniques and technology and those who embraced the emerging world of engineering surveying had begun.

---

52 Ibid., p. 18.   **53** Ibid., p. 35.   **54** *Freeman's Journal*, 22 Sept. 1787.   **55** Delany, *The Grand Canal of Ireland*, p. 15.   **56** Ibid., p. 51.   **57** 13 Jun. 1806 (DCA WSC/Mins/20), p. 114.

19 'From thence to the quays': charts of Dublin Bay and harbour, 1671–1803

In the eighteenth century, the sea represented Dublin's gateway to the world. Positioned next to one of the world's greatest maritime powers, Britain, and having easy access to markets in Europe, North America and further afield, Dublin's bay and harbour were of great importance to the economic wealth and survival of the city. The bay is both large and offers good shelter for ships from adverse weather and sea conditions. The sea floor is prone to excess silting, however, which reduces shipping to a channel continuous to the River Liffey. Given the reliance on sea travel in the eighteenth century and the regular changes brought to the layout of the sea floor of Dublin Bay by the deposition of sediment, which frequently affected shipping lanes, Dublin's bay and harbour feature prominently in eighteenth-century Irish mapping. Indeed, more original charts of Dublin Harbour were produced during this period than city plans of Dublin.

Dublin port and harbour were legally the responsibility of Dublin Corporation by charter of Queen Elizabeth I. In 1708,[1] the Ballast Board Act was enacted, creating a body, the Ballast Board, responsible for the maintenance of Dublin Harbour and bay, and through this body many maps were created and preserved, providing an illustrated history of the same area, covering the entire eighteenth century. Early marine charts of Dublin Bay included John Seller's *The English pilot* (London, 1671),[2] and Thomas Philips' 'An exact survey of the city of Dublin and part of the harbour' (1685), which detail the labyrinth of navigable passages from the open sea to the Liffey. It was these passages through the sandbanks that became the overriding theme of most eighteenth-century charts of the harbour, as accurate mapping of these routes would enable profitable sea trade. Resections and intersection surveys appear to have been popular methods of establishing sounding positions and coastal layouts.[3]

One of the first eighteenth-century engineering maps of Dublin Harbour was the work of Dublin surveyor Gabriel Stokes in 1725. His manuscript map focused on the mouth of the River Liffey and was produced at a time of heightened interest in possible engineering projects to improve the port's efficiency. One of the main proponents of this initiative was Captain John Perry. Perry had previously been employed by Tsar Peter II of Russia (1672–1725) on inland navigation and the improvement of existing rivers. In September 1713, Perry conducted a survey of

---

1 '... in the sixth year of her late majesty Queen Anne (1707–8) ... appointed conservator of the port of Dublin ... 20 Mar. 1760': Gilbert (ed.), *Ancient records*, x, p. 409. **2** Gerald Daly, 'George Semple's chart of Dublin Bay, 1762', *PRIA*, 93:3 (1993), 81–105. Seller was also the author of the navigational treatise *Practical navigation* (London, 1669). **3** Alexander Dalrymple, *Essay on the most commodious methods of marine surveying* (London, 1771), p. 6.

Dublin Harbour at the request of the corporation before departing for England to conduct similar work. In 1725, he submitted a report to Dublin Corporation entitled *A method proposed for making a safe and convenient entrance to the port of Dublin* (Dublin, 1725). Describing the shoals of Dublin Bay as 'beyond all memory accompanied with distress', Perry suggested the construction of a canal from Sutton, near the north of the bay, to the north bank of the Liffey.[4] Addressing the problem of tides and their effect on the proposed canal water level, Perry gave this suggestion:

> Fix a sluice towards the outward part of the canal where the ground is best for the purpose, by which to keep up such head of water from thence to the city as may at all times of the tide answers the service of boats … with expedition and safety going from thence to the quays, on occasion of loading and unloading large ships lying below the sluice that have not sufficient depth of water for coming up to the quay.[5]

The estimated cost of this proposal was £36,606 16s. 9d., which, after consultation with the merchants and shipmasters of Dublin, was decided by the council to be too costly and Perry's scheme was rejected.

Perry's scheme was only one of a number of engineering works at the time being conducted for Dublin shipping. Brooking's *A map of the city and suburbs of Dublin* (London, 1728) shows the continuation of Dublin's Liffey walls out to Ringsend on the south bank and an equal distance on the northern bank. Brooking's reference to the land enclosed by the north wall as 'walled in but as yet overflow'd by ye tide' indicates that this was a work in progress and his panorama of the city shows the areas behind the new north and south walls as yet uninhabited.

Despite Brooking's strong indications that the area behind the north wall was waterlogged, the area had been mapped and divided into lots in 1717. An anonymous map,[6] possibly originating from Gabriel Stokes, given the similarity to his style, presents this walled area as a series of lots, distinguished by each owner's name and the area of each lot in acres, perches and roods. This may indicate that the reclamation work behind the north wall had either not been as successful as originally planned or had suffered a setback between 1717 and 1728. Another possibility is that the overall enclosed area was known in 1717 and the map was a proposed plan of the area once it had been finally drained. Regardless, the anonymous map shows that there was a demand for land reclaimed from the Liffey and Dublin Bay.

Perry was not finished with his work on Dublin Bay after his initial canal proposal in 1725. Three years later, he, along with Surveyor General Thomas Burgh, produced a map of the bay with a concentration of depth readings at the mouth of the Liffey. Burgh and Perry, 'in company with persons appointed by the Ballast

---

4 Gilbert (ed.), *Ancient records*, vii, p. xvii (n.d.).   **5** Ibid.   **6** Entitled *A map of ye strand of north side of ye river Anna Liffe as it was granted and set out in Easter assembly 1717 by ye Rt Hon. Thomas Bolton esq., lord mayor of the city of Dublin* (Dublin, 1717).

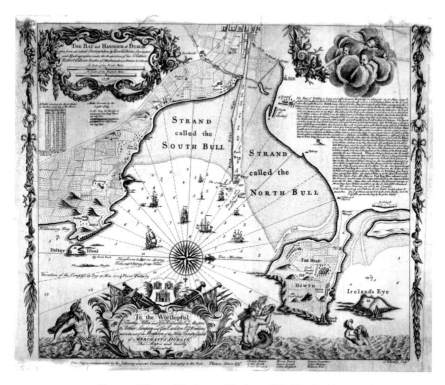

19.1 George Gibson, *The bay and harbour of Dublin* (Dublin, 1756)
(courtesy of the Board of Trinity College Dublin).

Office',[7] utilized Brooking's recently published map for their representation of Dublin city, thus making their production an accurate version of both city and harbour from surveys conducted in the same year. What appears to be Perry's canal is represented as a deep channel running from Sutton to just outside the city, indicating that he had not entirely abandoned his recommendations presented earlier to the corporation. An important feature of the Perry/Burgh map is its representation of soundings, strongly indicating that an intersection was used, probably from two sets of shore-based surveyors, to map the physical path they travelled during the survey. Despite the presence of soundings in many other eighteenth-century charts of Dublin Bay, few give as strong evidence of the survey techniques used in Burgh and Perry's 1728 map.

The 1750s and 1760s witnessed another flurry of surveying activity in Dublin Bay. Eminent surveyors such as George Gibson, John Rocque, Bernard Scalé and engineer George Semple all produced detailed surveys of the area, highlighting a distinct change in map artwork and greater investigation of the sea floor.

Gibson's *The bay and harbour of Dublin* (Dublin, 1756) is a good example of the

---

7 Thomas Burgh and Captain John Perry, *Dublin Bay* (London, 1728).

change in decorative fashion in native Irish mapping between the early and mid-eighteenth century (fig. 19.1). The edges of Gibson's maps are highly decorated, including representations of Neptune supporting the cartouche, baroque vignettes and a higher concentration of ships in the harbour than is found in earlier maps. Gibson surveyed the area under the supervision of his father, Robert, and the amount of detail, both written and visual, contained within the map strongly indicates that the entire work was by Gibson's own hand. Aside from a wider area covered by sounding readings than seen in earlier eighteenth-century maps, Gibson provided a detailed account of the bay, indicating that he was familiar with navigation or had consulted Dublin's ship captains: 'the bay of Dublin is large and affords good anchorage in all parts. In it ships may be sheltered from the S to NE …winds. The best anchorage is from 3 to 7 fathoms on S side'.[8] Useful navigations aids, such as the position of sunken rocks, highly visible buildings onshore that could be used as landmarks, the level and time of high water at the mouth of the Liffey, and the position of the stationary light ship to guide ships into port, make Gibson's map very practical for sailors. Gibson was keen to state his Irish origin, highlighting in the map's scale bar that his father was a 'native and citizen'. His cartographic detail is relatively basic and typical of Irish mapping produced in the early to mid-eighteenth century.

John Rocque's representation of Dublin Harbour was of a higher cartographic quality than previous maps. Rocque's representation of Dublin Bay,[9] included as part of his 1757 survey of Dublin's environs, showed a large number of sloops, brigs and other sailing ships. While never producing a dedicated map of the harbour, Rocque is known to have surveyed the mud-flats around Ringsend,[10] and his inclusion of the depth readings, the stationary 'light ship', a 'quarantine sloop' and the 'pacquet moorings' indicate that he had performed additional survey work in the area.

While Rocque's work on Dublin Bay may only have been cursory in comparison with his work inland, his apprentice and brother-in-law, Bernard Scalé, gained far more experience in its ebbs and flows in the 1760s. Published jointly with William Richards in 1765, Scalé's *Directions for navigation into the bay of Dublin* (Dublin, 1765) was a detailed examination of the best shipping lanes between Wicklow Head and Balbriggan, with comments on water depth, places to shelter from storms, and the location of dangerous shoals and sunken rocks. The two surveyors were employed by the pilot committee, who were interested in producing what amounts to an eighteenth-century equivalent of a risk assessment evaluation, considering 'the fatal accidents that ships and vessels, trading to or from the port of Dublin, would be liable to, in case of any mistakes or inaccuracies that hurry or inadvertency might have produced'.[11]

As an added assurance to the book's purchasers, the pilot committee had insisted that the publication be delayed until their own 'haven-masters' and 'pilot masters' had confirmed the depth readings and bearings produced by the two surveyors during

---

8 George Gibson, *The bay and harbour of Dublin* (Dublin, 1756).   **9** Rocque, *The city, harbour, bay and environs of Dublin*.   **10** *Dublin Journal*, 14 Sept. 1754.   **11** Bernard Scalé and William Richards, *Directions for navigation into the bay of Dublin* (Dublin, 1765), postscript.

the course of their 'useful work'. The head of the pilot committee, Nathanael Card reported:

> with that ingenuity, judgement and fidelity which the committee as lovers of trade, and ... encouragers of navigation, cannot, upon the occasion, omit recommending this chart to all masters of ships trading to this port, as they are fully satisfied that within the limits of this survey many dangers are now pointed out, that were hitherto totally unknown.[12]

MARITIME SURVEYING

Reviewing period survey treatises, there is a notable lack of advice or specifics directly related to maritime surveying. One could argue that such maritime charts were normally the work of navigators, however the surviving maps of Dublin Bay from the eighteenth century demonstrate that Dublin's surveyors were active in mapping this area. This neglect by authors was masterfully summed up in a seminal 1774 publication by British surveyor Murdoch MacKenzie:

> No branch of practical geometry has been so little considered by men of science as maritime surveying. This subject has never been particularly treated of by any author, nor taught by a master; nor have surveyors given any account of their operations and procedure in such surveys. To this reserve of writers, and silence of practitioners, it may be ascribed, that an art of such great importance in navigation has hitherto received so little improvement; that in practice little or no distinction is made between land-surveying and coast-surveying, though they differ essentially from each other in their nature and circumstances.[13]

MacKenzie was one of the very few authors to tackle this subject directly, and he published an entire treatise dedicated to maritime surveying. Land and maritime surveying shared many elements and techniques, such as geometry and trigonometry, determination of latitude, calculation of intersection measurements and working with instruments like the theodolite and circumferentor. There were, however, several unique methods involved in maritime surveying. MacKenzie documented how distances could be estimated using the flash and sound of a gun being fired, how to assess the usefulness of harbours[14] and how prominent coastal features, such as church steeples, could be used to act as control points while taking depth measurements.[15] Another method unique to this branch of surveying was tide measurement:

---

12 Ibid.   **13** Murdoch MacKenzie, *A treatise of maritime surveying* (London, 1774), preface.
14 Ibid., p. 101.   **15** Ibid., p. 69.

The perpendicular rise of spring and neap tides varies sensibly according to the distance and position of the moon with respect to the earth; and of the earth and moon with respect to the sun, and also by winds and weather; [and] the depths of the water.[16]

MacKenzie's practical advice, particularly relating to the sort of vessel and personnel that were required for conducting such surveys, was also unmatched by Irish surveying authors of the era. For coastal surveys he recommended

a vessel about 120 tons burden, pretty broad in the beam, and full in the bows ... Her complement of men (besides the surveyor, his assistant and two servants) to be a master, a purser, a mate, a midshipman, a carpenter ... fourteen able seamen before the mast and a pilot for the coast. A larger vessel cannot go into small creeks, which will often retard the service, and be found very inconvenient on a survey: a vessel much less, cannot keep sea well, nor carry provisions and other stores sufficient for the season; which is likewise a disadvantage.[17]

MacKenzie was not the only author on maritime surveying,[18] however his obvious extensive experience in the area helps highlight the sparse attention that maritime surveying received from many of his fellow surveying authors. Given Dublin's presence in maritime charts and maps, and its prominent role as a major port, it seems strange that such Irish authors such as Gibson and Noble failed to include the subject of maritime surveying in their treatises.

MAPPING SILT

Silt deposition was an ongoing problem for shipping in Dublin Bay and was regularly featured in maps of the area. The extension of the Liffey walls, as shown in Brooking's 1728 map, had channelled the river's force to reduce sediment build-up at the mouth of the river, but it was not a sufficient or permanent solution. If the silting up of the Liffey continued, the viability of Dublin as a sea port would be greatly diminished. Writing in 1780, Robert Poole and John Cash highlighted the situation in Dublin Bay: 'Dublin would have had a commodious and secure station for shipping if the entrance of the bay had not been so choked up, that vessels of birthen [*sic*] cannot come over the bar'.[19] Contemporary writers understood the physics behind this problem; Charles Vallancey noted that

16 Ibid., p. 97.   **17** Ibid., p. 107.   **18** Dalrymple, *Essay on the most commodious methods*, p. 6.
19 Robert Poole and John Cash, *View of the most remarkable public buildings ... in the city of Dublin* (Dublin, 1780), p. 7.

the entrance or mouths of rivers are commonly the shallowest, because the
velocity of the water is here so diminished, by the little fall of the bed, and by
its spreading and widening, that it deposits mud, sand &c. whenever it over-
flows.[20]

It was to address this challenging situation that George Semple, the city's resident
problem solver, approached the Ballast Board in 1762. Using existing maps of Dublin
Bay and harbour, he had charted the changing depth and position of the bay's sandbanks and believed he had several solutions to improve the economic capability of
the harbour. In a letter to the board, Semple stated the work he had already undertaken and the objectives of his project:

> I have in the following work industriously endeavoured to collect and care-
> fully laid down some of the most authentick surveys of this harbour for some
> hundred years past down to the present time; wherein by inspection may
> easily be discover'd the great loss the river was at for want of a direction into
> the bay, and I have given the sundry shiftings and changes of the sands and
> taken new and exact soundings through the whole bay ... which doth most
> evidently demonstrate the happy effects of erecting the New Pier, together
> with two different designs for completing the safe and commodious harbour
> ... And I humbly apprehend that these maps and plans ought to be carefully
> perused ... to give present and general satisfaction to the publick, particularly
> the members of both the House of Parliament in time being as a convincing
> proof that the indefatigable labours of your board is already productive.

Semple had previously worked in Kingstown[21] for a board similar to the Ballast
Office, and included his plans of Kingstown Harbour as part of his proposed
improvements of Dublin Bay: 'tho it dos' not come under your inspection yet as it
properly belongs to and is part of this harbour [Dublin] I have also given it a place
in this work'.[22] Semple's proposals comprised eight maps, some with newly surveyed
soundings but none of which consisted of new surveys of Dublin Bay or harbour.
He collated the previous works of Burgh and Philips,[23] Stokes,[24] and Rocque,[25]
and compared them to each other and to his own depth readings. These initial
comparative maps appear to be an attempt to show the worsening situation in relation to sediment build-up in Dublin Harbour, however those copied from Rocque
and Stokes show fewer sounding readings than the originals, while the map copied
from Burgh and Philips included the original surveys for a canal from Sutton to the

20 Vallancey, *A treatise on inland navigation*, p. 84.   **21** Modern day Dun Laoghaire.   **22**
George Semple, 'Letter to chairman ... of the Ballast Office' (Dublin, 1762), quoted in full
in Daly, 'George Semple's charts of Dublin Bay', 83.   **23** Semple, 'Letter to chairman', maps
ii, iii.   **24** Ibid., maps iii, v.   **25** Ibid., maps vi, v: both copies of Rocque, *The city, harbour,
bay and environs of Dublin.*

19.2 Captain William Bligh by Jean Condé, after John Russell engraving, 1792 (© National Portrait Gallery, London).

city, which had been abandoned decades previously, leaving its presence a mystery in the 1762 copy.

Semple also proposed that two large sea walls be built, one extending from 'Buters Town'[26] [Booterstown] in the south and one from Sutton in the north. Each was to extend into Dublin Bay for over a kilometre, until they met the Liffey's main channel, at which point they would meet the north and south wall respectively of the river's banks, which would also have to be greatly extended. The proposed northern walled section would contain 2,444 plantation acres and the southern section would cover 1,266 – calculated by Daly to be a total of 2,291 acres.[27] Such an undertaking would have added a massive area of reclaimed land to the city.

The engineering logic supporting this endeavour is questionable. Considering that modern Bull Island, which was created by sedimentary deposition accelerated by the construction of the North Bull Wall and which occupies approximately the same

26 Semple, 'Letter to chairman', map vii.   **27** Daly, 'George Semple's charts of Dublin Bay', 97.

area as the northern section of Semple's reclaimed land, the amount of physical work
and financial backing required for Semple's project would not be justifiable. Semple's
ideas were never taken up by the Ballast Board, but his mapping project not only
demonstrates the gradual silting up of Dublin Bay over the seventeenth and eighteenth centuries, but also shows that engineers were actively using existing mapping.

The dawn of the nineteenth century saw a renewed interest in the mapping of
Dublin Bay and, like the 1750s, witnessed the changing of cartographic styles and the
evolution of map production. Two charts of the bay were published in a three-year
period; one by John Cowan in 1800 and the other by Captain William Bligh (1754–
1817) of HMS *Bounty* infamy (fig. 19.2).

Bligh's representation of the bay is a highly advanced work of cartography for the
first years of the nineteenth century (fig. 19.3). Like the change in attitude towards
surveying and mapping caused by Rocque's arrival in the 1750s, Bligh's work also
indicated that the future of cartography in Ireland would be radically different.

Bligh had had a tumultuous career before his 1803 survey of Dublin Bay. Having
served in the Caribbean as a midshipman in the Royal Navy, he was recommended
at the age of 22 by none other than Lord Sandwich, first lord of the admiralty, to join
Captain James Cook's third voyage to the Pacific in 1776.[28] Bligh's four-year voyage
with Cook on HMS *Resolution* allowed him to map large portions of the Pacific,
from the tropics to the Bering Sea, and also gave him his first command, upon Cook's
death in Hawaii in 1779. Bligh was a talented navigator, however he was also known
for his sharp tongue and poor sense of humour, commenting on the jovial 'crossing
of the line' ceremony on board the *Resolution* as 'a vile practice … to afford some
fun'.[29] Bligh had the unusual misfortune of having three mutinies occur under his
command during the course of his military career. The most famous of these was in
1787 when the crew of HMS *Bounty* rebelled against Bligh's overly strict command,
and set him and several of his supporters adrift in the Pacific Ocean. He again found
himself with a rebellious crew during the mass mutiny by Royal Navy sailors at the
Nore anchorage, Thames Estuary, in 1797 – although this one was not triggered by
Bligh. The sailors in this incident were protesting over their wages. In 1805, shortly
after his work in Dublin, Bligh was appointed governor of New South Wales,
Australia. Three years later, due to ongoing conflicts with colonists and a deterio-
rating relationship with the local military, he was forcibly detained by the New South
Wales Corps and was held for two years under house arrest. This incident later
became known as the Rum Rebellion.[30]

Bligh's map of Dublin Bay was extremely detailed and clearly laid out in comparison to maps and charts of the same area produced throughout the eighteenth
century. The coastline of the entire bay was highly detailed, with a large and tight
concentration of soundings recorded around the area of modern Dun Laoghaire

28 Richard Hough, *Captain James Cook* (London, 1994), p. 333.   29 Hough, *Captain James Cook*, p. 429. 'Crossing of the line' was a traditional naval ceremony commemorating a sailor's first crossing of the equator.   30 A.W. Jose et al. (eds), *The Australian encyclopedia* (Sydney, 1927), pp 171–2.

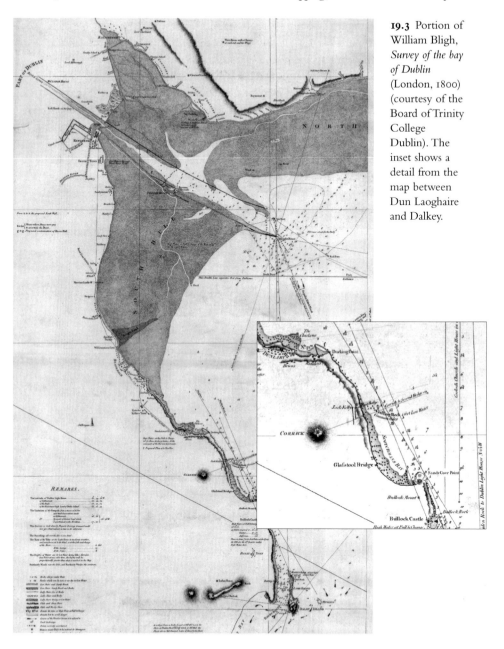

19.3 Portion of William Bligh, *Survey of the bay of Dublin* (London, 1800) (courtesy of the Board of Trinity College Dublin). The inset shows a detail from the map between Dun Laoghaire and Dalkey.

Harbour,[31] Howth Head and the entrance to Dublin Harbour and the Liffey. It was precise, it was informative, it was clean and clear. Like Burgh and Perry's map of 1728, the course Bligh took across Dublin Bay is identifiable, as a string of sound-

31 Modern Dun Laoghaire.

ings indicate that he employed the same techniques as had been used in previous surveys of the harbour. Devoid of any non-cartographic decoration or artistic cartouche, Bligh's map was a taste of the standardization that was to be introduced by the Ordnance Survey in the 1820s.

The charts and maps of Dublin Bay and harbour differ from plans of the city produced in the eighteenth century. They recorded an area virtually devoid of human interference. They are a good example of how a group of surveyors and engineers could vary in their representations of the same natural feature – the sea bed and shore. While the maps mentioned in this chapter are not the only ones produced for Dublin Bay during this period, they highlight the vital connection between the city and the sea.

Conclusions

Dublin's eighteenth-century land surveying is interwoven into the very streets, walls, paths and feel of the city. Dublin's surveyors did not finance the redevelopment of the city during the eighteenth century, nor bring political influence to make such changes possible, but they held the key position of linking the great designs and plans of Dublin's most powerful and wealthiest individuals with the real world. The surveyors of that era told the story of the development of eighteenth-century Dublin.

The surveying population had a greatly disproportionate influence on the city in comparison to their relatively small numbers. Aside from their obvious impact in the construction of the main thoroughfares and avenues with the Wide Streets Commission, their work affected the city's population in a more subtle and often mundane manner. Dublin's surveyors left an unprecedented record of the city's rapid growth over the eighteenth-century and how its antiquated infrastructure was gradually replaced due to the ever-increasing demands placed upon it. Speed, Brooking and Rocque, each in his own way, still influence how Dublin of that era is seen. Such major mapping projects, accompanied by the thousands of period estate maps that survive, create a picture of a complex and vibrant urban environment and help document the lives of both the poor and the rich.

The tenants of Dublin, both rural and urban, were intrinsically linked to the products of land surveyors. Surveyors' measurements played a key role in establishing the value and potential output of the country's main economic resource – land – either through agricultural produce or rents. Such measurements had a fundamental impact on the citizens of Dublin, from the residents of the dense urban core to tenant farmers throughout the county. Surveyors determined rents and rates, boundaries and borders.

Where they led, the city followed. Surveyors played an elemental role in transferring into a real world environment plans and designs of areas of the city now considered quintessentially Georgian and characteristically Dublin. They helped the city shed its medieval past and begin its journey into the modern era.

The city equally had an impact on its surveyors. It provided them with employment and a commercial market. It gave focus to a scattered and fragmented industry. It brought surveyors into competition, and occasionally conflict, with each other, and provided an environment within which real and long-lasting commercial networks could be forged. The city's newspapers provided them with a forum in which to advertise, complain, announce and promote. The city exposed them to the trends and fashions that were influencing not only cartography but all decorative arts. It was their home.

The city needed surveyors in order to grow and evolve into its modern form; the surveyors needed the city and its citizens to provide them with a living. This symbiotic relationship still exists. At the beginning of this book, it was said that the work of Dublin's period surveyors is part of the city's living heritage. It is found in the streets, parks, lanes and avenues that make up the capital of Ireland. A jewel in the city's Georgian heritage, Merrion Square bears the hallmarks of Byron, Barker and Roe. O'Connell Street, the main thoroughfare not only of the city, but also of the nation, follows the path set out for it by Sherrard. Tourists enjoying the view of the neoclassical masterpiece of City Hall from Parliament Street can do so thanks to the work of Semple. The picturesque views along the Grand Canal are in a small way due to Vallancey and Brownrigg. The ferries and ships that sail through Dublin Bay pass over the same areas surveyed in superb detail by Gibson and Bligh. The city is alive with the work of its eighteenth-century surveyors.

In the end, for all their financial successes and failures, their often distinct and occasionally clashing personalities, their professionalism, their precision, their accuracy, at the heart of this story lies a small group of men, often overlooked by history, but whose impact is felt everyday by the citizens of Dublin city.

Bibliography

PRIMARY SOURCES

SURVEY TREATISES AND MANUALS

'A civil engineer', *The present practice of surveying and levelling* (London, 1848).

Adams, George, *Geometrical and graphical essays* (London, 1803).

Burgh, Thomas, *A method to determine areas of right-lined figure universally* (London, 1724).

Callan, Peter, *A dissertation on the practice of land surveying in Ireland* (Drogheda, 1758).

Castle, Richard, *Essay on artificial navigation* (Dublin, 1730).

Dalrymple, Alexander, *Essay on the most commodious methods of marine surveying* (London, 1771).

Delande, Joseph, *Exposition du calcul astronomique* (Paris, 1762).

Douglas, James, *The surveyor's utmost desire fulfilled* (London, 1727).

Fenning, Daniel, *The young measurer's complete guide or a new and universal treatise of mensuration* (London, 1772).

Gardiner, William, *Practical surveying improved* (London, 1737).

Gibson, Robert, *The theory and practice of surveying* (Hartford, CT, 1839).

Gibson, Robert, *Treatise of practical surveying* (Dublin, 1752).

Green, John, *The art of land-measuring explained* (London, 1757).

Halley, Edmond, *Theories of the variation of the magnetic compass* (London, 1683).

Hammond, John, *The practical surveyor* (London, 1765).

Hood, John, *Tables of difference of latitude and departure for navigators and land surveyors* (Dublin, 1772).

Hopton, Arthur, *Speculum topographicum* (London, 1611).

Jess, Zachariah, *A compendious system of practical surveying* (Wilmington, 1799).

Langley, Batty, *Practical geometry* (London, 1726).

Leigh, Valentine, *The most profitable and commendable science of surveying* (London, 1577).

MacKenzie, Murdoch, *A treatise of maritime surveying* (London, 1774).

Martindale, Adam, *The country-survey-book* (London, 1702).

Meade, Braddock, *The construction of maps and globes* (London, 1717).

Nesbit, A., *Treatise on practical surveying* (York, 1824).

Noble, Benjamin, *Geodæsia Hibernica* (Dublin, 1768).

Norden, John, *The surveyor's dialogue* (London, 1607).

Poussant, Louis, *Traité de topographie* (Paris, 1807).

Robertson, John, *A treatise of mathematical instruments* (London, 1775).

Roy, William, *An account of the measurement of a base on Hounslow-Heath* (London, 1785).

Scalé, Bernard, *Tables for the easy valuing of estates* (Dublin, 1771).

Vaughan, John, *The gentleman and farmer's pocket assistant* (Shrewsbury, 1795).

Waddington, J., *A description of instruments used by surveyors* (London, 1773).

Whiston, William, *New laws of magnetism* (London, 1750).

Wing, Vincent, *Geodaetes practicus redivicus* (London, 1699).

Wyld, Samuel, *The practical surveyor* (London, 1725).

Manuscript primary sources

Bannan, John, 'Bills for surveying, Rolleston estate' (1810–17), NLI MS 13794.

Barker, Jonathan, 'Maps of Dundrum and all its subdivisions' (1762), NAI 2011/2.

Brownrigg, John, 'A book of maps of the several estates of the Rt Hon. and Rt Rev. dean of and chapter of Christ Church, Dublin' (1800), NLI MS 2789.

Dublin 'City surveyors' book of maps' (1695–1827), DCA.

Kendrick, Roger, 'Map book of the Liberty of Saint Patrick's, Dublin' (1741), Marsh's Library.

Kenny, Michael, 'Book of maps of the estate of Charles Domville, Dublin' (1778), NLI MS 21F107.

Longfield, John, 'Book of maps of the estates of Christ Church, Dublin' (1812), NLI MS 2789–90.

Longfield, John, 'Map collection' (*c.*1770–1840), NLI MS 21F32 – 21F49.

Longfield, John, 'Maps and plans of estates, Dublin' (1724–1847), NLI MS 21F86–90.

Minute books of the Paving Board of Dublin, vols 1–32 (1774–97), DCA.

Minute books of the Wide Streets Commission, vols 1–22 (1757–1812), DCA.

Orr, James, 'Map book of the estate of Edward Brice' (1751), NLI MS 19,848.

Roe, John and Stokes, W., 'Manuscript maps of the estate of Lord Cloncurry in Dublin' (1795–1842), NLI MS 16. G. 50.

Vallancey, Charles, 'Letters Paris' (14 March 1789), NLI MS 1614.

Various, Manuscript maps of the Domville estate in Dublin city, Dublin county and Meath (1655–1816), NLI MS 11,937.

Various, Manuscript maps of the Hatch estate, NLI MS 21F112.

Various, Palmer estate, county Dublin (1766–1830), NLI MS 21F141.

Wide Streets Commission maps (1758–1851), DCA.

PRINTED PRIMARY SOURCES

Anon., *A refutation of the 'Remarks on the agreement between the commissioners for making wide streets and Mr Ottiwell'* (Dublin, 1795).

Anon., *An impartial view of the conduct of the commissioners of wide-streets, in their bargain with Mr Henry Ottiwell* (Dublin, 1796).

Anon., *Remarks on the agreement between the commissioners for making wide streets and Mr Ottiwell* (Dublin, 1794).

Anon., *Dublin and its vicinity in 1797* (London, 1797).

Anon., *Observations on a pamphlet lately published entitled a description of the rival lines for inland navigation &c.* (Dublin, 1756).

Arrowsmith, Aaron, *Memoir relative to the construction of the map of Scotland* (London, 1809).

Badeslade, Thomas, *Chorographia Britanni* (London, 1742).

Bosse, Abraham, *Traicté des manières de graver* (Paris, 1645).

Campbell, R., *The London tradesman* (London, 1747).

Chambers, Ephraim, *Cyclopaedia* (2 vols, Dublin, 1741).

Donn, Benjamin, *An epitome of natural and experimental philosophy including geography and the uses of the globes* (London, 1769).

Faithorne, William, *The art of graving and etching* (Dublin, 1702).

Gent, Thomas, *Life of Mr Thomas Gent, printer of York* (London, 1832).

Gough, Richard, *British topography* (London, 1780).

Green, John, *Remarks in support of the new chart of North America in six sheets* (London, 1753).

Hutton, Charles, *A philosophical and mathematical dictionary* (London, 1815).

Leybourn, William, *The works of Edmund Gunther* (London, 1662).

Lloyd, Edward, *A description of the city of Dublin* (London, 1732).

Lynch, James, *Observations on Mr Freeman's paper* (Dublin, 1806).

Moll, Herman, *A set of twenty new and correct maps of Ireland* (London, 1728).

Morres, Redmond, *Letters on the Grand Canal* (Dublin, 1773).

Petty, William, *Hiberniae delineatio* (1685).

Petty, William, *The history of the survey of Ireland*, ed. T.A. Larcom (Dublin, 1851).

Poole, Robert and Cash, John, *View of the most remarkable public buildings ... in the city of Dublin* (Dublin, 1780).

Report from select committee on survey and valuation of Ireland, p. 73 [445], H.C. 1824, viii.79.

Rocque, John, *An exact survey of the city and suburbs of Dublin* (Dublin, 1756).

Scalé, Bernard and Richards, William, *Directions for navigation into the bay of Dublin* (Dublin, 1765).

Scalé, Bernard, *An Hibernian atlas* (London, 1776).

Semple, George, *A treatise of building in water* (Dublin, 1786).

Semple, George, *Hibernia's free trade* (Dublin, 1780).

Shelly, Mary, *Frankenstein* (London, 1818).

Sherrard, Thomas, *Extracts from the minutes of the commissioners* (Dublin, 1802).

Smith, John, *The art of painting in oil* (London, 1701).

Stokes, Gabriel, *A scheme for effectually supplying every part of the city of Dublin with pipe-water* (Dublin, 1735).

Swift, Jonathan, *Gulliver's travels* (London, 1726).

Taylor, George and Skinner, Andrew, *Maps of the roads of Ireland* (Dublin, 1778).

Vallancey, Charles, *A report on the Grand Canal* (Dublin, 1771)

Vallancey, Charles, *A treatise on inland navigation* (Dublin, 1763).

Wight, Joshua, 'Diary' (Friends Library, Dublin).

Wilson, William, *Wilson's Dublin directory* (Dublin, 1769–99), multiple editions.

Young, Arthur, *A tour of Ireland* (2 vols, London, 1780).

NEWSPAPERS

Belfast News Letter (1760).
Cork Evening Post (1767–83).
Drogheda Journal (1796).
Dublin Chronicle (1788–91).
Dublin Evening Post (1785–95).
Dublin Gazette (1729–60).
Dublin Journal (1750–1801).
Dublin Mercury (1767).
Dublin Weekly Journal (1729).
Exshaw's Magazine (1760).

Finn's Leinster Journal (1773–1801).
Freeman's Journal (1769–88).
Hibernian Chronicle (1786).
London Daily Journal (1728).
Public Gazette (1760–67).
Saunders' Newsletter (1792).
Strabane Journal (1786).
Universal Advertiser (1753–60).
Walker's Hibernian Magazine (1804).

SECONDARY SOURCES

Aiskew, Thomas (ed.), *The history of the survey of Ireland* (Dublin, 1851).

Ambrosoli, Mauro, *The wild and the sown: botany and agriculture in Western Europe, 1350–1850* (Cambridge, 1992).

Andrews, J.H., 'Mean piratical practices, the case of Charles Brooking', *IGSB*, 23:3/4 (1980), 33–41.

Andrews, J.H., 'New light on three eighteenth-century cartographers: Herman Moll, Thomas Moland and Henry Pratt', *IGSB*, 35 (1992–3), 17–22.

Andrews, J.H., 'The French School of Dublin land surveyors', *Irish Geography*, 5 (1967), 275–92.

Andrews, J.H., *Maps in those days* (Dublin, 2009).

Andrews, J.H., *Plantation acres* (Omagh, 1985).

Andrews, J.H., *The queen's last map maker: Richard Bartlett in Ireland, 1600–3* (Dublin, 2008).

Andrews, J.H., *Two maps of eighteenth-century Dublin and its surroundings by John Rocque* (Dublin, 1977).

Bendall, Sarah, *Dictionary of land surveyors and local map makers of Great Britain and Ireland, 1530–1850* (2 vols, London, 1997).

Bennett, J.A., *Divided circle* (London, 1988).

Black, Jeremy, *The Hanoverians* (London, 2004).

Brady, John and Simms, Anngret (eds), *Dublin, c.1660–1810* (Dublin, 2001).

Bryan, Michael, *Dictionary of painters and engravers* (London, 1904).

Casey, Christine (ed.), *The eighteenth-century Dublin town house* (Dublin, 2010).

Casey, Christine, *The buildings of Ireland: Dublin* (London, 2005).

Clark, Mary, *The book of maps of the Dublin city surveyors, 1695–1827* (Dublin, 1983).

Clark, Mary and Smeaton, Alastair (eds), *The Georgian squares of Dublin* (Dublin, 2006).

Clarke, H.B., *Dublin part 1, to 1610* (Irish Historic Towns Atlas, no. 11, Dublin, 2002).

Colley, Mary, 'A list of architects, builders, surveyors, measurers and engineers extracted from Wilson's Dublin directories, 1760–1837', *IGSB*, 34 (1991), 7–68.

Daly, Gerald, 'George Semple's chart of Dublin Bay, 1762', *PRIA*, 93:3 (1993), 81–105.

Danson, Edwin, *Weighing the world* (Oxford, 2006).

Delany, Ruth, *The Grand Canal of Ireland* (Dublin, 1973).

Evans, E., *Historical and bibliographical account of almanacs, directories etc. etc. published in Ireland from the sixteenth century* (Dublin, 1897).

Fagan, Patrick, 'The population of Dublin in the eighteenth century', *Eighteenth-Century Ireland/Iris an dá chultúr*, 6 (1991), 121–56.

Fairclough, R.H., 'Sketches of the roads in Scotland, 1785: the manuscript road book of George Taylor', *Imago Mundi*, 27 (1975), 65–72.

Fennell, Geraldine, *A list of Irish watch and clock makers* (Dublin, 1963).

Ferguson, Kenneth, 'Rocque's map and the history of nonconformity in Dublin: a search for meeting houses', *Dublin Historical Record*, 58 (2005), 129–65.

Figgis, Nicola, *Irish artists in Rome in the eighteenth century* (London, 2001).

Gebbie, J.H., *An introduction to the Abercorn letters as relating to Ireland, 1736–1816* (Omagh, 1972).

Gilbert, J.T. (ed.), *Calendar of ancient records of Dublin* in the possession of the municipal corporation (19 vols, Dublin, 1889–1944).

Gillespie, Raymond, *The first chapter act book of Christ Church Cathedral, Dublin, 1574–1634* (Dublin, 1997).

Goodison, N., *English barometers, 1680–1860* (London, 1977).

Harley, J.B., Petchenik, B. and Towner, L., *Mapping the American revolutionary war* (Chicago, 1978).

Hodge, Anne, 'A study of the rococo decoration of John Rocque's Irish maps and plans, 1755–1760' (BA, NCAD, 1994).

Horner, Arnold, 'Cartouches and vignettes on the Kildare estate maps of John Rocque', *IGSB*, 14: 4 (1971), 57–71.

Horner, Arnold, *Maynooth* (Irish Historic Towns Atlas, no. 7, Dublin, 1995).

Hough, Richard, *Captain James Cook* (London, 1994).

Hunter, David, 'Copyright protection for engravings and maps in eighteenth-century Britain', *Library*, 9:2 (1987), 28–47.

Jacob, Christian, *The sovereign map* (Chicago, 2006).

Kelly, James, *That damn'd thing called honour: duelling in Ireland, 1570–1860* (Dublin, 1995).

Lennon, Colm and Montague, John, *John Rocque's Dublin: a guide to the Georgian city* (Dublin, 2010).

Lennon, Colm, *Dublin part 2, 1610 to 1756* (Irish Historic Towns Atlas, no. 19, Dublin, 2008).

Marshall, D.W., 'Military maps of the eighteenth century and the Tower of London drawing room', *Imago Mundi*, 32 (1980), 21–44.

Mary, Colley, 'A list of architects, builders, surveyors, measurers and engineers extracted from Wilson's Dublin directories, 1760–1837', *IGSB*, 24 (1991), 7–68.

Maxwell, Constantia, *Dublin under the Georges* (Dublin, 1936).

McCullogh, David, *1776* (London, 2005).

McCullough, Niall, *Dublin, an urban history: the plan of the city* (Dublin, 2007).

McParland, Edward, 'The Wide Streets Commissioners: their importance for Dublin architecture in the late 18th-early 19th century', *IGSB*, 15 (1972), 1–31.

Morrison-Low, A.D. and Burnett, J., *Scientific instrument making in Dublin, 1700–1830* (Dublin, 1991).

Mosley, Charles (ed.), *Burke's peerage, baronetage and knightage* (107th ed., 3 vols, Wilmington, 2003).

Murdoch, T., *The quiet conquest: the Huguenots, 1685–1985* (London, 1985).

Murtagh, Harman, *Athlone* (Irish Historic Towns Atlas, no. 6, Dublin, 1994).

O'Brien, G., *The economic history of Ireland from the Union to the Famine* (London, 1921).

O'Dwyer, Frederick, 'Building empires: architecture, politics and the Board of Works, 1760–1860', *IGSB*, 5 (2002), 108–75.

O'Reilly, William, 'Charles Vallancey and the military itinerary of Ireland', *PRIA*, 106C (2006), 125–217.

O'Sullivan, Harold, *Dundalk* (Irish Historic Towns Atlas, no. 16, Dublin, 2006).

Parks, S. (ed.), *English publishing, the struggle for copyright and the freedom of the press, 1666–1774* (New York, 1975).

Pedley, Mary Sponberg, *Commerce of cartography* (Chicago, 2005).

Pedley, Mary Sponberg, *Map trade* (Chicago, 2000).

Prunty, Jacinta, *Maps and map making in local history* (Dublin, 2004).

Refaussé, Raymond and Clark, Mary, *A catalogue of the maps of the estates of the archbishops of Dublin, 1654–1850* (Dublin, 2000).

Severns, Kenneth, 'A new perspective on Georgian building practice: the rebuilding of St Werburgh's Church, Dublin (1754–1759)', *IGSB*, 35 (1992), 3–16.

Sims, Richard, *A manual for the genealogist, topographer, antiquary and legal professor* (Oxford, 1856).

Skelton, R.A., *County atlases of the British Isles* (London, 1970).

Smyth, William, *Map making, landscape and memory* (Cork, 2006).

Thomas, Avril, *Derry* (Irish Historic Towns Atlas, no. 15, Dublin, 2006).

Turner, Jane (ed.), *The dictionary of art* (34 vols, New York, 1996).

Varley, John, 'John Rocque, engraver, surveyor, cartographer and map-seller', *Imago Mundi*, 5 (1948), 83–91.

Whiteside, Lesley, *A history of the King's Hospital* (Dublin, 1975).

Withers, Charles, *Geography, science and national identity: Scotland since 1520* (Cambridge, 2001).

Woodward, David (ed.), *Art and cartography* (Chicago, 1987).

Woodward, David (ed.), *Five centuries of map printing* (Chicago, 1975).

Index